Creative Work Beyond the Creative Industries

Creative Work Beyond the Creative Industries

Innovation, Employment and Education

Edited by

Greg Hearn

Ruth Bridgstock

Ben Goldsmith

and

Jess Rodgers

Australian Research Council Centre of Excellence for Creative Industries and Innovation, Creative Industries Faculty, Queensland University of Technology, Australia

Edward Elgar

Cheltenham, UK • Northampton, MA, USA

Published by
Edward Elgar Publishing Limited
The Lypiatts
15 Lansdown Road
Cheltenham
Glos GL50 2JA
UK

Edward Elgar Publishing, Inc.
William Pratt House
9 Dewey Court
Northampton
Massachusetts 01060
USA

A catalogue record for this book
is available from the British Library

Library of Congress Control Number: 2013958026

This book is available electronically in the ElgarOnline.com
Business Subject Collection, E-ISBN 978 1 78254 570 5

ISBN 978 1 78254 569 9

Typeset by Servis Filmsetting Ltd, Stockport, Cheshire
Printed and bound in Great Britain by T.J. International Ltd, Padstow

Contents

Figures

Tables

Contributors

Greg Hearn is Research Professor in the Creative Industries Faculty at the Queensland University of Technology. His work focuses on policy development and R&D for new technologies and services in the Creative Industries. He has authored or co-authored over 25 major research reports and books, including *The Knowledge Economy Handbook* (Edward Elgar, 2005 and 2012), *Knowledge Policy: Challenges for the 21st Century* (Edward Elgar, 2008) and *Eat Cook Grow: Mixing Human–Computer Interactions with Human–Food Interactions* (MIT Press, 2013, in press). Hearn is the leader of the Creative Workforce 2.0 Program in the Australian Research Council Centre of Excellence for Creative Industries and Innovation (CCI).

Ruth Bridgstock is Senior Lecturer and Senior Research Fellow in the Creative Workforce Program at the Australian Research Council Centre of Excellence for Creative Industries and Innovation (CCI), and co-ordinator of the core program of the Bachelor of Creative Industries course at the Queensland University of Technology. She researches various aspects of creative careers, creative entrepreneurship, capability development for the Creative Industries, and higher education policy and practice. Her most recent work is concerned with the development of effective entrepreneurship curricula for emerging creative professionals. Bridgstock is author of *The Protean Careers of Artists: Exploring Skill and Attitude Predictors of Success* (Lambert, 2011).

Ben Goldsmith is Senior Research Fellow and part of the Creative Workforce Program at the Australian Research Council Centre of Excellence for Creative Industries and Innovation (CCI). His research interests include Australian cinema and television, media production and globalization, media and cultural policy, and the Australian apps development industry. He has previously worked at the University of Queensland, the Australian Film, Television and Radio School, and Griffith University. He has written several books, including *Rating the Audience* (with Mark Balnaves and Tom O'Regan, Bloomsbury, 2011), *The Film Studio* (with Tom O'Regan, Rowman & Littlefield, 2005) and *Local Hollywood* (with Susan Ward and Tom O'Regan, University Of Queensland Press, 2010).

Jess Rodgers is Research Associate for the Creative Workforce 2.0

Program at the Australian Research Council Centre of Excellence for Creative Industries and Innovation (CCI). Rodgers has extensive research assistance experience in the School of Justice and the Creative Industries Faculty at the Queensland University of Technology, and has taught in the School of Journalism, Media and Communication and the School of Public Health there. Rodgers is published in queer theory and queer history, with a PhD thesis that examined 'Australian Queer Student Activists' Media Representations of Queer'.

———————————————

Dawn Bennett is a Distinguished Research Fellow and Director of the Creative Workforce Initiative at Curtin University in Perth, Australia. Research interests include work and career in the creative sector, the role of identity development in student engagement, music education at post-secondary level, and the impact of research frameworks on the academic workforce. In 2010 Bennett became an Australian Learning and Teaching Council Fellow, extending her work on identity development and student engagement to students across multiple disciplines. A viola player, she serves on several editorial boards and assessment panels. She is on the board of directors for Music Council of Australia and is a commissioner for the ISME World Commission on Education of the Professional Musician.

Jane Coffey is Discipline Leader, Director International Programs and Senior Lecturer in Employee Relations and Human Resources at the School of Management, Curtin Business School. She has extensive academic and industry experience as a consultant, practitioner, researcher and youth arts board member in Western Australia. Coffey is co-author of the Australian HRM textbook, *Human Resource Management: Strategy and Practice* (Cengage Learning Australia, 2010). She researches and publishes in the areas of youth career expectations, attraction and retention in the performing arts, youth education and performance management while continuing her industry involvement in both the human resource and arts management sectors.

Stuart Cunningham is Distinguished Professor of Media and Communications, Queensland University of Technology, and Director of the Australian Research Council Centre of Excellence for Creative Industries and Innovation. His most recent books are *Digital Disruption: Cinema Moves Online* (edited with Dina Iordanova, St Andrews Film Studies, 2012), *Key Concepts in Creative Industries* (with John Hartley, Jason Potts, Terry Flew, John Banks and Michael Keane, Sage, 2013), *Hidden Innovation: Policy, Industry and the Creative Sector* (University of

Queensland Press, 2013), and *Screen Distribution and the New King Kongs of the Online World* (with Jon Silver, Palgrave Macmillan, 2013).

Scott Fitzgerald is a Research Fellow with the Graduate School of Business at Curtin University. His research and teaching interests encompass the political economy and sociology of communications and culture, as well as political sociology, international political economy and labour studies. His book, *Corporations and Cultural Industries*, was published by Rowman & Littlefield in 2011.

Alan Freeman is author of the 2008 Cultural Audit. A former cultural economist with the Mayor of London, he is a Visiting Professor at London Metropolitan University and a Research Fellow of the Queensland University of Technology. With Hasan Bakhshi and Peter Higgs, he co-authored Nesta's *Dynamic Mapping* report on the Creative Industries in the UK. With Radhika Desai, he edits the 'Future of World Capitalism' book series. He now lives in Winnipeg, Canada.

Janet Pagan is a retired academic who has undertaken research at CSIRO, the Australian National University and the University of Rochester in New York, publishing extensively in microbial bioenergetics and nitrogen fixation. On returning to Australia, she provided research and policy advice to the Australian government in relation to science, innovation and the information and communications industry. In 2007 she became a researcher at the Queensland University of Technology. She is also a visual artist.

Peter Petocz is Associate Professor in the Department of Statistics at Macquarie University, Sydney. He divides his time between professional work as an applied statistician, mostly in health-related areas, and pedagogical research in statistics and mathematics education. He has authored textbooks and video-based resources for statistics learning, written widely in the field of statistics pedagogy, and held a position as editor of *Statistics Education Research Journal* for several years. His and his team's investigations of the process of moving *From Expert Student to Novice Professional* and *Becoming a Mathematician* have culminated in the recent publication of research monographs by Springer (2011 and 2012).

Aneta Podkalicka is a Research Fellow at the Swinburne Institute of Social Research, Swinburne University of Technology in Melbourne. Her work has focuses on social innovation in the area of media, everyday consumption and sustainability. She has published on digital media, media translation and consumption practices in a number of major academic media and cultural studies journals, and is currently co-writing (with Ellie Rennie) a book on media projects for social change.

Jason Potts is Professor of Economics at the School of Economics Finance and Marketing at the Royal Melbourne Institute of Technology (RMIT) in Melbourne. He is an evolutionary economist who also works on creative industries economics. His current research is on innovation commons. His latest book is *Creative Industries and Economic Evolution* (Edward Elgar, 2011).

Al Rainnie is Professor and Director of Research at the Graduate School of Business at Curtin University. He was previously Director of Research at the Centre for Labour Market Studies at Leicester University, UK, and Director of the Monash University Institute for Regional Studies. Rainnie has researched and written extensively in the political economy of work and employment and regional development. He has studied, *inter alia*, small firms and industrial relations, highly qualified workers, the film industry, creative workers and regional development, trade unions and community unionism. His latest field of research and publication is concerned with spatiality work and employment.

José H.P. Rodrigues has a degree in Sport Science/Management and a Master's in Dance – Artistic Performance from the Faculty of Human Kinetics at the Technical University of Lisbon, Portugal. He is a PhD candidate, researching pedagogical dance expertise, at the School of Exercise and Nutrition Sciences at the Queensland University of Technology, in Brisbane. His research interests include the ecological dynamical theoretical framework applied to the study of neurobiological cognition and action.

Tarecq Shehadeh is a freelance cross-disciplinary researcher who uses data science and computational social science methods to explore and analyse large-scale databases. He has worked extensively on government policy, investment management and investment banking. In the course of pursuing his interests in investment and design, Shehadeh has consulted to leading advertising and design firms on how to best model and leverage the commercial value of their creative output and to behave in an entrepreneurial and commercially valuable way. Among his other interests are behavioural economics, game theory, political economy and innovative business models that can improve the coordination and collaborative capacity of individuals.

Dan Swan is a PhD student at the Queensland University of Technology and the Australian Research Council Centre of Excellence for Creative Industries and Innovation (CCI) in Brisbane. In addition to academic study he is a seasoned digital professional with over 18 years' experience in innovation and remains involved in the industry as both adviser and investor to several start-up businesses. He has been involved with many successful technology start-ups and listed companies in the US, the UK and Australia. His experience in innovation spans the full digital project lifecycle, with enterprise technology, tier-one product development and consecutive awards in digital marketing. He has a BA (Hons) in Sociology from Ruskin University, Cambridge, together with a Master's in Interactive Media (MIM) from University of Technology Sydney.

Oksana Zelenko is a Research Fellow at the Young and Well Collaborative Research Centre, Institute of Biomedical Health and Innovation, at the Queensland University of Technology, leading design research for six evidence-based e-health applications promoting well-being in young Australians. She has led the design of e-health applications in use nationally and internationally and consults widely on the potential of interactive media for community resilience and leadership. For three years, Zelenko was Head of the Work Integrated Learning program at QUT's Creative Industries Faculty. She currently lectures in design practice and design research methods in the Creative Industries Faculty School of Design at undergraduate and postgraduate levels. Zelenko is the co-editor of an interdisciplinary anthology, *Design and Ethics: Reflections on Practice* (Routledge, 2012).

Acknowledgements

This book was made possible by funding through the Australian Research Council Centre of Excellence for Creative Industries and Innovation (CCI), within the Creative Workforce Program. We thank CCI Director Professor Stuart Cunningham for his encouragement in this project. We would also like to thank anonymous reviewers for their feedback and the editorial expertise at Edward Elgar. Finally, we thank all family and friends (human and otherwise) for their patience and support.

1. Creative work beyond the Creative Industries: an introduction

Greg Hearn, Ruth Bridgstock, Ben Goldsmith and Jess Rodgers

Creative occupations exist across the entire economy. The creative worker's habitus cannot be discovered by looking only in film studios, games companies or artists' garrets. Work practices, evolved through the traditions of the creative and performing arts, are now deployed to create new services and products across all sectors, to develop process innovations, and to change the distribution thereof. Yet the bulk of academic study of creative work (both functionalist and critical), as well as the content of higher/ further professional education programs and everyday understanding of creative workers, focuses on one subset of the Creative Industries: those involved in the production of cultural goods or services (film, television, music etc.) for consumption by the general public. And further, the bulk of existing academic work focuses on those creative workers employed in Cultural Production industries. However, as recent work has shown, this focus misses both the large (and increasing) number of creative workers embedded in industries beyond the core Creative Industries (for example, manufacturing, banking, mining) and those creative workers and firms that supply services to business as well as to the general public, such as architects, technical writers and graphic designers (see Cunningham 2013; Potts and Cunningham 2008; Potts et al. 2008). This book focuses on this subset of very important, and yet under-recognized creative workers: embedded creative workers and providers of Creative Services into other sectors of the economy, as indicated in taxonomy shown in Table 1.1, which juxtaposes occupation and industry sector.

The first point to note in examining Table 1.1 is a simple one: the difference between 'an industry sector', defined in aggregate by its outputs measured via assessment of firms' outputs, and 'an occupation', defined by the work of individuals and measured via descriptions of that work. While the semantic descriptions of some industries and occupations may align (for example, film or marketing), 'industry' and 'occupation' are

Table 1.1   The focus of this volume

	Cultural Production occupations	Creative Services occupations
Creative Industries	Specialist Cultural Production workers	*Specialist Creative Services workers*
Other industries	*Embedded Cultural Production workers*	*Embedded Creative Services workers*

of course two distinct concepts, which are empirically separable. In line with the work of the Australian Research Council Centre of Excellence for Creative Industries and Innovation (hereafter CCI), we define the Creative Industries as consisting of: architecture, design and visual arts; music and the performing arts; film, radio and television; writing and publishing; advertising and marketing; and software and digital content. Occupational segments can be similarly classified. The term 'Creative Industries' can be segmented into two sub-categories, namely, 'Cultural Production' and 'Creative Services'. We use this terminology in relation to occupation in Table 1.1. The segments that define the terms 'Cultural Production' and 'Creative Services' are depicted in Table 1.2. The occupations in each of the segments are listed in Table 1.3.

The range of chapters showcased in this volume covers the neglected quadrants: those not concerned with producing cultural artefacts for consumption (movies, books, films, computer games, news content) and those that capture creative occupations and work practices used for other purposes. This includes Cultural Production workers and Creative Services workers embedded in other industries, as well as creative work in Creative Services firms who are contracted to other industries. We justify this focus not only because these occupations and work practices have been relatively neglected in academic studies, but also because there are

Table 1.2   Cultural Production and Creative Services segments

Cultural Production segments	Creative Services segments
Film, TV and Radio	Advertising and Marketing
Music, Visual and Performing Arts	Architecture and Design
Publishing	Software and Digital Content

Note: The architecture, design and visual arts sub-sector was split between the segments, with architecture and design going to Creative Services and visual arts to Cultural Production.

Table 1.3   Creative occupations by industry sectors under the Australian and New Zealand Standard Classification of Occupations (ANZSCO)

Creative occupation ANZSCO	Creative segment
Media Producer (excluding Video)	Film, TV & Radio
Radio Presenter	Film, TV & Radio
Television Presenter	Film, TV & Radio
Art Director (Film, Television or Stage)	Film, TV & Radio
Director (Film, Television, Radio or Stage	Film, TV & Radio
Film & Video Editor	Film, TV & Radio
Technical Director	Film, TV & Radio
Film, Television, Radio & Stage Directors nec	Film, TV & Radio
Television Journalist	Film, TV & Radio
Camera Operator (Film, Television or Video)	Film, TV & Radio
Production Assistant (Film, Television, Radio or Stage)	Film, TV & Radio
Arts Administrator or Manager	Music & Performing Arts
Actor	Music & Performing Arts
Dancer or Choreographer	Music & Performing Arts
Entertainer or Variety Artist	Music & Performing Arts
Actors, Dancers & other entertainers nec	Music & Performing Arts
Musician (Instrumental)	Music & Performing Arts
Singer	Music & Performing Arts
Light Technician	Music & Performing Arts
Make-up Artist	Music & Performing Arts
Sound Technician	Music & Performing Arts
Performing Arts Technicians nec	Music & Performing Arts
Book or Script Editor	Publishing
Newspaper or Periodical Editor	Publishing
Print Journalist	Publishing
Technical Writer	Publishing
Journalists & other writers nec	Publishing
Librarian	Publishing
Library Technician	Publishing
Library Assistant	Publishing
Proofreader	Publishing
Photographer	Architecture, Design & Visual Arts
Painter (Visual Arts)	Architecture, Design & Visual Arts
Architect	Architecture, Design & Visual Arts
Landscape Architect	Architecture, Design & Visual Arts
Fashion Designer	Architecture, Design & Visual Arts

Table 1.3   (continued)

Creative occupation ANZSCO	Creative segment
Industrial Designer	Architecture, Design & Visual Arts
Graphic Designer	Architecture, Design & Visual Arts
Interior Designer	Architecture, Design & Visual Arts
Urban & Regional Planner	Architecture, Design & Visual Arts
Architectural Draftsperson	Architecture, Design & Visual Arts
Jeweller	Architecture, Design & Visual Arts
Advertising & Public Relations Manager	Advertising & Marketing
Marketing Specialist	Advertising & Marketing
Advertising Specialist	Advertising & Marketing
Copywriter	Advertising & Marketing
Web Designer	Software & Digital Content
ICT Business Analyst	Software & Digital Content
Systems Analyst	Software & Digital Content
Web Developer	Software & Digital Content
Analyst Programmer	Software & Digital Content
Developer Programmer	Software & Digital Content
Software Engineer	Software & Digital Content
Software & Applications Programmers nec	Software & Digital Content
ICT Quality Assurance Engineer	Software & Digital Content
ICT Systems Test Engineer	Software & Digital Content
Web Administrator	Software & Digital Content

Note: nec = not elsewhere classified.

Source: Andrews, Yeabsley and Higgs (2009).

about four times as many creative workers across these quadrants as in the core Cultural Production sector alone. Moreover, with some exceptions, employment outside the Cultural Production sector is growing more strongly than within it, particularly in Creative Services. There are theoretical reasons for this focus as well. One important reason is that the context, conditions, contributions and education of creative labour cannot be fully understood by referring only to the Cultural Production sector. Another is that the dynamics of innovation in contemporary economies cannot be understood as deriving only from science and technology, but rather must include an understanding of the role played by those creative occupations that are engaged industrially.

The pursuit of this agenda has primarily been possible because of the detailed empirical apparatus established by the CCI, based on census statistics in Australia, the UK and New Zealand. The original intention of the examination of census data was to analyse the economic fundamentals of the Creative Industries, in terms of the size and growth of their contribution to gross domestic product (GDP). This task proved very difficult because of outdated industry classifications, which resulted in the need to disaggregate some sectors, such as computing services, which encompassed the emerging fields of games and web design. Researchers in CCI (see, for example, Cunningham and Higgs 2009) hit on the idea of using occupational data (ANZSCO or Standard Occupation Classification) as a proxy for the size of these sub-sectors, because occupational data provide much more fine-grained accounts of creative work than do industry data. It was this primary insight that led to the finding that there were more creative workers outside the Creative Industries than within them.

As a result of this work, we have come to realize that many kinds of theoretical problems can be approached using census data for occupations. These data are rigorously collected, very robust, not subject to sampling errors of primary surveys, and extend the value of ethnographies of creative work. Many of the chapters herein utilize CCI's occupational data approach, or other major databases (such as Household Income Labour Dynamics Australia), or are primary surveys. However, qualitative and theoretical expositions are also represented, and are very important to the task at hand.

The conceptual *raison d'être* for the book is a holistic consideration of creative work outside the Creative Industries. However, we were driven by three important debates. First, we wanted to make sense of why this kind of work has emerged in contemporary economies, and why it is growing. Second, we wanted to examine what this new empirical approach had to say about the issues of the precarity of creative labour – a debate largely shaped by considerations of the workers in the Cultural Production sector. Third, we wanted to understand the implications of this approach for the educational preparation and ongoing professional learning of workers in these occupations.

CREATIVITY, CREATIVE WORK AND INNOVATION

Why does creative work seem to be important to all sectors? At the macro level, there is a considerable amount of writing on the ways in which modern corporations have been shaped by the culturalization of economic life (Lash and Urry 1994). In fact, at least 50 per cent of GDP in modern economies is composed of personal consumption of goods and services. Increasingly this is directed not only towards the pursuit of cultural goods but also to the culturalization of all products and services. For example, manufacturing industry products, such as cars or furniture, or financial services, such as home loans or credit facilities are sold as lifestyles. Even health services include cosmetic procedures and aged-care lifestyles.

In addition, it can be argued that all economic activity is 'embedded' in the social sphere (see, for example, Granovetter 2005) and, we would add, that creative occupations are partially the agents of this embedding. That is, economic life depends on various sets of social relationships being enacted effectively, apart from the relationship with the consumer. For example, social networks play a key role in labour markets in terms of transmitting information about employers, employees and job flows. Many tasks in any value chain require serious cooperation from others. We suggest that digital media now facilitates these relationships – and creative digital workers are foremost in creating this 'infrastructure of embedding'. For example, Mudambi (2008) and Hearn and Rooney (2008) argue that there is creative input along the value chain in many sectors. This includes the use of design disciplines to capture value at the beginning of the value chain, and the use of digital and media disciplines at the end of the value chain to attempt to control the relationship with consumers via branding, advertising and, now, social media. Dell'Era et al. (2011) argue that designers are implicated throughout the product cycle. Designers may be involved in designing functionality, changing the meaning of a design, or creating new categories of product.

Stoneman's (2010) notion of 'soft innovation' also suggests why we might find the embedding of creative occupations throughout the economy. He proposes that the kind of innovation found in the Creative Industries is different from technical R&D (see also Bakhshi, Hargreaves and Mateos-Garcia 2013, 51–62; Cunningham 2013). Essentially soft innovation refers to aesthetic changes that are nevertheless economically important, including in sectors beyond the core Creative Industries. He offers the food industry and pharmaceutical industry, for instance, as sectors where aesthetic branding plays a part.

Cunningham (2013) and his collaborators (see, for example, Potts and Cunningham 2008; Potts et al. 2008) make a stronger case for the role of the creative sector in producing innovation across the economy as a whole. Cunningham (2013) suggests that creative sector innovation is not just aesthetic variation, but more intrinsic, particularly in the case of design. Potts and Cunningham (2008) go further, arguing that the growth in the Creative Industries is correlated with rising affluence, more specialized and larger stocks of human capital, the rise of ICT (information and communication technology) and globalization. Moreover, they propose that the Creative Industries are implicated in the growth of the whole economy. Beyond the adoption of new ideas and technologies, they may in fact be the engine of the higher-order cultural novelty driving economic evolution, and have led to steep changes in economic activity, such as the widespread adoption of the Internet, or the design-led innovation movement.

Although the testing of theory has not yet caught up with the empirical reality of embedded creative workers (Hearn and Bridgstock 2014), the ideas discussed above suggest that it is reasonable to look to their role in innovation as an explanation for this phenomenon. The next question the current volume asks is: if these workers are important to the process of innovation, are they rewarded commensurately in terms of their conditions and remuneration?

PRECARITY AND EMBEDDED CREATIVE LABOUR

Recent research has indicated that the labour conditions and experiences of the creative workforce in general have a number of distinct characteristics (Cunningham 2011). Most creative workers, it is argued, are contract labourers rather than permanent employees, are highly mobile in their place of employment, will typically experience 'portfolio careers' or multiple career pathways, and are less likely than in the past to be employed and trained through large, often public sector, agencies. At the same time, most creative employment has been found to occur outside the core Creative Industries, with design occupations in particular in demand outside the specialist design industry sectors.

In their analysis of creative labour in the publishing, music and television industries, Hesmondhalgh and Baker (2011) outline the 'remarkable fact' of the virtual absence until relatively recently of a focus on creative labour in studies of Cultural Production across three contrasting research paradigms: political economy of culture; organizational, business and management studies; and cultural studies (ibid., 55). The recent 'turn to labour' in cultural studies, of which Hesmondhalgh and Baker's work forms a part, tends to critique the conditions and experiences of workers in the core Creative Industries. This new focus has been in part a response to 'celebratory' accounts of the economic power of creativity and the Creative Industries that are also argued to have 'strategically ignored . . . the labor dimension essential to creative production' (Pang 2009, 55). The expansion of the Creative Industries, their popularity with policymakers, and the boosterism of commentators and consultants such as Florida (2002), Leadbeater (1999) and Howkins (2001) has, critics argue, contributed to a 'tendency to ignore or, conversely, sugarcoat the precarious employment situations prevalent in the [Creative Industries]' (de Peuter 2011, 418). Critical responses to 'creativity hype' (ibid.) have, therefore, begun to emphasize the precarious character of creative labour in the core Creative Industries (Neilson and Rossiter 2008; de Peuter 2011). New work in the emerging field of production studies has highlighted both the creativity and precarity of service workers in the Creative Industries (Mayer 2011). Many of these critiques draw on the autonomist tradition of Marxist labour theory, and in particular on the work of Hardt and Negri (2000), to position creative labour as the epitome of transformations of work in advanced economies 'away from stable notions of "career" to more informal, insecure and discontinuous employment' (Gill and Pratt 2008, 2). As Gill and Pratt relate, a variety of recent studies (see, for example, Banks 2010; Christopherson 2008; Hesmondhalgh and Baker 2011; Ross 2008; Pang 2009; de Peuter 2011) have highlighted a number of relatively stable features of [creative] work:

> a preponderance of temporary, intermittent and precarious jobs; long hours and bulimic patterns of working; the collapse or erasure of the boundaries between work and play; poor pay; high levels of mobility; passionate attachment to the work and to the identity of creative labourer (e.g. web designer, artist, fashion designer); an attitudinal mindset that is a blend of bohemianism and entrepreneurialism; informal work environments and distinctive forms of sociality; and profound experiences of insecurity and anxiety about finding work, earning enough money and 'keeping up' in rapidly changing fields. (Gill and Pratt 2008, 14)

But these studies, like almost all studies of creative labour, have tended to focus solely on the core Creative Industries: media, design, fashion, architecture and so on. While these studies have usefully directed attention to the particular conditions and experiences of creative workers, for the most part they have overlooked creative labour beyond the Creative Industries. This is despite the fact that a number of studies in different countries have shown that more creative workers are employed outside than within the core Creative Industries, and that employment of creative workers 'embedded' in other industries, or providing creative services to other sectors, is growing at a faster rate than employment within the Creative Industries (Pagan, Higgs and Cunningham 2008; Higgs and Freebody 2010; Higgs, Cunningham and Bahkshi 2008). This growth indicates innovation; new uses and applications are being found for creative skills and attributes across the broad range of industry sectors.

Data about embedded creatives produced first by the CCI, and subsequently by others adopting its Creative Trident methodology, contest some of the findings of studies of precarious creative labour. As one of the architects of the Creative Trident methodology, Cunningham, has noted, 'our studies suggest that embedded creatives do not generally exhibit the profiles attributed to creative labour by the precarity school of critical media and cultural studies. A great many creatives, we must assume, have managed precarity by working outside the creative industries' (Cunningham 2011, 38). The chapters in this book make important theoretical and empirical contributions to this debate, and help to tease out some of the issues raised both by proponents of the precarity perspective, and by other scholars of the Creative Industries.

EDUCATION FOR CREATIVE OCCUPATIONS

The education of the creative workforce is relevant to the discussion of innovation, precarity and the Creative Industries. Because the embedded creative workforce is involved in addressing the interaction, translation and synthesis of knowledge between and among scientific/technical, creative/cultural and business/entrepreneurial disciplines, and also between different sub-disciplines within each (for example, between aerospace engineering and astrophysics in the design and construction of new types of radio telescope) (Hearn and Bridgstock 2010), the processes of knowledge translation and synthesis for innovation require a range of high-level capabilities underpinned by transdisciplinarity, social networking capability and creative entrepreneurship. However, unlike domain-specific 'disciplinary' expertise, these creative workforce skills have yet to find general recognition and acceptance in higher and professional education (Hearn and Bridgstock 2010; Bridgstock and Hearn 2012). Educational approaches to the development of these skills also remain underconceptualized and underdeveloped. Traditional classroom or studio-based pedagogies tend to emphasize the skills required for performance in specialist and unidisciplinary creative work situations, rather than addressing the complex and varied requirements of transdisciplinary embedded and business-to-business services creative work.

A number of skilling, education and training implications also arise from the distinctiveness of creative labour. Labour oversupply, a well-established phenomenon in creative labour markets, particularly for graduate and entry-level positions (Menger 2006), has been observed to result in over-education among creative workers. Creative overeducation is suggested to occur because underemployed creatives acquire additional education and training in order to compete more effectively for scarce jobs, resulting in a mismatch between the qualifications needed for a creative position and the credentials of the incumbent. Indeed, some survey-based empirical studies confirm this pattern (for example, Caroleo and Pastore 2011).

The portfolio career and observations about precarity of creative labour further suggest that, in general, creative workers must ensure their own skill currency, and take personal responsibility for professional development (MKW 2001). Certainly, there are relatively few professional accreditation bodies or formal skill standards for creative occupations. Post-initial training skills acquisition seems primarily to occur through self-directed learning, via mechanisms such as formal and informal internships, and mentoring (Creative & Cultural Skills 2010). Creative workers are challenged to be what du Bois-Reymond (2004) calls 'trendsetter learners' (187), who set their own learning agendas in response to, or even in anticipation of, emerging industry and market developments. It is not immediately clear, however, how creative workers become trendsetter learners.

In terms of formal and initial education and training provision for creative occupations, there is significant evidence of skills shortages and gaps, particularly in terms of multiplatform and digital content, intellectual property and commercial acumen (Galloway et al. 2002; Creative & Cultural Skills 2010; Haukka 2011). In Haukka's (2011) survey of employers of graduates from creative disciplines, almost half reported having difficulty recruiting 'the right skills'. While some mismatches between employer expectations and graduate skills seem inevitable, and while educational institutions will always struggle to keep abreast of the latest digital tools of trade, empirical work suggests that creative graduates are fairly well equipped in terms of core disciplinary and broad generic employability skills (such as written communication, critical thinking and numeracy) (Ball, Pollard and Stanley 2010; Haukka et al. 2010). However, recent research indicates that there is a range of other high-level capabilities that are critical to success in creative work, namely, social network capability, disciplinary agility, enterprise and career self-management (Hearn and Bridgstock 2010; Bridgstock and Hearn 2012; Bridgstock 2013a, 2013b).

While higher and further education are adept at delivering conventional curricula for disciplinary and generic skill development, these four clusters of Creative Economy capabilities have not yet received general recognition and acceptance in post-secondary education (Hearn and Bridgstock 2010). Nor is it entirely clear which pedagogical approaches might prove most effective in developing capabilities, or how to assess for them. Further, while we may speculate how the Creative Economy capabilities required by embedded creative workers may be different from those required by creative workers who operate within the Creative Industries (for example, Hearn and Bridgstock 2014), little empirical work on this topic yet exists. Research may also reveal other capabilities as particularly important to embedded creative workers, or perhaps certain permutations of the creative economy capabilities presented herein will emerge as fundamental to the embedded creative worker's skill set. For example, an embedded creative designer might need well-developed enterprise opportunity recognition capability and social network capability in order to identify the most innovative specialist suppliers of design services. Two further questions relating to the education and training of embedded creatives are: how does tertiary education go about preparing students for the likelihood of embeddedness, given that beginning students often aspire strongly to specialist roles? And should there be special professional development and support mechanisms specifically for embedded creatives in different fields?

OVERVIEW

To pursue the issues raised above, the book is divided into three parts.

Part I explains the importance of creative work outside the Creative Industries and examines the role of this work in innovation. It also extends the precarity debate into the domain of embedded creative work. Part II comprises a series of case studies of embedded creative work and workers in a variety of industries and contexts. These help to identify embedded creative workers, what exactly they do and how they embed into particular industries. Part III examines education, skills and career issues for embedded creatives.

Part I   Foundational Issues

In the opening chapter of Part I, 'Creative labour and its discontents: a reappraisal', Stuart Cunningham provides a broad overview of the theoretical and measurement debates around the phenomenon of creative labour. Cunningham dissects the 'precarity' perspective, a body of cultural studies and labour studies scholarship that has had a particular interest in labour in the arts, cultural and Creative Industries. While acknowledging problems with the overly positive depictions of labour precarity in early commentary on the role of creativity in the modern economy, in particular in the work of writers such as Florida, Leadbeater and Howkins, as well as in his own early writing on the subject, Cunningham provides a number of responses to the criticisms of those writing from the precarity perspective. Cunningham points to the ways in which creative workers manage their precarious labour conditions, highlighting the degree of embeddness in creative occupations as a factor that tends to be ignored in precarity debates. Consequently, Cunningham notes that creative workers arguably face a less precarious future than their counterparts in other sectors, such as agriculture, mining or low-wage service sectors.

The second part of Cunningham's chapter discusses the development by the CCI (of which Cunningham is the Director) of its Creative Trident methodology for measuring the creative workforce. The Trident methodology divides the creative workforce into 'specialist', 'embedded' and 'service' occupations, and has contributed to substantial improvements in employment statistics and analyses of rates of change in the Creative Industries. The second iteration of the Trident methodology divides creative occupations into 'Cultural Production' and 'Creative Services' groupings, a development that has permitted even more fine-grained analysis of creative employment and the distinctiveness of this workforce. Cunningham's chapter thus provides an important introduction to the various discussions of embedded creative labour and Creative Services provision in the chapters that follow.

Jason Potts and Tarecq Shehadeh utilize the Household Income Labour Dynamics Australia (HILDA) survey panel to examine empirical evidence of the claim that the market for creative labour is precarious. They question the assertion of precarious employment, finding that it is only 'relatively' evident among creatives within Creative Industries and not at all evident among creatives embedded in other industries. The 'relative' precarity appears to be a function more of the industry, rather than occupational classification, and not systemic to creative employment as a whole. The data also reveal the significant variety of non-monetary compensating factors working to affect the relative desirability of work within the creative sector, such that precarity might actually be a dimension against which other terms of compensation are traded. The authors conclude that when these compensating differentials are factored in, employment in either Creative Industries and/or occupations is, in aggregate, neither better nor worse than employment in other sectors.

The next chapter by Dan Swan and Greg Hearn continues the focus on creative workers who are deploying their capacities in other sectors outside their core industry, through the contracting of Creative Services. They argue that one reason for the growth in creative digital services in particular, in relation to other industries, is that they are drivers of innovation. They present three case studies where creative digital services firms were deployed in companies in other sectors, namely, mining, education and manufacturing. They suggest that the integration of creative components into services or products in other sectors is not straightforward, and not always successful. The need to understand what makes a creative intervention 'interoperable' with products or services in other industries is a major finding of this chapter. Two processes arguably underlie this collaborative process. First, brokering was necessary for partnerships between host and digital creative firm to occur. In the subsequent embedded phases of discovery and incubation it was the bridging of knowledge systems that was then necessary for successful innovation. This raises important questions surrounding the nature and systems of shared language required for embedded creative digital knowledge. The evaluation of the case studies suggested that, without the intervention of programs that enable brokering and bridging, organizations struggle to engage the knowledge provided by creative digital companies in order to produce valuable creative outcomes.

Alan Freeman's discussion of London's creative workforce concludes Part I. Freeman opens his chapter with the example of the establishment of Nissan's design studio in the heart of London. He provides a valuable overview of the significance of creative occupations to the Creative Economy through a narrative that traces the development of researching London's Creative Industries against a governance and policy backdrop. London, as a world stage of creativity, is a key site for the emergence of Creative Industries policy and measurement. At the emergence of this area of interest there was no workable theory of how the cultural or Creative Economy functioned. For over a decade, research by a number of organizations sought to locate, define and measure the creative workforce in London, where and why it was growing, and where and why it clustered. Most recently the Creative Intensity model of defining creative occupations shifted from *a priori* taxonomies of industries and occupations to measurement by the characteristics of work (for example, whether the work can be mechanized). The indispensable input provided by such labour is precisely that which could not be replaced – its creativity. This approach found that creative intensity in the Creative Industries is 25 times greater than in the rest of the economy – with intensities ranging from 30 to 80 per cent – and helped to explain creative clustering. The creative intensity of industries is also shown to be a useful way to think about the notion of embedded creatives.

Part II   Case Studies of Embedded Creative Employment

To begin the case study section, Janet Pagan and Jess Rodgers update the 2008 *Getting Creative in Healthcare* report (Pagan, Higgs and Cunningham) by detailing the changes in embedded creative work in the Australian healthcare industry since the 2006 Census and considering reasons for the shape of creative work in this industry. Embedded creative workers form 0.5 per cent of the healthcare industry. The average for all industries is 1.6 per cent. The *Getting Creative in Healthcare* report found that creative contributions to healthcare occur in other ways as well, such as through contracted services or contributions from those who have no creative training. Between 2006 and 2011, creative employment embedded in healthcare increased at about the same rate as the total healthcare workforce – 19 per cent. The overall increase in embedded creative employment was driven by the 34 per cent growth of the largest segment, software and digital content. This chapter considers the types of contributions that the different segments make to healthcare and the industry contexts that influence different levels of creative employment. Primary contributions come from ICT analysts, web and software developers. Pagan and Rodgers also consider the role of allied health therapists who are not counted as creative workers in the Trident methodology.

In Chapter 7, Jess Rodgers examines embedded creatives in the Australian manufacturing industry. Embedded creative employees make up 2 per cent (17 635) of manufacturing industry employees. The average for all industries is 1.6 per cent. Given this higher presence of creative workers, the importance of manufacturing to the Australian economy, and the significance of innovation to manufacturing, Rodgers considers how embedded creative workers contribute to innovation in this industry. The architecture and design and advertising and marketing segments house the most embedded creative workers in manufacturing, at 45 per cent and 27 per cent respectively. Rodgers explores, through case study interviews, the type of companies these embedded creatives work for, the types of positions they hold, their contributions to innovation and the challenges they face. The embedded creative workers interviewed bring a variety of value-add propositions to their companies, including translation, reaching customers and product differentiation. However, the interviewees often feel that their creative input is not valued by their companies. Drawing on other research, Rodgers suggests that these experiences are not atypical and makes recommendations for interdisciplinary environments that foster innovation, and Creative Industries education.

In Chapter 8, 'Embedded digital creatives', Ben Goldsmith explores the different ways in which digital creative workers have featured in official reports and studies, and points out that these and other documents tend to display only limited understanding of the role of creative workers in the digital economy and in innovation, the issues they face, and their specific needs. Goldsmith's chapter poses a series of questions: who are digital creative workers? Where are they working? Where are their numbers growing? Using principally Australian Census data, Goldsmith then proposes a typology of digital creative occupations as a means both to estimate the size of the digital creative workforce and to better understand and assist planning for the needs and potential of this increasingly important group. The typology comprises three groups of occupations: 'Born Digital' creative occupations, such as software developers, whose work essentially did not exist before the digital age; 'Digital Migrants', such as television presenters, whose occupations existed before digitization but whose creative work is now entirely reliant on digital technologies or processes; and 'Semi-Digital creatives', or occupations in which digital technologies and processes may or may not be used, such as advertising and marketing professionals. These categories are then broken down into the Creative Trident II division between Cultural Production and Creative Services. Goldsmith's findings show that, while there is high growth in both specialist digital Cultural Production and Creative Services occupations, embedded digital creative occupations grew much more slowly. The findings also provide a sounder basis than previously available for estimating the size of both the digital creative workforce as a whole, and that of the specialist and embedded digital creative workforce.

In his second chapter in this volume, 'Embedded digital creative workers and Creative Services in banking', Goldsmith examines creative inputs into the banking industry through the optic of mobile applications (apps) development. Finance industries are particularly fertile ground for the analysis of digital and embedded creative work; in Australia, finance and insurance services industries employ both the highest proportion of embedded creative workers and the largest total number of software and digital content workers. The work of embedded digital creative workers and services provided by specialist creative firms are becoming increasingly important in the finance sector as Internet and mobile banking grows. Banks, in particular, are experiencing customer demand for mobile apps that enable a range of personal and corporate financial services. As Goldsmith demonstrates, this requires the deployment of a variety of digital creative workers in the design and development of innovative models and interfaces, the animation of icons, actions and services, and the development of image-based, graphically rich and user-friendly interfaces. Goldsmith describes the three models of bank apps development, with examples drawn principally from the Australian banking sector. These examples show that, while functionality and convenience are important attributes of financial services apps, so too are aesthetics and user engagement. Sharp growth in the use of mobile services and in the popularity of mobile banking indicates that the role of digital creative workers and specialist creative firms in the banking sector is likely only to grow in coming years.

In Chapter 10, 'Looking inside the portfolio to understand the work of creative workers: a study of creatives in Perth', Dawn Bennett and colleagues report on a survey-based study of the careers, work practices and skill needs of professional creatives in Perth, Western Australia. The chapter successfully problematizes neat distinctions between embedded and specialist creative categories and points to the complexities of the lived experiences of creative workers. There are complex and highly individual intersections and complementarities between specialist, embedded, support and 'non-creative' work within the careers of the creatives studied. Based on their findings, the authors argue that innovative and enriched creative practice is based in a much more diverse range of activities and experiences than previously acknowledged in the literature. The findings suggest that enriched practice often emerges from a multiplicity of creative and non-creative activities within and beyond the creative sector. Self-identification as a creative worker, self-organization of the portfolio career and personal meaning-making are all important underpinnings to the construction of creative work.

Part III   Education, Learning and Careers

The first chapter of Part III (Chapter 11) is a theoretical contribution that examines creative learning that takes place outside the formal education system. Such learning is not only of relevance to individual careers, but is equally important for the constitution of knowledge required to solve dynamic creative problems in many industry sectors. Although this type of learning has been studied extensively across many hi-tech and R&D contexts, few studies exist that specifically examine learning in Creative Services teams. These teams must become adept at routinely producing original and imaginative ideas that solve problems with quite fixed requirements from clients. Greg Hearn, José H.P. Rodrigues and Ruth Bridgstock theorize what might influence learning processes in teams composed of Creative Services occupations as identified in the current volume. They suggest that complex system theories can be applied to understand both learning about each individual problem brief (Type 1 Learning) and the process of learning to survive over the long term by cultivating creative assets and resources in the team (Type 2 Learning). In Type 1 Learning different kinds of creative outcomes are involved, ranging from aesthetic variation to business paradigm innovation. Further, they propose that quite different types of learning are required for generative, evaluative and optimization tasks. In Type 2 Learning, capability acquisition is the objective. This is enacted in a large and very dynamic social network milieu, comprising competitive and collaborative processes. Teams may survive by adaptation or by merging with other agents, scaling up through replication of solutions or operating methodologies, or by gaining competitive advantage through first-principles innovation.

Next, Aneta Podkalicka (Chapter 12) considers the benefit of creative education to a different cohort – marginalized youth. She examines the

Youthworx Media project, which provided accredited courses in Creative Industries alongside open-access multimedia workshops and independent one-on-one mentoring to young people in Melbourne, Australia. The chapter intersects with debates on non-linear youth transitions into education and employment (Furlong 2009; Fouad and Bynner 2008), and the role of creative production as an alternative educational site for skill development (Buckingham 2007; Sefton-Green and Nixon 2009). The aims of the students going into the course are considered, along with their post-course outcomes and the benefits that they obtained from Youthworx. The disparity between stated dream jobs and interest in media employment, on the one hand, and future education and employment plans, on the other, perhaps demonstrates recognition of the precarity of creative employment. Podkalicka shows that Youthworx enables students to engage in further education in the Creative Industries or in other fields, and to increase their confidence and general employment-related skills to seek work elsewhere. This speaks to the broader applicability of Creative Industries education and demonstrates how such education can contribute to the broader economy and social engagement, thus embedding creatives beyond the Creative Trident modes of employment.

Chapter 13, 'Developing agency in the creative career', by Oksana Zelenko and Ruth Bridgstock, breaks new theoretical ground by introducing a design-influenced pedagogy for creative internships. Such work-integrated learning experiences are aimed at developing in undergraduate Creative Industries practitioners the skills to navigate disciplinary boundaries and manage their emerging professional identities in response to an uncertain, dynamic and rapidly changing world of creative work. A new conceptual framework for work-integrated learning (WIL) is presented, based in principles of design practice, that affords the development of necessary agency, autonomy and reflective capacity for professional success through student co-design of the learning experience. The chapter includes a case study of an advanced-level undergraduate WIL course. The content of reflective blogs written by WIL students from four creative disciplines is used to document students' experiences in designing/shaping their embedded and specialist professional roles and identities.

Education for portfolio careers is one of the themes canvassed in the last chapter in the book (Chapter 14), 'Graduate careers in journalism, media and communications within and outside the sector: early career outcomes, trajectories and capabilities'. In this chapter, Ruth Bridgstock and Stewart Cunningham report findings from a tracking study of ten years of graduates from Queensland University of Technology's courses in journalism, media and communication studies. The study describes the graduates' employment outcomes, characterizes their early career movements into and out of embedded and specialist employment, and compares the skill requirements and degree of course relevance reported by graduates employed in the different Creative Trident segments. The chapter engages with broader creative labour precarity discussions, and also ongoing assertions of graduate oversupply. The authors conclude by considering how university programs can best engage with the task of educating students for a surprisingly diverse range of media and communication-related occupational outcomes within and outside the Creative Industries.

This book is intended as a summation of the program of research conducted in the CCI within the Creative Workforce Program. As such, the contributions have been deliberately chosen from collaborators within CCI's network. The main aim of the book has been to document the research undertaken within CCI. We believe that the significance of this work is two-fold. First, we showcase the substantial work that has been undertaken by CCI to build a robust, international, empirical foundation, using national occupational data, from which to interrogate many contemporary debates, build new theory and formulate practical policy interventions. Second, we believe that the focus on creative work outside the Creative Industries has demonstrated how significant a gap there is in current understandings of creative labour, both in terms of sheer numbers as well as in the sample of theoretically relevant contexts and conditions. However, we do not claim in any way to have produced a definitive account, nor spoken the final word on these matters, and we look forward to future engagement with researchers outside our immediate collaborators.

REFERENCES

Andrews, G., Yeabsley, J. and Higgs, P. (2009), *The Creative Sector in New Zealand – Mapping and Economic Role*, Wellington: New Zealand Trade & Enterprise, available at http://eprints.qut.edu.au/31133/ (accessed 29 July 2013).
Bakhshi, H., Hargreaves, I. and Mateos-Garcia, J. (2013), *A Manifesto for the Creative Industries*, London: Nesta.
Ball, L., Pollard, E. and Stanley, N. (2010), *Creative Graduates, Creative Futures*, London: Creative Graduates Creative Futures Higher Education Partnership and the Institute for Employment Studies.
Banks, M. (2010), 'Craft labour and creative industries', *International Journal of Cultural Policy*, **16** (3), 305–21.
Bridgstock, R. and Hearn, G. (2012), 'A conceptual model of capability learning for the 21st century knowledge economy', in D.J. Rooney,

G. Hearn and T. Kastelle (eds), *Handbook on the Knowledge Economy, Volume Two*, Cheltenham, UK and Northampton, MA, USA: Edward Elgar, pp. 105–22.

Bridgstock, R. (2013a), 'Not a dirty word: arts entrepreneurship and higher education', *Arts and Humanities in Higher Education*, **12** (2–3), 122–37.

Bridgstock, R. (2013b), 'Professional capabilities for twenty-first century creative careers: lessons from outstandingly successful Australian artists and designers', *International Journal of Art & Design Education*, **32** (2), 176–89.

Buckingham, D. (2007), *Beyond Technology: Children's Learning in an Age of Digital Culture*, Cambridge: Polity.

Caroleo, F.E. and Pastore, F. (2011), 'Talking about the Pigou Paradox: socio-educational background and educational outcomes of AlmaLaurea', IZA Discussion Papers 6021, Institute for the Study of Labor (IZA).

Creative & Cultural Skills (2010), *Sector Skills Agreement for the Creative and Cultural Industries: An Analysis of the Skills Needs of the Creative and Cultural Industries in England*, London: Creative & Cultural Skills.

Christopherson, S. (2008), 'Beyond the self-expressive creative worker', *Theory, Culture & Society*, **25** (7–8), 73–95.

Cunningham, S. (2011), 'Developments in measuring the "creative" workforce', *Cultural Trends*, **20** (1), 25–40.

Cunningham, S. (2013), *Hidden Innovation: Policy, Industry and the Creative Sector*, St Lucia, Queensland: University of Queensland Press and Lexington Books, an imprint of Rowman & Littlefield.

Cunningham, S. and Higgs, P. (2009), 'Measuring creative employment: implications for innovation policy', *Innovation: Management, Policy and Practice*, **11** (2), 190–200.

De Peuter, G. (2011), 'Creative economy and labor precarity: a congested convergence', *Journal of Communication Inquiry*, **35** (4), 417–25.

Dell'Era, C., Buganza, T., Fecchio, C. and Verganti, R. (2011), 'Language brokering: stimulating creativity during the concept development phase', *Creativity and Innovation Management*, **20** (1), 36–48.

du Bois-Reymond, M. (2004), 'Youth – learning – Europe: Ménage à trois?', *Nordic Journal of Youth Research*, **12** (3), 187–204.

Florida, R. (2002), *The Rise of the Creative Class: And How It's Transforming Work, Leisure, Community and Everyday Life*, New York: Basic Books.

Fouad, N.A. and Bynner, J. (2008), 'Work transitions', *American Psychologist*, **63** (4), 241–51.

Furlong, A. (2009), 'Revisiting transitional metaphors: reproducing inequalities under the conditions of late modernity', *Journal of Education and Work*, **22** (5), 343–53.

Galloway, S., Lindley, R., Davies, R. and Scheibl, F. (2002), *A Balancing Act: Artists' Labour Markets and the Tax and Benefit Systems*, London: The Arts Council of England.

Gill, R. and Pratt, A.C. (2008), 'In the social factory? Immaterial labour, precariousness and cultural work', *Theory, Culture & Society*, **25** (7–8), 1–30.

Granovetter, M. (2005), 'The impact of social structure on economic outcomes', *Journal of Economic Perspectives*, **19** (1), 33–50.

Hardt, M. and Negri, A. (2000), *Empire*, Cambridge, MA: Harvard University Press.

Haukka, S. (2011), 'Education-to-work transitions of aspiring creatives', *Cultural Trends*, **20** (1), 41–64.

Haukka, S., Brow, J., Hearn, G. and Cunningham, S. (2010), *60Sox Report Volume 2: From Education to Work in Australia's Creative Digital Industries: Comparing the Opinions and Practices of Employers and Aspiring Creatives*, Brisbane: Australian Research Council.

Hearn, G. and Bridgstock, R. (2010), 'Education for the creative economy: innovation, transdisciplinarity, and networks', in D. Araya and M.A. Peters (eds), *Education in the Creative Economy: Knowledge and Learning in the Age of Innovation*, New York: Peter Lang, pp. 93–116.

Hearn, G. and Bridgstock, R. (2014), 'The curious case of the embedded creative: managing creative work outside the creative industries', in S. Cummings and C. Bilton (eds), *Handbook of Management and Creativity*, Cheltenham, UK and Northampton, MA, USA: Edward Elgar.

Hearn, G. and Rooney, D. (2008), *Knowledge Policy: Challenges for the 21st Century*, Cheltenham, UK and Northampton, MA, USA: Edward Elgar.

Hesmondhalgh, D. and Baker, S. (2011), *Creative Labour: Media Work in Three Cultural Industries*, London: Routledge.

Higgs, P. and Freebody, S.P. (2010), *Auckland's Creative Workforce Report 2010*, Auckland: Auckland Tourism, Events and Economic Development Ltd.

Higgs, P., Cunningham, S. and Bahkshi. H. (2008), *Beyond the Creative Industries: Mapping the Creative Economy in the United Kingdom*, London: NESTA.

Howkins, J. (2001), *The Creative Economy*, Harmondsworth: Penguin.

Lash, S. and Urry, J. (1994), *Economies of Signs and Space*, London: Sage.

Leadbeater, C. (1999), *Living on Thin Air: The New Economy*, Harmondsworth: Penguin.

Mayer, V. (2011), *Below the Line: Producers and Production Studies in the New Television Economy*, Durham, NC: Duke University Press.

Menger, P.-M. (2006), 'Artistic labour markets: contingent work, excess supply and occupational risk management', in V.A. Ginsburg and D. Throsby (eds), *Handbook of the Economics of Art and Culture (Vol. 1)*, Oxford: Elsevier, pp. 765–811.

MKW (2001), *Exploitation and Development of the Job Potential in the Cultural Sector in the Age of Digitalization*, Munich: MKW Wirtschaftsforschung GmbH.

Mudambi, R. (2008), 'Location, control, and innovation in knowledge-intensive industries', *Journal of Economic Geography*, **8** (5), 699–725.

Neilson, B. and Rossiter, N. (2008), 'Precarity as a political concept, or, Fordism as exception', *Theory, Culture & Society*, **25** (7), 51–72.

Pagan, J., Higgs, P. and Cunningham, S. (2008), *Getting Creative in Healthcare: The Contribution of Creative Activities to Australian Healthcare*, Brisbane: Australian Research Council Centre of Excellence for Creative Industries and Innovation.

Pang, L. (2009), 'The labor factor in the creative economy: a Marxist reading', *Social Text*, **27** (299), 55–76.

Potts, J. and Cunningham, S. (2008), 'Four models of the creative industries', *International Journal of Cultural Policy*, **14** (3), 233–47.

Potts, J., Cunningham, S., Hartley, J. and Ormerod, P. (2008), 'Social network markets: a new definition of the creative industries', *Journal of Cultural Economics*, **32** (3), 167–85.

Ross, A. (2008), 'The new geography of work: power to the precarious?', *Theory, Culture & Society*, **25** (7–8), 31–49.

Sefton-Green, J. and Nixon, H. (2009), 'Reviewing approaches and perspectives on "digital literacy"', *Pedagogies: An International Journal*, **4** (2), 107–25.
Stoneman, P. (2010), *Soft Innovation: Economics, Design, and the Creative Industries*, Oxford: Oxford University Press.

PART I

Foundational issues

2. Creative labour and its discontents: a reappraisal[1]

Stuart Cunningham

INTRODUCTION

There is a tension at the heart of contemporary discussions of 'creative' labour. On the one hand, there is, in media, cultural and communication studies and neighbouring disciplines, a broadscale and growing critique of the 'precarious' conditions of labour in the creative sector. On the other, we find consistent evidence of the continued growth of the size of the Creative Industries as an industry sector and 'creatives' as a component of the workforce under conditions of the long-term 'aestheticization' or 'culturalization' of the economy (Lash and Urry 1994). These are ugly neologisms; nevertheless, they point to key structural changes in advanced post-industrial economies that tell a story of the mainstreaming of cultural and creative capability in contemporary work practices.

I regard the tensions that arise from such contrasting perspectives on what are often agreed objects (for example, the growth of the creative workforce is usually not in contention) as reflective of the fact that matters of consequence are at issue, and productive of genuine advances in understanding. In this broad overview chapter, I will canvass the general thrust and findings of what has come to be seen as the 'precarity' perspective, acknowledge that the early establishing rhetoric around the Creative Industries often bought into overly romantic accounts of creative labour, and engage with some of the complexity of measuring the creative workforce with a brief exposition of the Australian Research Council Centre of Excellence for Creative Industries and Innovation's (CCI) Trident methodology (leaving more detail to subsequent chapters). One of the key findings of CCI's research is that whole swathes of this workforce – the so-called embedded workforce and those rapidly growing parts of it supplying Creative Services to the rest of the economy – have rarely figured in the debate, on either the quantitative (statistical) or qualitative (types and conditions of work) side.

What the Trident methodology does is decouple the human capital/

creative workforce dynamics from the fortunes of the Creative Industry sectors as such. What the precarity critics tend to do is conflate creative employment with industry – as if the only significant location of creative labour is in the Creative Industries. Given the repeated findings that there are more creatives outside the Creative Industries than inside, and that growth is occurring more significantly in this embedded workforce and in Creative Services to the rest of the economy, this would seem a significant conflation.

The continual – and contestable – recourse to data around growth should not be principally about size *per se*. The question of size has been one of the enduring, possibly unfortunate, legacies of the early Creative Industries mapping interventions in the UK, giving rise to early and regular criticisms that collocating what until that point had been called the cultural industries with information and communications technology (ICT) was a cynical and unsustainable move (for example Garnham 2005) (I will return to this collocation later). There are numerous segments of contemporary national workforces that are much bigger than the creative workforce, but their future prospects, judged on relative rates of growth or decline, may be bleak. The high rate of growth of the creative workforce is an indicator of structural change in the economy as the services of creatives are called on more broadly. In classical Smithian terms, as well, divisions of labour – for instance, the rapidly multiplying sub-segments of design – are an indicator of increasing economic efficiency and sophistication.[2]

It is important to grasp that the growth of the embedded workforce and of Creative Services is evidence of 'culturalization' in so far as this demonstrates a specific call on these particular attributes and skills where they have not been needed before. New problems and opportunities present themselves across the economy; creatives can help to solve these problems and grasp these opportunities. To illustrate this, while moving beyond statistical knowledges, this book offers case studies of creatives in the health, manufacturing, finance, education and mining industries.

THE PRECARITY PERSPECTIVE

A rapidly burgeoning literature has developed around the notion of precarious labour – much of it focused on the specific condition of creative labour in the arts, cultural and Creative Industries (for example McRobbie 2002; Terranova 2004; Deuze 2007; Scholz 2008; Rossiter 2007; Gill and Pratt 2008; Ross 2002, 2007, 2009). This debate has largely been conducted in the mode of a wide-ranging ideology critique. Criticisms of the presumed overly celebratory accounts of the increased significance of creative labour in contemporary economies have focused on ostensibly neoliberal concepts of human capital and of labour that inform panglossian endorsements of glamorous and attractive, but volatile and precarious, forms of work.

Indeed, in his panoramic overview of the state of play in media and cultural studies, Miller (2010) characterizes the future of these disciplines as lying in just such a focus on labour. Characterizing the dominant paradigms as 'misleadingly functionalist on its effects and political-economy side', and 'misleadingly conflictual on its active-audience side', Miller argues that

> Work done on audience effects and political economy has neglected struggle, dissonance, and conflict in favour of a totalizing narrative in which the media dominate everyday life. Work done on active audiences has over-emphasized struggle, dissonance, and conflict, neglecting infrastructural analysis in favour of a totalizing narrative in which consumers dominate everyday life. (2010, 50)

Miller's third mode 'should synthesize and improve' the dominant paradigms by its analytical concentration on the status of labour. He reminds us in the most ringing of tones, 'There would be no culture, no media, without labour. Labour is central to humanity' (ibid.).

It is not hard to see why this focus has developed. It goes to the heart of Marxism's theory of labour as constitutive of surplus value. This analysis, based on increasing immiseration of the masses through decreasing returns to scale, and so powerful in the mid-nineteenth century when the Industrial Revolution was wreaking its greatest 'creative destruction', has not largely been borne out. While later versions of Marxist analysis have theorized immiseration being pushed out first to the imperial world's colonies, then more generally to the developing world, the labour force in the developed West has largely, if unevenly, benefited from the growth of the capitalist 'pie'. It is, therefore, essential for the Marxist theory of labour that aggregate improvements in the conditions for labour be interrogated to reveal their hitherto hidden precarity.

The precarity perspective describes a world where poor pay and overwork have grown apace and where the relative absence of hierarchical organization in favour of autonomous and flexible work produces individualized workers who believe themselves personally culpable if they fail and singularly responsible for 'life' decisions both taken and not taken (McGuigan 2010; Gregg 2011). Such individualization exposes workers to the stresses associated with broader economic conditions over which they have no control (Ross 2002, 2007, 2009; McGuigan 2010), and penalizes a workforce in consistent oversupply (Ross 2007, 2009). Consequently, the creative worker is obliged to accept low pay and insecure forms of employment (unpaid internships, self-employment, freelance work or short-term contracts) (Arvidsson, Malossi and Naro 2010). This is an arrangement that, in the West, also tends to favour those who can most afford to support themselves outside the work milieu (Lee 2011).

The conditions historically associated with low-wage sectors, such as short-term or casual contracts, increasingly become the norm as they filter through occupational levels to a broad spectrum of knowledge workers in high-wage occupations (Ross 2009). The precariousness of creative work means that the virtually continuous hunt for the next job has become the norm, and that workers are increasingly reliant on the reputations and social networks they have cultivated, or are prepared to work for very little, or both (Arvidsson, Malossi and Naro 2010; McGuigan 2010). Much so-called creative work is routine and repetitive – marketing, event production, retail design and the production and promotion of consumer 'experiences' – and tends to resemble other sectors of the service or knowledge industries (Arvidsson, Malossi and Naro 2010). Opportunity is often based not on merit but on cronyism, as formal recruitment procedures are bypassed in favour of network relationships.

Indeed, an integral part of creative work consists in deploying generic social skills in the construction and maintenance of productive networks, which function as a means of sharing tacit knowledge, fostering relationships within flexible working environments, and building competitive advantage (Lee 2011). Lee (ibid.) argues that, while important in terms of finding work and developing a career, such social networks also serve as a mechanism of exclusion, hierarchy and discrimination that favours individuals with high levels of cultural and social capital. Such social capital becomes manifest in a blurring of work and life into a world with its own standards of value and its own definition of reality. For example, Gregg (2011) argues that, while new media technologies are marketed as devices that enhance the freedom to work and play when and where we want, they consequently collapse the distinction between them.

The 'consistent findings' of this work, as summarized by Banks and Hesmondhalgh (2009), include that

> creative work is project-based and irregular, contracts tend to be short-term, and there is little job protection; that there is a predominance of self-employed or freelance workers; that career prospects are uncertain and often foreshortened; that earnings are usually slim and unequally distributed, and that insurance, health protection and pension benefits are limited; that creatives are younger than other workers, and tend to hold second or multiple jobs; and that women, ethnic and other minorities are under-represented and disadvantaged

in creative employment. All in all, there is an oversupply of labour to the creative industries with much of it working for free or on subsistence wages. (Ibid., 420)

The negative academic critique of creative labour arises largely in response to the overly sanguine accounts given of it in early work to establish the provenance of the role of creativity in the modern economy. Leadbeater's (1999) *Living on Thin Air* and Howkins's *The Creative Economy* (2001), for example, were early paeans of praise for creative labour, as indeed was Florida's (2002) very influential account of the so-called creative class, which was held to comprise fully one-third of the US workforce. Howkins's spin is full on: 'For these people, betting their creative imagination against the world may appear a more secure proposition, and certainly more fun, than becoming a little cog in a big organisation or another bit in the information society' (2001, 125). Leadbeater's language is more measured, but it is still about the normalization of the working life of the independent knowledge worker: 'self-employed, independent, working from home . . . armed with a laptop, a modem and some contacts' (1999, 1). Partly this is a matter of genre: these are 'business' books that, according to their genre, are breezy reads with lashings of what Adorno would scorn as 'affirmative' culture thrown in. It is also partly because Florida is a genre-bender – mixing his business pitch with straight academic social science research – that he has attracted a great deal more academic criticism. Some early humanities academic engagement also tended to over-egg the creative pudding. My early writings on the subject (Cunningham 2002), for example, gave the impression that the movement from arts and cultural industries to Creative Industries was a teleological, progressive movement of eclipse rather than a matter of accretion and overlay. I have sought to correct this impression in more recent work (for example Cunningham 2013).

But it is important not to lose sight of the fact that even some of the most strident critics also affirm the potential for 'good work' that creative labour represents in the modern economy and the undeniable attraction of (relatively) autonomous labour that it promises (Banks and Hesmondhalgh 2009, 419; Banks 2010; Hesmondhalgh and Baker 2010). This is a recurring theme, registered as a paradox by some (for example Arvidsson, Malossi and Naro 2010), but unfortunately often downplayed as false consciousness by others (hopeful entrants can be 'seduced'; thus critical social science must 'expose': Banks and Hesmondhalgh 2009, 418, 419). Nevertheless, such congruencies keep the lines of communication in the creative labour debate open.

STATISTICS, DAMNED STATISTICS AND THE 'CREATIVE TRIDENT'

Meanwhile, parallel to these debates – only rarely touching on them, but highly relevant for them – there has been significant work done on improving statistical parameters for more clearly defining the creative workforce. One of the field's major writers, Ross, considers that '[s]tatistics generated about the sectors have been legion' (2009, 31) and pleads for more work on 'quality of work life'. His call has undoubtedly been answered – there is by now, as we have seen, a mini-industry exploring the social and psychic dimensions of creative labour and precarious labour more generally. Quantitative analysis will not capture the texture of emotional labour, the challenging nature of portfolio work, or the psychic difficulties attendant on securing an initial foothold in the job market. But the need to continue to work on statistics matters.

It was the size and growth rates of the creative sector that kick-started the Creative Industries idea in the late 1990s, and 'the necessary (but seemingly interminable) debate' (Banks and O'Connor 2009, 366) remains hotly contested. As I said at the beginning, greater-than-standard growth is *prima facie* evidence of culturalization. More than a dozen years on from their first 'mapping' document, in 2011 the UK's Department of Culture, Media and Sport (DCMS) made a substantial change to their methodology that sees the Creative Industries account for only 2.9 per cent of gross value-added (GVA), far lower than the previous estimate of 5.6 per cent, with creative employment down from 2.3 million to 1.5 million, and the number of creative enterprises changed from 182 000 to 107 000. This followed the Department's removal of two 'standard industrial codes' from the definition of the software sector and a 'scaling adjustment' that it used to apply to the estimate of whole-economy GVA. Such big changes by the bureaucracy 'are unlikely to do much for the sector's credibility' (BOP 2011). They may be a symptom of ongoing lack of resourcing and attention to a fully professional approach to definition, method and data collection (Bakhshi and Freeman 2012). And there has been a strong, considered response to the move (Bakhshi, Freeman and Higgs 2013) – about which I shall say more later. One thing is certain: much is at stake in stabilizing the statistical base in this emerging sector.

Interrogating the welter of statistics is also paramount if we are to adequately differentiate among creative sectors and modes of labour engagement in terms of their capacity to support decent labour conditions. The deep financial crisis confronting the West since 2008 has generated claims, especially in the US, that the so-called creative class is a downright 'lie' (Timberg 2011), based on the difficulties faced by workers in threatened industries such as writing and publishing, journalism and video retailing. Florida's (2011) answer, pointing to steep rises for other members of the creative 'class' (producers and directors, art directors, graphic designers, audio and video technicians), reminds us to try to be specific whenever large categories like creative labour and precarity loom. This chapter takes this as one of its central purposes.

The imprecision of official statistics is a part of the broader challenges of effectively measuring domains undergoing substantial change through the rapid convergence of the computer, communication, cultural and content industries. This 'megatrend' has been the subject of a significant academic and policy literature (for example UNESCO Institute for Statistics 2009; Pratt 2008; Roodhouse 2001, 2006; Wyszomirski 2008; Pattinson Consulting 2003). New hybrid occupations and industry sectors that do not comfortably fit into standard statistics classifications emerge. The ten-to-15-year gap between updates of these classification schemes means that there are almost no comprehensive, standardized employment or industry data available during the critical emergence period of many sectors. Measuring the production and purchasing of physical products is difficult enough, but measuring the number, 'size' and value of the delivery of services is an order of magnitude more difficult. The challenges in seeking to measure the flow-on impact of, for instance, emergent digital Creative Industries services to other sectors of the economy are even greater.

This is a widely recognized problem that, in other instances of emergent or difficult-to-define sectors (such as ICT, environment, unpaid household work or tourism), has resulted in the creation of satellite accounts.[3] Without such an initiative for the Creative Industries, many statistical authorities and agencies have endeavoured to improve our quantitative understanding following the original *Creative Industries Mapping Study* by the UK DCMS (1998; see, for an overview, Higgs and Cunningham 2008).

This work has proceeded over the first decade of the 2000s as the problems of definition posed by the original DCMS (1998) mapping of the Creative Industries have been addressed in various ways. Overall, this work can be regarded as having made a useful contribution to advancing debate in these fields, because during this time there has emerged, if not a consensus (which is highly unlikely), then a broad pathway forward on the statistical parameters and routines for generating whatever definition of the creative sector that policymakers, program designers and researchers need. We focus here on the contribution that the CCI has made to this ongoing international project. It is one approach that addresses the imprecision of official statistics in grasping the emergent nature of the Creative Industries and the creative workforce. In the following exposition, Australian data are used although the Trident methodology has been applied in other jurisdictions (see Higgs and Cunningham 2008; Higgs, Cunningham and Bakhshi 2008; Higgs 2010).

CREATIVE TRIDENT MARK I: INDUSTRY AND OCCUPATION

The work of the CCI has focused on the development and application in several jurisdictions of the 'Creative Trident' methodology. The metaphor of the trident is used because it points to three parts of an employment quadrant composed of an occupation/industry matrix of two rows and two columns. This is the total of creative occupations within the core Creative Industries (specialists), plus the creative occupations employed in other industries (embedded), plus the business and support occupations employed in Creative Industries, which are often responsible for managing, accounting for and technically supporting creative activity (support). Simply put, the number of people employed in the 'Creative Economy' is the total of Creative Industries employment plus embedded employment (see Figure 2.1). This can be summarized as in Table 2.1.

The Trident is based on the recognition that the size and significance of

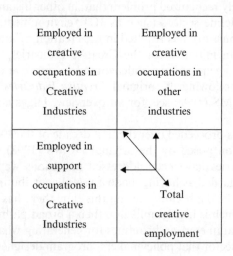

Source: (Higgs and Cunningham 2008, 26).

Figure 2.1   Figurative view of the Creative Trident

Table 2.1   Tabular view of the Creative Trident

	Employment in Creative Industries	Employment in other industries	Total
Employment in creative occupations	Specialist creatives	Embedded creatives	Total employment in creative occupations
Employment in other occupations	Support workers		
Total	Total employment in Creative Industries		Total creative workforce

Source: Adapted from Centre for International Economics (2009, 20).

Creative Industries cannot be accurately measured by using the industry activity codes alone. When counting only industry sectors, we surmise that previous studies have underestimated the employment impact of some creative sectors by up to 40 per cent, and the pre-2006 versions of some industry classification systems produce significant errors in sizing, possibly up to 25 per cent.

This approach to the creative workforce is similar to, but also substantially different from, high-profile and highly criticized work, such as that of Florida (2002; Florida and Tinagli 2004). Florida promiscuously and implausibly corralled all white- and no-collar workers into the orbit of the creative class, even as he very helpfully highlighted the importance of those in creative occupations being studied in their own right, rather than focusing narrowly on industries in which they work. Our approach is a much more constrained and carefully defined categorization of the creative workforce (defined as a group of occupational categories much narrower than in Florida), but much wider than traditional arts and culture: advertising and marketing; architecture, design and visual arts; film, TV and radio; music and performing arts; publishing; and software and digital content.

Nevertheless, the Trident approach can be customized for virtually any slice of the creative workforce: the arts, digital content, cultural industries or other segments (Higgs and Cunningham 2008, 23ff.). By adopting a rigorous, but methodologically disinterested, approach to 'which slice', it goes some way to addressing the 'tortuous and contorted definitional history' of the arts, cultural and Creative Industries (Roodhouse 2001, 505) to which many scholars and policy officials have addressed themselves.[4]

The methodology was first applied to Australian Census data from 1996 to 2001 and updated with the release of the 2006 and 2011 Census data. Results included much bigger totals for the creative workforce (5.3 per cent) and significantly higher estimates of income (over AU$36 billion, almost 7 per cent of earnings of the total workforce in 2011) than had previously been estimated based on standard classification categories.

The analysis also showed that the strong growth in creative employment experienced between 1996 and 2001 (4.2 per cent per annum as against 1.2 per cent for the workforce as a whole) had slowed considerably between 2001 and 2006 (1.7 per cent) but picked up again to 2.8 per cent between 2006 to 2011, a rate above that of the workforce's growth rate (2 per cent). Embedded employment was well off its traditional pace, growing at 'only' 2.7 per cent, while the specialist Creative Industries experienced a healthier 3.2 per cent growth.

The Trident methodology has been applied to the employment data-sets of the UK, in collaboration with the National Endowment for Science, Technology and the Arts (NESTA) (Higgs, Cunningham and Bakhshi 2008), and New Zealand, in collaboration with the New Zealand Institute for Economic Research (for New Zealand Trade and Enterprise) (Andrews, Yeabsley and Higgs 2009). Detailed data on embedded creatives have been generated, and extensive work has been done on time-series data based on groups of census data in national jurisdictions that have been the basis for key claims about growth of the creative workforce.

This methodology has also produced a 'Financial Creative Trident' (see Higgs and Cunningham 2008, 18ff.) that tracks personal incomes of the creative workforce based not on the turnover of organizations within the industry, but on the gross amount received by labour as declared on a census form or through a labour force survey. A consistent finding from repeated applications of the Financial Creative Trident is that creative workers have incomes above national averages, and in some cases considerably above, except for music and performing arts, which typically aggregate below national averages.

Indeed, a customized 'Arts Trident' was conducted based on Australian Census data (see Cunningham and Higgs 2010) and it was no surprise to learn that those in the arts are relatively poorly paid and losing further ground when compared with the total workforce. In real terms, while the arts mean personal annual incomes have increased between 1996 and 2006, the gap between that mean and the average of the workforce has also increased from a relative income gap of minus AU$5200 in 1996 to a relative income gap of minus AU$6400 in 2006.

The Creative Trident represents an advance on previous Creative Industries mapping approaches because: it avoids the tendency to overreach; it disaggregates creative employment effectively and with resulting insight; it allows for the decomposition of specialist and support employment within Creative Industries; and whenever possible it uses population-based data sources rather than surveys.

But this methodology is no silver bullet. Like all deployments of official census data sources, this approach shares the limitation that it accounts only for the respondent's main source of income at a given time. This is a particular limitation for the creative workforce, as a great deal occurs through 'second' jobs, cash-in-hand, volunteer and amateur activities (but see Higgs, Cunningham and Bakhshi 2008, 65 for some estimates of the impact of second jobs on creative employment figures; and see Chapter 10 in this volume, for a discussion of creative employment that looks beyond main occupation). The fact that census data significantly underestimate the full amplitude of creative activity is an endemic problem. Additionally, as the Centre for International Economics (CIE) points out, the Creative Trident approach is limited to capturing employment, because there are no reliable measures of output by occupation: 'It is therefore not possible to estimate the contribution embedded creatives make to the output of the industries in which they are employed' (CIE 2009, 20). Such a contribution must be approached qualitatively, as is done in this book with its case studies chapters. But also, because the Trident methodology mixes the concepts of industries and occupations, 'employment estimates are not really comparable to traditional industries. Estimating a Creative Trident across all industries would result in significant double counting' (ibid.). Moreover, a full suite of standard economic indicators for the Creative Industries must include contribution to gross domestic product (GDP) (or its sub-national constituent parts), productivity, GVA and export data. As the CIE also points out, each of these core indicators requires more fine-grained analysis than standard official statistics can provide.

We will gather up these findings (that there are more creatives found outside the Creative Industries than inside them, that income levels are uniformly above average, except for music and performing arts, and that sector growth rates are consistently above average) later. First, we need to disaggregate growth rates to a finer level of detail – the rate of growth, as I have argued, is the key.

TRIDENT MARK II: FOCUS ON RELATIVE GROWTH RATES

It is possible to congregate creative activity to a higher level than the traditional sub-segments, thereby producing three groups: Cultural Production,

Creative Services and the embedded workforce. Cultural Production covers those sectors and occupations that focus on the production of cultural products and experiences for final consumption, and include film, television and radio, publishing, music, performing arts and visual arts. Creative Services are business-to-business (B2B) activities such as design, architecture, software and digital content, advertising and marketing. The original six sub-segments (architecture, design and visual arts; music and performing arts; film, radio and television; publishing; advertising and marketing software and digital content) used by CCI Trident Mark I found a home in one or the other cluster. However, we needed to split the architecture, design and visual arts sub-sector, with architecture and design going to Creative Services and visual arts to Cultural Production. Nearly all the above-average growth in the creative workforce has been generated within Creative Services, either in Creative Service industries (support and specialists) or Creative Service occupations embedded in other industries (embedded in Cultural Production industries as well as non-Creative Industries); see Table 2.2.

It is not hard to see why there should be such relatively high growth patterns in Creative Services and Creative Service occupations embedded in other industries. The progressive embedding of the Internet and associated digital applications and services into the general economy, especially since the first correction of the dotcom boom and bust more than a decade ago, has seen rapid rises in demand for website design and online visual communication, as well as online and digital advertising, and software data basing, automation and business applications. Additionally, there are widespread converged digital technologies of reproduction and dissemination (digital cameras, digital video, digital audio creation, sharing online in social platforms) and a growing design-and-communication skill base and consciousness that supplies people, ideas and applications into the economy, and creates increasingly sophisticated demand in consumers (some of whom are co-producing and disseminating content).

The original critique by figures such as Garnham (2005) of the cynical collocation under the Creative Industries banner of the 'cultural' industries and ICT looks less powerful as data on the evolution of the sector point to increasing interdependence and interconnection. Recent research by Nesta and the CCI

> confirms that the creative industries bring together a particular combination of content and ICT skills; their integrity as an emerging economic entity relies on this combination, and if we attempt to define or measure these industries by omitting either component, the results make a lot less sense. (Bakhshi, Freeman and Higgs 2013, 45)

Table 2.2 Creative Economy employment figures based on 2011
Australian Census data

Organizations	Industries/sectors		
	Cultural Production	Creative Services	Other industries
Cultural Production	51 906	4 873	31 593
Creative Services	9 895	82 310	
Support organizations	67 189	153 699	Rest of economy 9 526 201
		Total employment	% of total employment
Cultural Production	Film, TV & Radio; Publishing; Music, Performing & Visual Arts	160 583	1.6
Creative Services	Architecture & Design; Advertising & Marketing; Digital Content & Software	370 361	3.7
Total, Creative Economy		530 944	5.3

Technical note: When calculating the totals (Cultural Production; Creative Services; total Creative Economy), the intersection zones between Cultural Production and Creative Services are not counted twice to avoid double counting. This means that Cultural Production occupations found within Creative Services industries are counted in the Creative Services total, and Creative Services occupations found within the Cultural Production industries are counted in the Cultural Production total.

Source: CCI analysis of custom extracts of the ABS Australian Census of Population and Housing 2011 under ANZSIC06 and ANZSCO classifications.

Creative Services activity and Creative Services occupations embedded in other industries are not as subject to the exceptionalist rules of supply and demand governing the Cultural Production sector, which classic studies, such as that of Caves (2000), analyse. Incomes for creatives in specialist Creative Services or Creative Services occupations in other industries are both higher and more evenly spread. Demand for their services is also more evenly spread and more consistently expressed across the economy: every town and city, big or small, needs architects. Almost all businesses, government departments and agencies, community organizations and non-government organizations need a web presence and experts to maintain and update them. Most pay for advertising and communications. And so on. On the other hand, Cultural Production is typified by the 'A list/B list', 'nobody knows' and 'arts for arts sake' dicta so named by Caves (2000). What is more, the consumption of Cultural Production is tied to discretionary income such that demand is not as great or as consistent. It may still be seen as 'icing on the cake' rather than the cake itself. The 'cake' economy is better represented by high-demand Creative Services.

Tables 2.3 and 2.4 show that the growth is found in Creative Services at around 3.8 per cent. This is almost twice the growth of the rest of the economy, which grew at 2 per cent from 2006 to 2011. It is important to note that this growth in Creative Services occupations (the designers, content developers, communicators and so on) is not restricted to the Creative Services sector itself, populated by many small-to-medium enterprises. The level of growth in the employment of Creative Services occupations within other industry sectors – the embedded workforce (such as designers employed by manufacturers, architects by construction firms and so on) at 2.5 per cent was also above the growth rate of the workforce.

It is a different story for Cultural Production, where overall employment

Table 2.3   Creative Economy employment growth rates based on 2006 and 2011 Australian Census data

| | Industries/sectors | | |
Organizations	Cultural Production	Creative Services	Other industries
Cultural Production	2.6%	3.5%	−0.8%
Creative Services	1.7%	4.8%	2.5%
Support occupations	−0.2%	4.3%	rest of economy 2.0%

		5 yr Average Annual Growth
Cultural Production	Film, TV & Radio; Publishing; Music, Performing & Visual Arts	0.6%
Creative Services	Architecture & Design; Advertising & Marketing; Digital Content & Software	3.8%
Total, Creative Economy		2.8%

Source: CCI analysis of custom extracts of the ABS Australian Census of Population and Housing 2011 and 2006 under ANZSIC06 and ANZSCO classifications.

Table 2.4 Average annual growth rate in employment by segment, 2006–2011

Creative sector	Creative segment	Total creative employment (%)	Creative Industries			Plus embedded (%)
			Total creative Industries (%)	Specialists (%)	Support staff (%)	
Cultural Production	Film, TV and Radio	2.1	2.4	3.5	1.2	−0.2
	Music, Visual and Performing Arts	1.8	3.2	3.9	2.3	−2.2
	Publishing	−1.1	−1.5	0.0	−2.4	0.4
	Total	0.6	1.0	2.5	−0.2	−0.8
Creative Services	Advertising and Marketing	2.8	2.0	5.4	−0.2	3.3
	Architecture and Design	3.1	3.3	4.4	1.7	2.8
	Software and Digital Content	4.6	5.6	4.8	5.9	1.3
	Total	3.8	4.5	4.7	4.3	2.5
Total		2.8	3.2	3.8	2.8	1.8

Source: CCI analysis of custom extracts of the ABS Australian Census of Population and Housing 2011 and 2006 under ANZSIC06 and ANZSCO classifications.

Table 2.5   *Average annual growth in inter-segment specialist employment, 2006–2011*

Sector	Occupation segment	Cultural Production industries (%)	Creative Services industries (%)	Total Creative occupations (%)
Cultural	Film, TV and Radio	3.8	3.7	3.8
Production	Music, Visual and Performing Arts	3.1	0.6	3.0
occupations	Publishing	1.1	5.5	1.4
	Total	2.6	3.5	2.7
Creative Services	Advertising and Marketing	3.1	7.3	6.1
occupations	Architecture and Design	–0.5	4.3	3.8
	Software and Digital Content	6.5	4.7	4.7
	Total	1.7	4.8	4.5
Total creative occupations		2.5	4.7	3.8

Source: CCI analysis of custom extracts of the ABS Australian Census of Population and Housing 2011 and 2006 under ANZSIC06 and ANZSCO classifications.

has plateaued at 0.6 per cent (a decline in the context of the workforce's 2 per cent rate of growth) almost solely because of the decline in embedded employment (–0.8 per cent) – the first time our data have shown a decline in embedded employment since the 1996 Census. It would appear that those in Cultural Production occupations have concentrated in specialist roles within either the Cultural Production or Creative Services industries.

As Table 2.4 shows, specialist music, visual and performing arts has grown 3.9 per cent and film, television and radio has grown 3.5 per cent. Publishing, on the other hand, declined in real terms (–1.1 per cent), driven mainly by the shedding of support staff (–2.4 per cent) and the below-average workforce growth of embedded at 0.4 per cent. Table 2.5 shows the annual growth rate in intersegment specialist employment. It shows, for example, that film, TV and radio specialist employment grew in Cultural Production industries (3.8 per cent), as would be expected, but equally in Creative Services industries (3.7 per cent) – mostly the advertising and software and digital content segments. Music, visual and performing arts had strong growth in Cultural Production industries (3.1 per cent) and almost none in Creative Services (0.6 per cent).

If it is defensible, while acknowledging evident problems with definitions, boundaries and data, to define the creative workforce as inclusive of the high-growth as well as the static and relatively declining segments, then we can present a more balanced picture of the fortunes of creatives in contemporary economies. It is important to grasp that the growth of the embedded workforce and of Creative Services is an indicator of 'culturalization' in so far as this demonstrates a specific call on these particular attributes and skills where they have not been needed before. As I have pointed out before (Cunningham 2008, 231), it might be interface designers who contribute to revolutions in the finance industry, technical writers in online education export industries, or simulation and games experts who make training environments for mining operations or defence departments. New locations of creative labour are co-evolving with new needs and opportunities across the economy.

BACK TO PRECARITY – CREATIVE CAREERS

As fields typical of much knowledge work today, creative careers are characterized by the increasing occurrence of contract labour requiring high degrees of mobility, by multiple career pathways, and by an increasingly internationalized labour market. They are challenged by the diminution of the market organizer roles played by many large (often public sector) agencies in mentoring, apprenticeships and structured whole-of-career pathways for creative workers. In most cases, 'learning-by-doing' apprenticeship opportunities, such as these organizations used to provide, have declined significantly.

Certainly, the creative workforce is distinctive along some key axes. Of all the people employed in the Australian Creative Industries at the 2011 Census, for example, 13 per cent are sole practitioners compared with 6 per cent for the overall workforce. Almost 60 per cent of employment in the industry classification for creative artists, musicians, writers and performers is self-employment (56 per cent). There are four other Creative Industry classifications having self-employment rates at least twice the Creative Industry average: professional photographic services (46 per cent), music and other sound-recording activities (34 per cent), other specialized design services (30 per cent) and craft jewellery (26 per cent).

This might support claims for distinctive precarity, but other findings complicate this picture. Compared with other employment, particularly in the traditional professions, creative employment disproportionately occurs outside the Creative Industries themselves. In other words, creatively trained people are more likely to be working outside the specialist

Creative Industry sectors than inside them, and this is the case in the countries we have studied, and has been the case for a long time. The degree of embeddedness is greatest in the many 'design' occupations: 60 per cent of the employment for design occupations in Australia occurs outside specialist design industry sectors.

The Australian data show that, while there had been a slowing of growth between 2001 and 2011, when viewed over a longer time period the Creative Industries have continued to grow at a significantly faster pace than the aggregate economy and to account for approximately 5.3 per cent of all employment in 2011 – a reasonably steady increase from the 4.6 per cent share held in 1996. Growth is spread across a broad range of industry sectors and creatives are relatively well paid (all segments are above the national average, except for music and the performing arts). The creative workforce also has higher average levels of formal qualification than the workforce as a whole.

If we can generalize at all from these data, it would be to conclude that the creative workforce shares a number of the characteristics of knowledge workers generally. While the creative workforce may be clearly distinctive in the degree of 'flexibility' seen in its labour market, creatives are also generally remunerated well for their services. This significantly complicates the picture usually painted of creative workers based on the typicality of the independent artist. Most creative workers have 'options' and mobility due to their qualification levels and experience in project-based work. However, this, as we saw in the discussion of the Arts Trident, in no way obviates the need to address the endemic problem of artists' incomes.

A more holistic picture of precarity in contemporary labour would balance these characteristics of the creative workforce against the problems faced by those working in sectors with declining demand for labour (agriculture), in sectors with major restructuring due to long-term challenges such as climate change (mining), or in sectors where exploitation is the norm due to low qualification and wage structures (such as low-wage service sectors). It is arguable that these sectors of the workforce face a much more precarious future than do creatives. As Hesmondhalgh (2007) – himself very much a critic of Creative Industries 'boosterism' – points out, the precarity school runs the risk of over-generalizing from the conditions of work both for traditional artists and in 'secondary' labour markets (low-wage, insecure, menial work; see Flew 2012, 104). In addition, the CCI studies summarized in this chapter suggest that embedded creatives and those engaged in Creative Services do not generally exhibit the profiles attributed to creative labour by the precarity perspective.

A great many creatives, we might surmise, manage precariousness by balancing between a range of labour conditions – for example, by pursu-

ing a precarious artistic practice while holding down more secure employment, or by pursuing both 'self-generated' and 'client-driven' projects
within the one specialist firm or sole-trading operation (see Chapter 10
in this volume). Many creatives in the Cultural Production end of the
Creative Industries manage precarity over a career life cycle by moving
outside the Creative Industries – often into teaching (Throsby and Zednik
2011) or, as Oakley, Sperry and Pratt (2008) show, by moving from the
core arts into the Creative Industries. We need to know much more about
creative labour in its full range of manifestations.

This volume begins to draw out these manifestations by exploring
embedded creatives and Creative Services. The volume covers wider
questions around measurement, the contribution of embedded creatives
and Creative Services to innovation, their roles in various industries, and
modes of employment and education.

NOTES

1. An earlier version of this chapter was first published in S. Cunningham (2013), *Hidden Innovation: Policy, Industry and the Creative Sector*, St Lucia, Queensland: University of Queensland Press and Lexington Books, an imprint of Rowman & Littlefield.
2. Design has a rapidly growing series of sub-sectors. Wikipedia divides design into five meta-groupings: product and industrial design; communication design; fashion design; interaction design; and 'other' (which embraces major fields such as architecture, interior and urban design). Grouped under these categories are – at the last count – 35 sub-sectors (Wikipedia 2013).
3. Satellite accounts, as defined by the Australian Bureau of Statistics, in discussing tourism, 'allow an expansion of the national accounts for selected areas of interest while maintaining the concepts and structures of the core accounts . . . However, while all the products that are produced and consumed in meeting tourism demand are embedded in the core accounts, they are not readily apparent because "tourism" is not identified as an industry or product in international statistical standards' (Australian Bureau of Statistics 2008).
4. The work of Paul Owens, Andy Pratt and Calvin Taylor for *The Revised 2009 UNESCO Framework for Cultural Statistics* (UNESCO Institute for Statistics 2009) stands out as significantly addressing these issues.

REFERENCES

Andrews, G., J. Yeabsley and P. Higgs (2009), *The Creative Sector in New Zealand – Mapping and Economic Role*, Wellington: New Zealand Trade & Enterprise, available at http://eprints.qut.edu.au/31133/ (accessed 29 July 2013).
Arvidsson, A., G. Malossi and S. Naro (2010), 'Passionate work? Labour conditions in the Milan fashion industry', *Journal for Cultural Research*, **14** (3), 295–309.
Australian Bureau of Statistics (2008), *5249.0 – Australian National Accounts:*

Tourism Satellite Account, 2007–08 Explanatory Notes, available at http://www. abs.gov.au/AUSSTATS/abs@.nsf/Lookup/5249.0Explanatory%20Notes12007-08?OpenDocument (accessed 29 July 2013).

Bakhshi, H. and A. Freeman (2012), 'How big are the UK's creative industries?', *NESTA Creative Economy Blog*, available at http://www.nesta.org.uk/blogs/ creative_economy_blog/how_big_are_the_uks_creative_industries (accessed 29 July 2013).

Bakhshi, H., A. Freeman and P. Higgs (2013), *A Dynamic Mapping of the UK's Creative Industries*, London: NESTA.

Banks, M. (2010), 'Autonomy guaranteed? Cultural work and the "art–commerce relation"', *Journal for Cultural Research*, **14** (3), 251–69.

Banks, M. and D. Hesmondhalgh (2009), 'Looking for work in creative industries policy', *International Journal of Cultural Policy*, **15** (4), 415–30.

Banks, M. and J. O'Connor (2009), 'After the creative industries', *International Journal of Cultural Policy*, **15** (4), 365–73.

BOP (2011), 'DCMS publishes Creative Industries Economic Estimates for 2011', *BOP Consulting's Culture and Creative Industries Blog*, available at http://bop. co.uk/blog/culture-and-creative-industries/dcms-publishes-creative-industries-economic-estimates-for-2011 (accessed 29 July 2013).

Caves, R.E. (2000), *Creative Industries: Contracts between Art and Commerce*, Cambridge, MA: Harvard University Press.

Centre for International Economics (CIE) (2009), *Creative Industries Economic Analysis Final Report*, prepared for Enterprise Connect and the Creative Industries Innovation Centre, available at http://www.enterpriseconnect. gov.au/OurServices/Documents/Economic%20Analysis_Creative%20Industri es_Final%20Report_240909.pdf (accessed 29 July 2013).

Cunningham, S. (2002), 'From cultural to creative industries: theory, industry, and policy implications', *Media Information Australia Incorporating Culture & Policy*, **102**, 54–65.

Cunningham, S. (2008), *In the Vernacular: A Generation of Culture and Controversy*, St Lucia, Queensland: University of Queensland Press.

Cunningham, S. (2013), *Hidden Innovation: Policy, Industry and the Creative Sector*, St Lucia, Queensland: University of Queensland Press and Lexington Books, an imprint of Rowman & Littlefield.

Cunningham, S. and P. Higgs (2010), *What's Your Other Job?: A Census Analysis of Arts Employment in Australia*, Surry Hills, New South Wales: The Australia Council for the Arts, available at http://www.australiacouncil.gov.au/__data/ assets/pdf_file/0009/79074/What_is_your_other_job_the_census_study.pdf (acc-essed 29 July 2013).

Department of Culture, Media and Sport (DCMS) (1998), *Creative Industries Mapping Document 1998*, London, DCMS. available at http://webarchive.nation alarchives.gov.uk/+/http://www.culture.gov.uk/reference_library/publications/ 4740.aspx (accessed 29 July 2013).

Deuze, M. (2007), *Media Work*, Cambridge: Polity Press.

Flew, T. (2012), *Creative Industries: Culture and Policy*, London: Sage.

Florida, R. (2002), *The Rise of the Creative Class: And How It's Transforming Work, Leisure, Community and Everyday Life*, New York: Basic Books.

Florida, R. (2011), 'The creative class is alive', *The Atlantic: Cities Place Matters*, 6 October, available at http://www.theatlanticcities.com/jobs-and-economy/2011/10/creative-class-alive/252/ (accessed 29 July 2013).

Florida, R. and I. Tinagli (2004), *Europe in the Creative Age*, Pittsburgh, PA and London: Carnegie Mellon Software Center and Demos.

Garnham, N. (2005), 'An analysis of the implications of the "creative industries" approach to arts and media policy making in the United Kingdom', *International Journal of Cultural Policy*, **11** (1), 15–29.

Gill, R. and A. Pratt (2008), 'The social factory?: Immaterial labour, precariousness and cultural work', *Theory, Culture and Society*, **25** (7–8), 1–30.

Gregg, M. (2011), *Work's Intimacy*, Cambridge: Polity.

Hesmondhalgh, D. (2007), 'Creative labour as a basis for critique of creative industries policy', in G. Lovink and N. Rossiter (eds), *My Creativity Reader: A Critique of Creative Industries*, Amsterdam: Institute of Network Culture, pp. 59–68.

Hesmondhalgh, D. and S. Baker (2010), '"A very complicated version of freedom": conditions and experiences of creative labour in three cultural industries', *Poetics*, **38** (1), 4–20.

Higgs, P.L. (2010), 'Auckland's Creative Workforce', Auckland: Auckland City Council, available at http://www.aucklandcreatives.com/pdfs/Aucklands CreativeWorkforce.pdf (accessed 29 July 2013).

Higgs, P. and S. Cunningham (2008), 'Creative industries mapping: where have we come from and where are we going?', *Creative Industries Journal*, **1** (1), 7–30.

Higgs, P., S. Cunningham and H. Bakhshi (2008), *Beyond the Creative Industries: Mapping the Creative Economy in the United Kingdom*, London: NESTA, available at http://www.nesta.org.uk/library/documents/beyond-creative-industries-report.pdf (accessed 29 July 2013).

Howkins, J. (2001), *The Creative Economy*, Harmondsworth: Penguin,

Lash, S. and J. Urry (1994), *Economies of Signs and Space*, London: Sage.

Leadbeater, C. (1999), *Living on Thin Air: The New Economy*, Harmondsworth: Penguin.

Lee, D. (2011), 'Networks, cultural capital and creative labour in the British independent television industry', *Media Culture & Society*, **33** (4), 549–65.

McGuigan, J. (2010), 'Creative labour, cultural work and individualisation', *International Journal of Cultural Policy*, **16** (3), 323–35.

McRobbie, A. (2002), 'Clubs to companies: notes on the decline of political culture in speeded up creative worlds', *Cultural Studies*, **16** (4), 517–31.

Miller, T. (2010), 'A future for Media Studies: cultural labour, cultural relations, cultural politics', in B. Beaty, D. Briton, G. Filax and R. Sullivan (eds), *How Canadians Communicate III: Contexts of Canadian Popular Culture*, Edmonton: Athabasca University Press, pp. 35–53.

Oakley, K., B. Sperry and A. Pratt (2008), *The Art of Innovation: How Fine Arts Graduates Contribute to Innovation*, London: NESTA, available at http://www.nesta.org.uk/publications/reports/assets/features/the_art_of_innovation (accessed 29 July 2013).

Pattinson Consulting (2003), *The Measurement of Creative Digital Content*, Canberra: Department of Communications, Information Technology and the Arts, available at http://www.archive.dcita.gov.au/__data/assets/pdf_file/0018/21708/measuring_digital_content.pdf (accessed 29 July 2013).

Pratt, A.C. (2008), 'Locating the cultural economy', in H. Anheier and R.Y. Isar (eds), *The Cultural Economy: The Cultures and Globalization Series 2*, London: Sage, pp. 42–51.

Roodhouse, S. (2001), 'Have the cultural industries a role to play in regional regeneration and a nation's wealth?', in J. Radbourne (ed.), *Proceedings of AIMAC 2001: 6th International Conference on Arts and Cultural Management*, Queensland, Australia: Faculty of Business: Queensland University of Technology, pp. 457–66.

Roodhouse, S. (2006), 'The creative industries: definitions, quantification and practice', *Conference Proceedings: Cultural Industries: The British Experience in International Perspective*, Berlin: Centre for British Studies, Humboldt University, available at https://www.leuphana.de/fileadmin/user_upload/PER SONALPAGES/Fakultaet_1/Behnke_Christoph/files/literaturarchiv/roodhouse-CI.pdf (accessed 29 July 2013).

Ross, A. (2002), *No-Collar: The Humane Workplace and its Hidden Costs*, New York: Basic Books.

Ross, A. (2007), *Fast Boat to China: Corporate Flight and the Consequences of Free Trade-Lessons from Shanghai*, New York: Vintage.

Ross, A. (2009), *Nice Work If You Can Get It: Life and Labor in Precarious Times*, New York: New York University Press.

Rossiter, N. (2007), *Organized Networks: Media Theory, Creative Labour, New Institutions*, Rotterdam: NAi Publishers.

Scholz, T. (2008), 'Market ideology and the myths of Web 2.0', *First Monday*, **13** (3), n.p. Available at http://firstmonday.org/ojs/index.php/fm/article/view/2138/1945 (accessed 29 July 2013).

Terranova, T. (2004), *Network Culture: Politics for the Information Age*, London: Pluto Press.

Throsby, D. and A. Zednik (2011), 'Multiple job-holding and artistic careers: some empirical evidence', *Cultural Trends*, **20** (1), 9–24.

Timberg, S. (2011), 'The creative class is a lie', *salon.com* (1 October) available at http://entertainment.salon.com/2011/10/01/creative_class_is_a_lie/singleton/ (accessed 29 July 2013).

UNESCO Institute for Statistics (2009), *The 2009 UNESCO Framework for Cultural Statistics (FCS)*, Montreal: UNESCO Institute for Statistics, available at http://unesdoc.unesco.org/images/0019/001910/191061e.pdf (accessed 29 July 2013).

Wikipedia (2013), *Design*, available at http://en.wikipedia.org/wiki/Design (accessed 29 July 2013).

Wyszomirski, M.J. (2008), 'The local creative economy in the United States of America', in H. Anheier and Y.R. Isar (eds), *The Cultural Economy: The Cultures and Globalization Series 2*, London: Sage, pp. 199–212.

3. Compensating differentials in Creative Industries and occupations: some evidence from HILDA

Jason Potts and Tarecq Shehadeh

INTRODUCTION

We interrogate the Household Income Labour Dynamics Australia (HILDA) survey panel for evidence supporting the claim that the market for creative labour is precarious. We find that the assertion of precarious employment is probably overblown, being only relatively evident among creatives within Creative Industries and not at all evident among creatives embedded in other industries. The 'relative' precariousness appears more to be a function of the industry, rather than occupational classification, and not systemic to creative employment as a whole. The data also reveal the significant variety of non-monetary compensating factors working to affect the relative desirability of work within the creative sector such that precarity might actually be a dimension against which other terms of compensation are traded. We conclude that, when these compensating differentials are factored in, employment in either Creative Industries and/ or occupations is, in aggregate, neither better nor worse than employment in other sectors.

COMPENSATING DIFFERENTIALS AND THE EFFICIENT LABOUR MARKETS HYPOTHESIS

The idea that the jobs in one industry or sector are better or worse than those in other sectors on some dimension is commonly held. For example, jobs in mining or construction are more physically hazardous than those in finance or design, while jobs in advertising or fashion might be more fun and glamorous than jobs in agriculture or healthcare. And then there is the notion that jobs in some sectors pay more than jobs in others. Those working in finance do, on average, earn more money than those working in tourism, for example. The Creative Industries or creative occupations are widely perceived to offer both enjoyable and interesting work, the prospect of very large pay-offs (Potts 2006), but also considerable 'precarity' in employment (see, for example, Ross 2009; Banks and Hesmondhalgh 2009).

So are some sectors better than others to work in, and what are the very best jobs to have? Are those in the Creative Industries among them? Economic theory makes a very specific prediction on this point. Supposing that labour markets are price 'efficient', which means that pertinent information about the attributes of each job, including compensation, is public or symmetrically distributed, and that there is free mobility of entry into jobs or into the training required to enter them (that is, no discrimination), then all jobs across all sectors will provide compensation packages (or portfolios) that, while different, are relatively equal in tradable value to their alternatives.[1]

This is obviously a statistical argument that applies only beyond the short run. But what we may call the 'efficient labour markets hypothesis' is an application of the so-called 'efficient markets hypothesis' (Fama 1965), which is usually applied in finance to say that the price of an asset (for example a stock or a bond) reflects all available information, and so supernormal returns cannot be traded systematically. The equivalent of 'supernormal returns' in labour markets is the notion of a job that really is better than all the others. For this to be true, there must be either special insider information, unaccounted frictions, inexplicable privilege or uncompensated barriers to entry. In the long run, and under the condition of free entry and perfect information, something must be corrupt or institutionally broken for a non-equilibrium result to emerge where some jobs would offer sustained supernormal returns.

The term for this equalizing phenomenon in labour economics is 'compensating differentials' (Rosen 1986). The idea is simply about unpacking the monetary and non-monetary elements of a wage. We assume that such wages are determined in markets (rather than by some other mechanism, such as tradition or parliamentary decree) and that they reflect the marginal value product, or the additional value the worker produces. This is an aggregate statistical observation rather than something that applies to each agent. We also assume that people make decisions about whether or not to work, and about what type of work to do based on an evaluation of their own preferences, of the wages on offer, and their assessments of the compensating differentials – maximizing their utility in the process. We assume, in essence, that there is a labour market operating on both supply and demand in the Creative Industries. Our interpretation of the HILDA results rests entirely on this assumption.

According to this theory, any job consists of a bundle of attributes, including wages, risk of injury, opportunity for fame, quality of work environment, learning opportunity, skills required, amount of flexible time, stimulation, risk of redundancy, leave provisions, sociality, self-actualization, perks and so on. The logic is that there is a 'reservation wage' that brings you into the labour market compared to your next-best alternative (for example, self-employment, welfare) and from there you choose based on compensating differentials. If a job is more dangerous, you will require a higher wage to be bid into that market, and similarly so if it requires more training to enter. If the job is very boring, you might also require a higher wage to induce you to enter. But this also goes in the other direction, namely if a job is fun and exciting, or has great flexible working opportunities, you will require a lower wage to be at the same level of inducement to enter.

Overall, the theory of efficient labour markets and the theory of compensating differentials predict that (on average, in equilibrium) we can expect compensation to adjust to relative shortages and excess entry into different sectors and jobs, such that all differences balance out, and/or at least tend in that direction. A specific prediction is that, when one class of jobs or sector has a characteristic that is systematically valued, whether positively or negatively (such as paid maternity leave, or risk of injury), these non-wage benefits or non-wage costs should eventually be reflected in wage compensation (Edwards 2006). Obviously this is another statistical equilibrium argument, and many of the assumptions may at best hold only weakly, and so perhaps the most we would expect to see is a tendency toward this. Also, this is an equilibrium outcome for a given distribution of skills, competences and investments.

We can endeavour to test this prediction that creative occupations and employment in the Creative Industries conform to this pattern. What we expect to observe is perhaps very different assessments of the relative costs and benefits of different degrees of precarity, of workplace flexibility, of expectations of various non-wage benefits or costs, and maybe even large differences in wages between the Creative Industries and other occupations; all of these differences may well be observed. But what the theory of efficient labour markets and the mechanism of compensating differentials specifically predicts is that overall satisfaction with a job should be, eventually and indeed invariably, equalized across all sectors. The argument we are making here is textbook neoclassical economics. In industry, if there are supernormal profits, they are eventually competed or arbitraged away by new entrants. The same process also operates in the labour markets.

METHOD AND RESULTS

Our analysis uses the Household Income and Labour Dynamics In Australia panel (see Wooden and Watson 2007), a large survey panel tracking in excess of 20000 individuals since 2001. The survey asks a detailed set of questions about household employment, spending, income, education, happiness and health, and includes many questions relating to satisfaction with various aspects of work and household life, conveniently framed on a 10-point Likert scale. Each of the mean observations calculated has high statistical significance, possessing a very low standard error. The HILDA panel is an ideal instrument for addressing the question we seek to pose here about the relative quality of employment in Creative Industries and occupations.

The analysis sample was constructed through a sequence of simple steps. It was limited to those in employment, and every individual was sorted by both their industrial and occupational standard classifications. Each employed individual in the HILDA panel is classified within the 4-digit Standard Occupational Classification (SOC) code and also as part of the 4-digit Standard Industrial Classification code (SIC). Following the Trident methodology developed by the Centre for Creative Industries and Innovation (Higgs, Cunningham and Pagan 2007), the Creative Industries (SIC) and Creative Occupational (SOC) classifications from Higgs and Cunningham (2007) were used. Each individual in the panel was thus classified by both their occupation (creative or not), and industry (creative or not); see Table 3.1.

Structural differences in both industry and occupational categories are evident among the types of contracts that characterize the job (see

Table 3.1   Classification by occupation and industry

	Employment in Creative Industries	Employment in other industries	Total
Employment in creative occupations	Specialist creatives	Embedded creatives	Total employment in creative occupations
Employment in other occupations	Support workers		
Total	Total employment in Creative Industries		Total creative workforce

Source: Adapted from Centre for International Economics (2009).

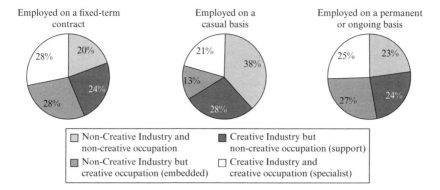

Figure 3.1 showing three pie charts:

Employed on a fixed-term contract: 20%, 24%, 28%, 28%

Employed on a casual basis: 21%, 38%, 28%, 13%

Employed on a permanent or ongoing basis: 23%, 24%, 27%, 25%

Legend:
- □ Non-Creative Industry and non-creative occupation
- ■ Creative Industry but non-creative occupation (support)
- ■ Non-Creative Industry but creative occupation (embedded)
- □ Creative Industry and creative occupation (specialist)

Figure 3.1   Employment type by industry and occupation

Figure 3.1). From Figure 3.1 we can see that those engaged in creative occupations were more likely than those not in creative occupations to have the security of either permanent or ongoing employment, or fixed-term contract engagements. Those in non-creative occupations (NCO) were much more likely to be employed on a contingent or casual basis. The preponderance of fixed-term contracts among those in creative occupations may reflect the nature of creative projects with specific beginnings and ends.

While those in creative occupations seem to have the most secure employment, the specialists within the Creative Industries (CI) report less job security than their counterparts – the embedded creatives – working in other industries.[2] From other questions, we can see that specialists were also about twice as likely to consider themselves independent contractors and less likely to be satisfied with their pay, and were significantly less sanguine about their chances of finding another job 'at least as good' as the one they held. This is an indication that they perceived themselves in a somewhat privileged position. This stands in contrast to the embedded creatives, who report significant satisfaction with a range of factors related to their employment. A composite graph of both creative occupation and industry was also compiled. Arithmetic mean results are presented in Table 3.2. There is a relatively even balance between those questions that reveal information about a respondent's occupation and those that reveal information about a respondent's industry sector. We look for those where we find a categorical distinction among the specialist, support or embedded occupations versus the rest of the labour force.

Further analysis would be required to uncover whether the lower level of security is a function of employment within smaller-sized employing firms, and whether there is a relationship between firm size and

Table 3.2   *HILDA survey comparing mean creative and non-creative responses*

	Non-Creative Industry and non-creative occupation	Creative Industry but non-creative occupation	Non-Creative Industry but creative occupation	Creative Industry and creative occupation
Total number of respondents	137 690	1 315	1 855	1 593
Satisfaction – your financial situation	6.3	6.5	6.8	6.4
Satisfaction – the amount of free time you have	6.7	5.8	5.9	6.1
Satisfaction – how satisfied with your life are you?	7.9	7.8	7.8	7.8
Satisfaction – your employment opportunities	7.0	7.4	7.5	7.3
Total pay satisfaction	6.9	6.9	7.0	6.4
Job security satisfaction	8.0	7.5	7.7	7.2
The work itself satisfaction	7.6	7.5	7.7	7.8
The hours you work satisfaction	7.2	7.1	7.2	6.9
The flexibility to balance work and non-work commitments satisfaction	7.4	7.8	7.8	7.6
Overall job satisfaction	7.7	7.6	7.6	7.5
I fear that the amount of stress in my job will make me physically ill	3.5	3.8	3.6	3.7
I get paid fairly for the things I do in my job	6.6	6.7	6.8	6.5
I have a secure future in my job	7.1	6.7	7.0	6.5
My job often requires me to learn new skills	6.4	6.7	7.0	7.2

I worry about the future of my job	4.0	4.4	4.5	4.7
My job requires me to do the same things over and over again	6.7	6.2	5.6	5.9
My job provides me with a variety of interesting things to do	6.6	7.0	7.4	7.7
My job is complex and difficult	5.5	6.2	6.5	6.7
I have a lot of freedom to decide how I do my own work	6.7	7.5	7.7	7.7
Percent chance I will find and accept job at least as good as current job	87.8	80.1	81.2	72.3
Percent time spent in jobs in last financial year	61.6	94.2	96.1	95.5
Percent time spent unemployed in last financial year	3.7	2.3	1.5	1.8
Percent time spent not in the labour force in last financial year	34.7	3.5	2.4	2.7
Percent chance of losing job in next 12 months	11.6	17.6	12.9	13.5

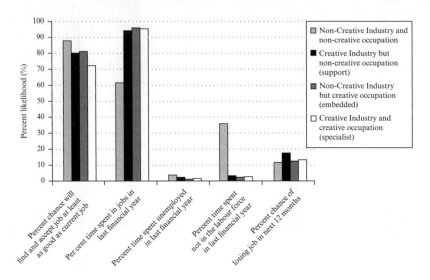

Figure 3.2   Job security by industry and occupation

job security. Generally, firms in Creative Industries are small and particularly susceptible to cyclical trends in the economy. Tellingly, those
in support occupations within the Creative Industries self-report the
highest chance of 'losing their jobs in the next 12 months' (see Figure 3.2).
We also find that, on average, those not employed in either a Creative
Industry or creative occupation (those outside the creative workforce)
spent more time unemployed and so by that measure experience greater
precarity than those in either/both a Creative Industry or/and occupation, yet reported greater confidence in finding a job at least as good as
the one they had (see Figure 3.2). While cyclical economic factors might
account for higher levels of job uncertainty at certain times, because the
survey has been conducted over a ten-year period, effects of cyclicality
have been dampened.

For some questions there is more noticeable divergence than for others,
yet, for the most part, there are no unexpected anomalies indicating much
higher levels of satisfaction in one cohort above all others. One of the most
interesting and somewhat surprising observations is the extent to which
creative occupations are characterized as complex and difficult, time
intensive, interesting and varied, and knowledge intensive. The specialists
report higher levels of satisfaction with 'the work itself', but lower levels of
satisfaction with total pay, yet overall each group is equally satisfied with
their job. Given the overall satisfaction, we might surmise that the work is
to some extent its own reward – and that such work is rare. As mentioned

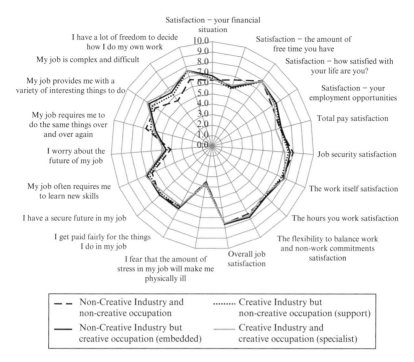

Satisfaction – your financial situation

I have a lot of freedom to decide how I do my own work

My job is complex and difficult

My job provides me with a variety of interesting things to do

My job requires me to do the same things over and over again

I worry about the future of my job

My job often requires me to learn new skills

I have a secure future in my job

I get paid fairly for the things I do in my job

I fear that the amount of stress in my job will make me physically ill

Overall job satisfaction

Satisfaction – the amount of free time you have

Satisfaction – how satisfied with your life are you?

Satisfaction – your employment opportunities

Total pay satisfaction

Job security satisfaction

The work itself satisfaction

The hours you work satisfaction

The flexibility to balance work and non-work commitments satisfaction

– – Non-Creative Industry and non-creative occupation	······· Creative Industry but non-creative occupation (support)
—— Non-Creative Industry but creative occupation (embedded)	——— Creative Industry and creative occupation (specialist)

Note: Several questions are similar (for example, about 'job security satisfaction' and 'I have a secure job in my future'). The questions about 'overall job satisfaction' and 'I get paid fairly for the things I do' would also be expected to correlate strongly, as indeed they do. These are standard ways of checking the robustness of a question by pitching it differently and eliminating framing bias.

Figure 3.3   Job satisfaction and security by industry and occupation

above, specialists report the lowest (72 per cent) confidence in being able to find another job at least as good at their current job (see Figure 3.2). By contrast, embedded creatives enjoy high satisfaction with their total pay, reporting greatest satisfaction with the statement that they 'get paid fairly for their work' (see Figure 3.3).

Psychologist Csíkszentmihályi's theory of Flow (Csíkszentmihályi, Abuhamdeh and Nakamura 2005) might provide some account as to why, despite lower levels of satisfaction with pay, job security and hours, those in creative occupations or industries experience a level of overall job satisfaction in line with others. Csíkszentmihályi's theory refers to a desirable psychological state where people are peak-performing. One of the conditions for this state is as follows: 'One must have a good balance between the perceived challenges of the task at hand and his or her own perceived skills. One must have confidence that he or she is capable to do the task at hand' (Csíkszentmihályi, Abuhamdeh and Nakamura 2005, 601). Since specialists or embedded creatives are more likely to be challenged by their work (complex and difficult) in a way that is both interesting and varied, we might expect them to achieve the state of Flow more frequently than their counterparts engaged in non-creative occupations or industries. Despite the possibility of this group achieving Flow, the associated happiness we ought to find as a result is not apparent: against the variable 'How satisfied with life are you?' we see convergence of results among all the groups, suggesting that no one group is significantly happier with life than any other.

So what do these results show? First, we should appreciate that this is a large panel. While not as large as a population survey (for example, a national census), such surveys do not include the kind of specific questions about decomposed satisfactions to enable the kind of inference derived here. So these results are as good as the data allow. Second, it is not just a survey of Creative Industries or occupations, but an economy-wide panel, enabling comparisons to be made. Our analysis can be extended to more specific industry comparisons; however, there are some statistical constraints. Overall, the results we find are not unexpected, and indeed confirm intuitive perceptions of employment in the creative workforce as offering, on average, more satisfying than secure employment.

The differences between the creative and non-creative cohorts broken down by industry, occupation and both seem to be relatively minor, and all of them tend in the same direction. There is slight evidence that the occupational differences are the smallest, which is also what we would expect given that this is where the impact of mobility and specialization would be greatest.

The embedded creatives show the highest levels of permanent or ongoing employment (they have the lowest incidence of independent contracting) and similarly report the highest levels of entitlement to paid leave, for either sickness or maternity. They do not, however, report the highest levels of flexibility for start/finish times or home-based work (something that is highest in the non-creative roles within the Creative Industries); see Figure 3.4.

Those employed inside the Creative Trident are more than twice as likely as those outside it to have the opportunity to work from home. Similarly, non-Trident workers are 20 per cent less likely to have the convenience of flexible start and finish times at work; see Figure 3.4.

Specifically, total pay satisfaction is 6 per cent lower for specialist creatives, as opposed to their embedded counterparts, and similarly lower on dimensions of 'Job security' and 'Hours worked'. Satisfaction with

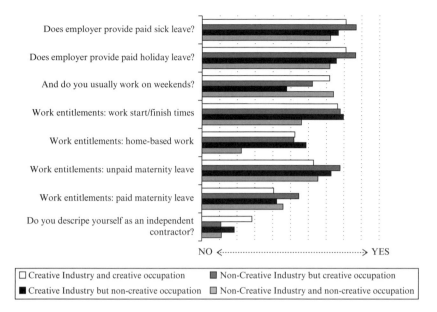

Figure 3.4   Employment conditions by industry and occupation

number of hours worked is about only 3 per cent lower, suggesting that this is partially chosen. Specialists indicate higher levels of satisfaction than embedded creatives with the amount of free time they have. There is an elevated expectation that work stress will lead to sickness, which is consistent with longer hours and greater precarity. And there is also a sense that pay satisfaction is lower than average. This statistic, however, needs to be carefully interpreted with respect to comparable sectors, rather than an economy-wide average, as there is substantial variation. But overall, these are significant differentials that suggest, based on these factors, that employment in Creative Industries is not as good as in other industries. That being said, outside the Creative Industries the embedded creatives indicate the highest levels of satisfaction with their financial situation and job security.

But if different parts of the table are read, another story emerges. While these differences are less pronounced, they suggest that creative occupations are more satisfying than average (for example, 'the work itself'), enable greater lifestyle flexibility, and allow people to work the hours they want. Interestingly, the baseline indicator of 'satisfaction with your own life' (Figure 3.3) tips a little towards suggesting that there are systemic differences in the type of people who choose this sector in the first place.

The main result we want to highlight, and which supports the compensating differentials argument, is the statistics on overall job satisfaction and 'I get paid fairly for what I do', both of which are within the same range as 'Overall, how satisfied are you with your life?' This means that, while there is some evidence of precarity and stress in Creative Industries, there is equal evidence of compensating factors, whether these relate to the perks of the job, to wages, or to flexibility, or to something else.

CONCLUSIONS

This brief report has presented the results of an interrogation of the HILDA panel looking for systematic differences between creative and non-creative employment as classified by creative occupation or not, by Creative Industries or not, or by creative occupation in the Creative Industries or not. Our motivation for this enquiry was to examine whether creative employment is as precarious and uncertain as many critics and commentators from political economy and media and cultural studies have alleged (see, for example, Ross 2009; Banks and Hesmondhalgh 2009), but also to enquire whether there was evidence that this was a problem overall.

   We have approached this question from within the framework of labour economics and with respect to the theory of compensating differentials. This argues that any occupation that has characteristics that are especially odious or unpleasant will have compensating differentials, most likely in wages, but possibly in other perquisites, that balance out and equalize differences across occupations or industries. Similarly, these compensating differentials can take the form of pleasant working conditions, small prospects of great fame or fortune, and so on. In the absence of these compensating differentials, where some jobs are systematically unpleasant or enjoyable, we would expect shortages or queues to form, driving wages up or down until an equilibrium (an indifference among jobs) is restored. The evidence we found (specifically in terms of 'overall job satisfaction' and 'I get paid fairly for what I do') is that the theory of compensating differentials seems to fit the Creative Industries labour market, both within the sector and across creative occupations.

   What this means, in other words, is that, even though there is substantial evidence of precarity, job insecurity and higher levels of job stress, this is not necessarily something that we should worry about. Put differently, suppose you could magically wave a legislative wand and make precarity go away in this sector. Would you do it? The theory of compensating differentials, and the evidence gathered here, suggest probably not, because it would lead to a new equilibrium in which other factors changed to balance the increased attractiveness of jobs in this sector. A likely implication would be lowered wages or some wage equivalent.

The point we seek to make here is that, when people argue about the problem of employment precarity in the Creative Industries, they invoke the notion that its elimination would be a good thing. If precarity is bad, then its elimination will be good. But simple economics explains why this attitude is wrong. If there is basic freedom of people to move between jobs, and if there is basic information about what different jobs offer and involve, then we would expect some manner of equilibrium tendency. In essence, precarity trades off against other factors that constitute a creative job, whether embedded or specialist. The logic by which this process works out is the economics of compensating differentials, and what our exercise here in comparative HILDA-based analysis shows is that this does seem to hold also in the Creative Industries and for creative occupations.

NOTES

1. Of course, we acknowledge that efficient labour markets are not necessarily reality and inequities influence employment access.
2. This is not to say that they reported job insecurity, just that they reported less security than their counterparts.

REFERENCES

Banks, M. and D. Hesmondhalgh (2009), 'Looking for work in creative industries policy', *International Journal of Cultural Policy*, **15** (4), 415–30.
Csíkszentmihályi, M., S. Abuhamdeh and J. Nakamura (2005), 'Flow', in A.J. Elliot and C.S. Dweck (eds), *Handbook of Competence and Motivation*, New York: Guilford Press, pp. 598–608.
Edwards, R. (2006), 'Maternity leave and the evidence for compensating differentials in Australia', *Economic Record*, **82** (259), 281–97.
Fama, E. (1965), 'The behavior of stock market prices', *Journal of Business*, **38** (1), 34–105.
Higgs, P. and S. Cunningham (2007), *Australia's Creative Economy: Mapping Methodology*, Brisbane: Australian Research Council Centre of Excellence for Creative Industries and Innovation.
Higgs, P., S. Cunningham and J. Pagan (2007), *Australia's Creative Economy: Basic Evidence on Size, Growth, Income and Employment*, Brisbane: Australian Research Council Centre of Excellence for Creative Industries and Innovation.
Potts, J. (2006), 'How creative are the super-rich?', *Agenda*, **13** (4), 139–50.
Rosen, S. (1986), 'The theory of equalizing differences', in O. Ashenfelter and

R. Layard (eds), *The Handbook of Labor Economics* (vol. 1), New York: Elsevier, pp. 641–92.

Ross, A. (2009), *Nice Work if You Can Get It: Life and Labor in Precarious Times*, New York: New York University Press.

Wooden, M. and N. Watson (2007), 'The HILDA survey and its contribution to economic and social research (so far)', *Economic Record*, **83** (261), 208–31.

4. Creative digital services in education, mining and manufacturing: pursuing innovation through interoperability*

Dan Swan and Greg Hearn

INTRODUCTION

Increasingly, creative workers are deploying their capacities in other sectors outside their core industry, either through the provision of Creative Services, or as employees embedded in other sectors (Hearn et al., Chapter 1 in this volume).[1] Furthermore, in most cases, the highest numbers of people in these embedded creative occupations work in digital content and software (Goldsmith, Chapter 8 in this volume). Mirroring this need for digital creative workers across all industries, growth in the provision of creative digital services to other industries is part of a longer-term, sharp growth of knowledge-intensive business services (see, for example, Miles 2005, 2008). The provision of creative digital services (including the creation and utilization of middleware) is now recognized by Screen Australia as an important diversification strategy for the games industry (Screen Australia 2011). Similarly, Australia's broadband strategy notes that 'the use of networked, digital technology spreads across all industry sectors' (Department of Broadband, Communications and the Digital Economy 2009, 3). The Australian Interactive Media Industry Association's 2009 *Digital Services Index* also noted the continuing rise of digital services to all industry sectors in Australia. This chapter examines a program where creative digital services were paired with other businesses for mutual benefit. Situating our discussion in the context of the Creative Economy, we describe the case studies and how the partnerships were beneficial. We argue that this mutual interaction and integration of knowledge exchanges that foster innovation suggest a notion of 'interoperability'.

THE OPPORTUNITY: AN ENABLER OF INNOVATION IN OTHER INDUSTRIES

One reason for the growth in creative digital services to other industries is that they are drivers of innovation (Cunningham 2013). Innovation-based growth built on creative innovation carries with it the possibility of parallel growth in employment, and so it can be clearly distinguished from productivity increases that come from reducing the number of workers employed (Hearn and Mandeville 2005). Potts (2012) argues that Creative Industries affect all phases of innovation: the creation, adoption and retention of new products or services. A survey of 2000 European creative firms provides empirical support for this proposition (Müller, Rammer and Trüby 2009). The survey results showed that these companies helped create innovation across a variety of other sectors through their creative inputs. These included new products, supplementary products and services or marketing support. Software and advertising companies showed the strongest links to these innovations. However, as this chapter will argue, the integration of creative components into services or products in other sectors is not always straightforward. The need to understand what makes a creative intervention 'interoperable' with products or services in other industries is a major finding of the current study, to which we return in the conclusion.

THE INTERVENTION SCHEME[2]

A creative digital skills Intervention Scheme pilot system was funded (2010–2012) by the Australian and Victorian governments to identify and pilot models for addressing workforce development needs in the Australian games and creative digital media industries. The Intervention Scheme's purpose was to develop a pilot system to address the unmet demands for labour and skills reported by the Australian games (and broader digital services) industry, so that the industry might take full advantage of new market opportunities created through innovative applications of interactive media to other industries and public sectors. The emphasis was not just on providing standard interactive gaming and digital services but, through the pilot system, also driving innovations in the host companies (the non-creative companies with which the digital creative service companies were partnered).

Using a comparative case study approach, rich longitudinal descriptions of pilot projects were developed using three waves of interviews and other evidence sources over a six-month pilot system period to evaluate the pilot Intervention Scheme. Comparison case studies were developed over the same period using pre-test and post-test interviews. These comparative studies looked at projects that applied for funding as part of the scheme, but did not receive it nor participate in the pilot system. In the current chapter we focus on only the three integration cases that received funding in order to describe the embedding process and to postulate that 'interoperability', which we define later, is a key factor in the successful knowledge exchange and integration of digital creative teams in other industry sectors. The Intervention Scheme pilot system emphasized forming partnerships that 'explore how we can work together to help both our businesses benefit', rather than regular fee-for-service relationships where the digital creative business was subordinate to the host company. It is this reciprocal collaboration between the host company and the digital creative business that suggests the notion of 'interoperability' as the mutual interaction and integration of knowledge exchanges that enable innovation.

CASE STUDY SELECTION CRITERIA

Leading Australian firms and organizations were invited to participate by the Intervention Scheme through industry networks, public speaking forums and the Intervention Scheme public website, where expression-of-interest forms were made available. Host firms, from varying sectors, and digital services applicants submitted eligibility requirements, selection criteria and an application form, which the committee reviewed to arrive at a shortlist. Each application was then reviewed, assessed and matched (or discarded) by the Intervention Scheme Selection Committee. The Committee consisted of the project director, key stakeholders, together with the mentors identified for each project.[3] Final selection and one-to-one matching were arranged through interviews and meetings of the host business with the creative digital team for selection and contractual agreement (see Table 4.1).[4]

EDUCATION CASE STUDY

Edumedia, an educational digital services company, focuses on interactive education solutions, for not-for-profit and corporate clients Edumedia is a new micro-business with three core founders who possess a blend of technical, design, project management and classroom education capabilities. Although the depth of individual experience is vast, the business

Table 4.1 Case study companies and sectors

Intervention	Education		Mining		Manufacturing	
Pilot system firm	The Regional University, Neuro-Learning Research Centre	Edumedia	Pioneering Mining Innovations	Viz Dat	Rotation Systems	Excel Media
Pilot type	Pilot host	Pilot creative	Pilot host	Pilot creative	Pilot host	Pilot creative
Sector	Education (university)	Digital services (education)	Mining services (data)	Digital services (visualization)	Manufacturing	Digital services (gaming)
Product/service	Product	Service	Service & product	Service	Product	Service
Size	Large/SME (small to medium enterprise)	Micro	SME	Micro	SME	SME
Digital skills	Low	High	Medium	High	Low	High

Note: Size is graded by approximate full-time employee numbers (FTE) since numbers generally fluctuate between FTE and contractors, especially in the target Creative Services firms.

is in its 'start-up' phase of development. Edumedia was matched with the Neuro-Learning Research Centre, part of The Regional University. Specifically, the target project for the pilot system was the Research Centre's 'NeuroSmart' neuroscience-based research program, which has developed a product aimed at improving literacy and numeracy for under-achieving school students. Initially with the Intervention Scheme, The Regional University wanted to explore the concept of 'NeuroSmart in the Home', that is, moving from the school classroom and bringing its existing successful skills programs (such as the 'Flash Card' kit) to parents or carers at home, using interactive online gaming techniques. NeuroSmart has relied on grants and public funding projects and, with the combined help of the Intervention Scheme pilot system, the Research Centre has also been able to explore the online commercialization of NeuroSmart. This transformation relies on the ability to work with other industry groups (particularly creative media teams). Hitherto, prior to participation in the Intervention Scheme's pilot system, experience outside the Research Centre was limited to external schools and Research Services at The Regional University.

Through the Intervention Scheme pilot system, Edumedia's objectives were aligned to develop a proof-of-concept that fulfilled The Regional University's requirement of a 'minimal viable product' (MVP), and to develop and maintain an ongoing relationship with the wider university. During the early stages of the pilot system, the Intervention Scheme promoted a process of discovery. This was critical for defining the achievable outputs of the project and setting client expectations. 'Speaking the client's language' is an important aspect of Edumedia's business practice, and this aligned well with the Intervention Scheme's approach to the integration, facilitating communication between technical and non-technical entities. Through the approach of the pilot system, during the initial stages the only barriers to communication were the demanding schedules of all those involved. Edumedia reported that, without the support of the Intervention Scheme, working relationships would have been slower to form. Being a micro-business, Edumedia has been unable to plan process change and innovation strategy to align with project deliverables due to the multiple sources of regional, state and federal funding NeuroSmart has begun to attract. The Intervention Scheme business mentor helped Edumedia take steps towards creating a prototype roadmap and broader innovation processes, similar to the pilot system, for the Research Centre. For the discovery phase in particular, it was important that this included a formal process of relationship building with the external organization, that is, sharing the creative digital service process with the increasing number of interested stakeholders from The Regional University. At an early stage of the project, The Regional University and the Research Centre were able to broaden NeuroSmart objectives beyond those that were initially proposed to the Intervention Scheme. Without this phase, the Research Centre would have had narrower goals, employed a consultant, or relied on limited internal expertise, suppliers and networks.

The Regional University saw the Intervention Scheme's role as building the Research Centre's capacity to innovate online and cope with the growing demand for NeuroSmart that already existed in schools. Collectively it was recognized that a much broader program for 'NeuroSmart Online' was possible. NeuroSmart in the Home (learning for school children) grew also to become a prototype for 'NeuroSmart for Adults' (assisting, for example, learning for jobseekers). By recognizing this program path with the pilot system, the Research Centre saw that, with greater online access and faster networks, the need emerged to grow digital capabilities and extend relationships where skills were previously spread too thin. Edumedia identified that it had the necessary personnel and digital skills to help the Research Centre achieve goals during the very early stages of the incubation phase: its view was that it was small enough to react quickly and without internal conflict. Through the discovery phase and a number of incubation stages, Edumedia managed challenges that arose by maintaining its 'nimble' approach. For instance, in the initial stages of the discovery phase Edumedia had to adapt quickly to the loss of its pilot system creative partner East Digital Games, which presented additional skills gaps for project validation and delivery of prototyping.[5] In the course of the subsequent incubation stage, with the growth of NeuroSmart for Adults, Edumedia was able to adapt to the changing requirements and skills needed for development by engaging contract consultants, as well as student placements provided through the Intervention Scheme. While these unexpected management overheads were taxing for Edumedia, structural changes within the company (in terms of key personnel) were minimal. The key challenge for Edumedia was maintaining resources to match the project demands alongside cash flow. In this case, the pilot system provided sufficient mediation to limit the impact of additional project requirements and mitigate strain on working relationships.

As a result of the collaboration with Edumedia, The Regional University Research Centre realized the outcome of years of research: the faithful online translation of NeuroSmart. This outcome of a first-release prototype prompted a more widely funded project (outside the six-month pilot system project) of NeuroSmart Online, a formal 12- to 24-month product program in a national adult numeracy learning setting. The Regional University and the Research Centre are expecting to roll out the MVP early in 2014. Research Centre directors were gratified by the outcomes of the pilot system, in that not only do they have viable outcomes of the project – detailed functional specifications and proof-of-concepts that are testable – but they have also been able to extend their research, broaden the reach of NeuroSmart into new sectors, and develop a formal product with national government support. Learnings from involvement in the Intervention Scheme will be carried into all stages of future development. The process provided a common language needed to engage with digital creative teams, and the skills to articulate problems and solutions, not in technical (that is, IT) terms, but within their educational expertise. Edumedia has also learned key skills – managing projects with larger organizations as well as developing the company around a successful case study that has helped it to win new business. Both partners have achieved commercial outcomes, including new commercial applications for NeuroSmart Online, such as education in the Mining sector, which may see it break away from The Regional University into its own commercial entity.

MINING CASE STUDY

Viz Dat, the digital creative team for mining integration, is an award-winning interactive media and data visualization company, founded in 1999 by its CEO of 2013. Its focus is on traditional industries that have problems sharing information (such as large data sets) with their clients. As a micro-business (fewer than five full-time staff), Viz Dat offers fee-for-service tools and methodologies in data visualization, overall user interface, user experience and content creation. Established in 1998 also by its CEO of 2013, Pioneering Mining Innovations was the host business matched with Viz Dat. Pioneering Mining Innovations is a data services company for the mining industry, specializing in providing insights into mining equipment productivity, benchmarking and analysis of people, performance and potential productivity. As a small to medium enterprise (SME) of around 15 full-time employees, Pioneering Mining Innovations has limited capacity to innovate in house and grow. In addition to fiscal growth, a general goal for Pioneering Mining Innovations's business model is to balance business peaks and troughs.

The pilot system helped Viz Dat complete a project with a large data set, and it is hoped that the Intervention Scheme pilot system will function as a case study and model for other cross-industry partnerships, particularly (but not exclusively) in the mining industry. In the past, Viz Dat has recognized that some of its processes could improve, particularly when dealing with cross-industry information exchange and knowledge transfer. The

CEO saw the opportunity to branch out into R&D through the innovation processes brought by the pilot system. A specific goal was product creation in contrast to a more commoditized approach associated with relying on fee-for-service work. Without the pilot system, Viz Dat would have had a much more fragmented approach to R&D, which would have been funded and executed through individual projects, with additional funding from leveraging assets through bank capital (for example, non-investment loans).

Pioneering Mining Innovations defined success as achieving a deliverable and demonstrable product, not just a process. It had a specific business problem identified for the Intervention Scheme: it produces very detailed and precise paper-based reports to its mining sector clients. The quality and depth of these reports are beyond question, and can help the company's clients increase productivity by billions of dollars. However, due to their size and level of detail, the reports can be inaccessible and ineffective for communicating key learnings to vital team members (on-site supervisors, payload drivers etc.) beyond the first reading audience (senior managers). The solution conceived through the Intervention Scheme was an interactive online data visualization tool to enable users to transform data into concise and manageable reports in the form of visual graphics.

Pioneering Mining Innovations has previously worked with business coaches, consultants and, more recently, Opportunity Join, which introduced them to the Intervention Scheme to seek solutions for their business problem.[6] A challenge for Viz Dat was that Pioneering Mining Innovations had previously developed a possible solution: project 'SquidInk', a back-end product to assist on-site supervisors with methodology. Pioneering Mining Innovations partnered with a mine and took the project to the prototype stage; however, the mine changed its processes and so abandoned the prototype, resulting in a very expensive loss for the company. Pioneering Mining Innovations had a clear vision for its product when it joined the Intervention Scheme, but was unsure how to get there. Based on previous experiences, the company wanted to build a relationship and partnership to overcome issues by consensus. Hence, at the discovery phase, the pilot system encouraged Pioneering Mining Innovations to improve the structure of its decision-making process. This was a valuable step since, as a small business, Pioneering Mining Innovations was aware that it tended to react according to demand rather than develop new markets.

For Viz Dat, the early phase of the project caused no significant structural change to its organization even with the new joint venture agreement with Pioneering Mining Innovations. Viz Dat saw this phase as normal practice, realigning the pilot integration project goals by agreeing on intellectual property (IP) ownership and licensing models. This enabled Viz Dat to develop and validate the overall prototype approach and business model alongside Pioneering Mining Innovations, supported with the neutral advice of the Intervention Scheme business mentor assigned to this group. The approach also allowed Viz Dat to deliver iteratively, so that Pioneering Mining Innovations could test and assess in very specific stages. Because iterative deliverables were set alongside pilot system milestones, results were delivered quickly and aided both businesses to work with minimal conflict. Iterative development allows for quick assessment by all parties whereby the digital team frequently releases design and code segments for rapid assessment.[7] This process mitigates risk and increases quality of delivery by alleviating 'waste' caused by language issues often expected when managing data and visualization (that is, business/technical information aligning with creative/gaming presentation). The Intervention Scheme helped to set expectations during the discovery phase, but in particular it was the Intervention Scheme business mentor who played a large role in the project's success in developing a new business model to support the project outcome.

The discovery phase was where the Intervention Scheme was most able to 'broker' the relationship between Viz Dat and Pioneering Mining Innovations by identifying compatibilities and aligning relationships, business processes and outcomes. A tangible example of the pilot scheme's role in relationship building was the recommendation that both businesses seek legal advice on the IP brought to the project, the IP created through the pilot system, and the IP that fell outside these two scenarios. The Intervention Scheme mentors' experience in innovation and commercialization was integral to the discovery process, which included advice surrounding developing business models that would benefit both the host and creative business around the new joint venture.[8] The joint venture IP is a visualization tool that connects with Pioneering Mining Innovations's back-end data. It allows deep analysis and data mining through visual tools and techniques. As well as helping Pioneering Mining Innovations roll out the visualization tool, Viz Dat has also been talking with other sectors and companies that may take up the tool. Participation in the Intervention Scheme pilot system has helped stabilize its business, not only via tangible outcomes but also through rigid processes of delivery and development to a definable business (licensing) model.

Pioneering Mining Innovations's business model underwent significant structural change as a result of the Intervention Scheme pilot system. The discovery stages helped move its business beyond a scrvices and consultancy model to the creation of an entirely new business division called 'Pioneering Mining Innovations Data'. In the initial stages, Pioneering

Mining Innovations's goal was to open up its services, but this progressed to significant organizational change. Through the iterative development process, Pioneering Mining Innovations's understanding of Viz Dat's solutions improved and, as outcomes through the pilot system became much more apparent, so did broader possibilities. Pioneering Mining Innovations recognized that the pilot system could give it a framework and an engine for its whole product. As a result of very close work with the Intervention Scheme mentor, the licensing model developed was also validated through an external consulting group, Smith-Brown. As these tools develop and business grows, it is conceivable that Pioneering Mining Innovations Data will become the core business, and Pioneering Mining Innovations a more globally scalable company. International growth will also mean that Pioneering Mining Innovations gains expertise with new data sets and new markets from Australia and 'above-ground' mining to Asian 'below-ground' mining.

MANUFACTURING CASE STUDY

Excel Media, founded in 2008, is a media services company specializing in gaming, video production and digital media development. Its goal was a specific six-month development program through the Intervention Scheme, which it hoped would lead to a longer-term relationship with its eventual partner, Rotation Systems, and allow it to expand into government and as well as manufacturing sectors. With 12 full-time employees, most with creative digital skills, Excel Media's medium- to long-term goal was to separate the business into distinct services (consultancy) and product organizations (the latter owning IP) in order to help its highly creative culture become more business savvy. Rotation Systems is an independently owned family business that began manufacturing large turntables for exhibition events, and now produces turntables for numerous applications and sectors around the world. Rotation Systems specializes in rotational movement – leveraging, creating and saving space – through innovative design and manufacturing methods, such as laser-cutting technology. Family owned and operated, Rotation Systems values relationships as deeply important and, through the Intervention Scheme, was looking for a clear and reliable relationship network to understand and share its risk.

The discovery phase began with a two-day workshop at the host business (Rotation Systems) conducted to establish requirements and goals, and set expectations. This phase revealed a perceivable skills gap with the host: although the outcomes of the Intervention Scheme pilot system were viable, the creative team anticipated that the internal processes and systems of Rotation Systems would need to develop digitally to fully streamline its business. The aim of the Intervention Scheme pilot system for Rotation Systems was also less clearly defined. The company saw an opportunity to increase market share through digital showcasing of products, as well as using online distribution networks to gain entry to new markets. Without the Intervention Scheme, Rotation Systems would have pursued digital marketing to solve these solutions, due to a general lack of knowledge surrounding digital and online media. Upon reflection and through pilot system observations, Rotation Systems came to believe that digital marketing would either not have succeeded, or provided a much more limited outcome.

Before the Intervention Scheme partnership, Rotation Systems's cross-industry experience was limited to engineers, architects and some town planners. In all cases, interactions centred on raising awareness of product specifications and capabilities. Rotation Systems must understand its partners' processes in order to achieve a mutually agreeable outcome. A key obstacle was that, by its own admission, Rotation Systems lacked any specific digital creative experience internally or any previous external engagement in the area. Through the pilot system discovery phase, Excel Media developed new ways of engaging with Rotation Systems to form a strong partnership with the creative team. Notably, Excel Media ran onsite workshops designed to reveal the 'blue sky' ambitions of Rotation Systems. This had the effect of Excel Media coming to understand Rotation Systems's processes and operations, which it was able to align with realistic goals for the six months of the pilot system period.

As a result of the discovery phase of the pilot system, Rotation Systems underwent significant changes. The company has struggled with the logistics of getting people 'on the ground' quickly to maintain its products (for warranty and maintenance). To solve this, the company developed the goal that the platform prototype created with the pilot system would enable a service provider model, assisting distributors with supervision and installation. This model would free Rotation Systems to focus more on design and engineering value by outsourcing sales, servicing and maintenance of products to a global network of distributors via the online platform. The increasing cost of manufacturing in Australia is a major factor driving this change, and the pilot system assisted Rotation Systems to act more quickly to develop its new model. Eventually, the platform will include a back-end framework that will allow the company to select and attract distributors, assess security, perform due diligence and manage month-to-month dealings. This framework will also integrate the firm's internal customer relationship management information and enterprise resource planning systems, combining to form the overall 'platform'.

In the short term, Rotation Systems's goal in the acceleration phase will be to focus on outsourcing sales through an 'extranet' portal, and in the medium term, by redeploying resources to concentrate on product management and manufacturing innovation. The company hopes to open this up publicly to break into new sectors with higher margins, such as mining, defence and outdoor installations. In the long term, it will be looking for investors in specialist machinery to develop these innovations.

For Excel Media, the Intervention Scheme brought about structural change, as the business diversified into separate consultancy and IP ownership arms. Excel sees the online platform as an enabler for companies such as Rotation Systems that need self-replicating communications networks for distribution. Through the Intervention Scheme, Excel Media has also connected with one of the Intervention Scheme's non-selected pilot businesses, Brakes Inc. (part of the control group study). Brakes Inc. – a leading Australian aftermarket brake manufacture founded in 1955 and now part of an international aftermarket automotive group – initially proposed the creation of its own platform for training suppliers and distributors called 'CarWorkshop'. As part of a significant selection process of nine other competitors' suppliers, Brakes Inc. selected Excel Media based on the platform developed as part of the Intervention Scheme pilot system.

DISCUSSION

Hearn and Mandeville (2005) proposed two scenarios in which information and communications technology (ICT) improves productivity in different industries. The first is by improving efficiencies and reducing the number of people required. The second is by innovations that expand and multiply revenues through new products, markets or business models. Mudambi (2008) suggests that this is achieved through design at the beginning of the value chain, and creative brands and advertising at the consumption end of the value chain. Mudambi also argues that value is created through ways of organizing these creative resources in the value chain that are hard for other companies to replicate.

These Intervention Scheme pilot system projects exemplify the second type of innovation path identified by Hearn and Mandeville (2005) and referred to by Mudambi (2008). For example, in the case of Pioneering Mining Innovations, interactive online visualization tools enabled the development of a new service model (via subscription rather than fee-for-service), which expands the market of potential clients that can be serviced by the same team, as well as expanding the possibility of new international markets. In the case of Rotation Systems, the pilot system enabled the creation of an international network of alliance partners, a case of Mudambi's hard-to-replicate organizing mode. The rich case studies provided by the Intervention Scheme are thus very relevant to all Australian industries, but particularly SMEs vying to be competitive in the global economy.

These types of ICT deployments have been identified as components of 'High Performing Workplaces' (see Boedker et al. 2011). According to these authors,

> ICT in High Performing Workplaces also supports the organisation's business strategies and organisations that consider themselves to have good alignment between their business and ICT strategies are associated with higher levels of performance. In such instances, ICT can help to improve the quality of services and customer experience by allowing the organisation to analyse the nature of customer and stakeholder relations and by building new types of connectivity between the organisation and its environment. (Ibid., 55)

A key factor in the success of Intervention Scheme was the brokering process, which involved a combination of matching, individual facilitation and mentoring. As Browne and Hamouda (2010, 6) suggest,

> The success factors of Silicon Valley start-ups are stated to include their company founders learning through mentoring. It has been indicated that those firms can raise seven times more funding and have three and a half times more user growth than those without mentors. Furthermore, a balance of technical and business acumen in the firm facilitates those firms to raise thirty per cent more money, have almost three times more user growth, and are almost twenty per cent less likely to scale prematurely than technical or business-heavy founding teams.

Hearn and Rooney (2008) argue that, while the source of innovation will be mainly the private sector, there is a role for government in facilitating innovation. Third parties that facilitate innovation are very important. R&D outputs with reproducible qualities can clearly be validated by Intervention Scheme-like partner organizations as intermediaries. These intermediaries (such as the Intervention Scheme) are open innovation facilitators, who can help both sides of the market (Ollila and Elmquist 2011; Vanhaverbeke 2009).

> These innovation intermediaries actively connect the supply and demand sides of the market, forging links between firms searching for external ideas (innovation seekers) with communities of highly-qualified solution providers (innovation solvers). (Ibid., 2)

CONCLUSION

Research has also begun to explore the contribution of the Creative Industries to innovation in other sectors:

> The Creative Industries' contribution to innovation in other sectors of the economy is strongly linked to the concept of open innovation (see Chesbrough 2002; Laursen and Salter 2006). Successful innovation most often requires the combination of a firm's own innovative resources with external inputs. (Müller, Rammer and Trüby 2009, 158)

The cases presented here exemplify this thinking. Collaborative exchanges between sectors and systems are implied when creatives operate inter-organizationally across many industry sectors, whether as employees or as service providers. Two processes arguably underlie this collaborative process. First, the Intervention Scheme brokering was necessary for part-nerships between hosts and digital creative firms to occur. In the subse-quent embedded phases of 'discovery' and 'incubation' we suggest that it was the bridging of knowledge systems that was then necessary for success-ful innovation. In future analyses we intend to explore the role of shared language in this bridging and whether other facilitating activities – such as mentoring, playing-field neutrality and support toolkits – also depended on this foundation of shared language. This raises important questions surrounding the nature and systems of the shared language required for embedded Creative Industries knowledge. Much work already exists around complex systems and how organizational systems interoperate (Australian Government Information Management Office 2006; Palfrey and Gasser 2007; Pagano 2011; Lumsden, Hall and Cruickshank 2011; Gonçalves 2012; Spagnoletti and Za 2012). However, none satisfactorily explain, from either Creative Industries and/or open innovation perspec-tives, how knowledge flows, and how exchanges and transfers take place to innovate and appropriate value. Early research in information sharing, for example, placed much emphasis on technical systems interoperability. Now the drive by large organizations to open their systems for knowledge sharing has changed the emphasis of interoperability. It is no longer solely about technology compatibility or integration, but instead it is concerned with how systems can serve external markets and enable innovative business models. Müller, Rammer and Trüby (2009) suggest that, as producers of IP, the Creative Industries are an attractive external source for firms seeking open innovation. However, a formal evaluation of the Intervention Scheme showed that, without the intervention of programs that enable brokering and bridging, organizations struggle to engage with the knowledge provided by Creative Industries companies in order to produce valuable creative outcomes. We suggest that the idea of embedded creative interoperability, which encompasses brokering and bridging, is an explanatory concept worth exploring in future studies.

NOTES

* The research described in this chapter was funded by the Australian and Victorian Government.
1. Creative Services refers to those sectors that provide business-to-business services. Creative Service segments are categorized as such by the Australian Research Council Centre of Excellence for Creative Industries and Innovation: architecture and design; advertising and marketing; software and digital content.
2. The names of all participants, organizations and projects, including the Intervention Scheme itself, have been changed for the purposes of confidentiality and anonymity. It is the intention that any pseudonyms used are fictional and do not relate to any actual participant, organization or project. Any fictional name used that may in fact relate to a real identity or entity should be deemed coincidental. The authors may be contacted in writing for informed consent relating to the real identities of participants, organizations and projects, including details of the Intervention Scheme.
3. Each of the three Intervention Scheme pilot system projects was assigned an industry business mentor as a neutral mediator for both host and creative groups to consult independently and to provide advice on the overall project.
4. The host business provided cash funding for the pilot system project, whereas the digital creative team commitment was paid for by the Intervention Scheme and the host business; hence the latter two parties have the final veto on the selection.
5. East Digital Games and Edumedia were initially partnered by the Intervention Scheme for the pilot system as they were both small digital creative firms with complementary skills applicable for the project. East Digital Games, however, disbanded with the loss of one of its key designers.
6. Opportunity Join offers comprehensive, confidential advice and support to eligible Australian small and medium businesses to help them transform and reach their full potential.
7. Viz Dat used 'Lean Software Development', part of the Agile iterative methodology (Poppendieck and Poppendieck 2003).
8. The joint venture split is 75/25 in favour of the host business, Pioneering Mining Innovations.

REFERENCES

Australian Government Information Management Office (2006), *Australian Government Information Interoperability Framework*, available at http://agict. gov.au/files/2012/04/Information_Interoperability_Framework.pdf (accessed 27 August 2013).
Australian Interactive Media Industry Association (2009), *Australian Interactive Media Industry Association Digital Services Index: Measuring the Australian Digital Services Industry* (May).
Boedker, C., R. Vidgen, K. Meagher, J. Cogin, J. Mouritsen and R.M. Runnalls (2011), *Leadership, Culture and Management Practices of High Performing*

Workplaces in Australia: The High Performing Workplaces Index, Sydney, NSW: Society for Knowledge Economics.

Browne, A. and A. Hamouda (2010), 'A holistic view of "soft" support strategies for high-tech firms', presented at the Meeting of the Institute of Small Business & Entrepreneurship, Sheffield (November).

Chesbrough, H.C. (2003), *Open Innovation: The New Imperative for Creating and Profiting from Technology*, Boston, MA: Harvard Business School Press.

Cunningham, S. (2013), *Hidden Innovation: Policy, Industry and the Creative Sector*, St Lucia, Queensland: University of Queensland Press and Lexington Books, an imprint of Rowman & Littlefield.

Department of Broadband, Communications and the Digital Economy (2009), *Australia's Digital Economy: Future Directions*, Final Report. Canberra: Department of Broadband, Communications and the Digital Economy.

Gonçalves, R. (2012), 'Sustainability of systems interoperability in dynamic business networks', thesis, Faculdade de Ciências e Tecnologia, Universidade Nova, available at http://hdl.handle.net/10362/8582 (accessed 23 July 2013).

Hearn, G. and D. Rooney (2008), *Knowledge Policy: Challenges for the 21st Century*, Cheltenham, UK and Northampton, MA, USA: Edward Elgar.

Hearn, G. and T. Mandeville (2005), 'How to be productive in the knowledge economy: the case of ICTs', in D. Rooney, G. Hearn and A. Ninan (eds), *Handbook on the Knowledge Economy*, Cheltenham, UK and Northampton, MA, USA: Edward Elgar, pp. 255–67.

Laursen, K. and A. Salter (2006). 'Open for innovation: the role of openness in explaining innovation performance among U.K. manufacturing firms', *Strategic Management Journal*, 27 (2), 131–50.

Lumsden, J., H. Hall and P. Cruickshank (2011), 'Ontology definition and construction, and epistemological adequacy for systems interoperability: a practitioner analysis', *Journal of Information Science*, **37** (3), 246–53.

Miles, I. (2005), 'Knowledge intensive business services: prospects and policies', *Foresight*, **7** (6), 39–63.

Miles, I. (2008), 'Knowledge services', in G. Hearn and D. Rooney (eds), *Knowledge Policy: Challenges for the 21st Century*, Cheltenham, UK and Northampton, MA, USA: Edward Elgar, pp. 11–26.

Mudambi, R. (2008), 'Location, control, and innovation in knowledge-intensive industries', *Journal of Economic Geography*, **8** (5), 699–725.

Müller, K., C. Rammer and J. Trüby (2009), 'The role of creative industries in industrial innovation', *Innovation: Management, Policy & Practice*, **11**, 148–68.

Ollila, S. and M. Elmquist (2011), 'Managing open innovation: exploring challenges at the interfaces of an open innovation arena', *Creativity and Innovation Management*, **20** (4), 273–83.

Pagano, P. (2011), 'Data interoperability', paper presented at the GRDI 2020, Brussels, Belgium (October).

Palfrey, J. and U. Gasser (2007), 'Mashups interoperability and eInnovation', *Internet and Higher Education*, **10**, 196–203.

Poppendieck, M. and T. Poppendieck (2003), *Lean Software Development: An Agile Toolkit*, Reading, MA: Addison Wesley Professional.

Potts, J. (2012), 'Creative industries and innovation in a knowledge economy', in D. Rooney, G. Hearn and T. Kastelle (eds), *Handbook on the Knowledge*

Economy (vol. 2), Cheltenham, UK and Northampton, MA, USA: Edward Elgar Publishing, pp. 193–203.
Screen Australia (2011), *Playing For Keeps: Enhancing Sustainability in Australia's Interactive Entertainment Industry*, available at http://www.screenaustralia.gov. au/about_us/pub_gamesreport.aspx (accessed 19 August 2013).
Spagnoletti, P. and S. Za (2012), 'A design theory for e-service environments: the interoperability challenge', *Lecture Notes in Business Information Processing*, **103**, 201–11.
Vanhaverbeke, W. (2009), *How Innovation Intermediaries are Shaping the Technology Market? An Analysis of their Business Model*, Munich, Personal RePEc Archive, available at http://mpra.ub.uni-muenchen.de/27017/ (accessed 27 August 2013).

5. London's creative workforce

Alan Freeman

INTRODUCTION

In 2002, with Britain still bemoaning the loss of its traditional car industry and with manufacturing less than 10 per cent of the city's employment, Nissan opened a London design studio. 'The central London location in the rapidly developing area of the Paddington Basin was chosen because of its multi-cultural backdrop and the access it provides to important and influential sources in contemporary art, architecture, fashion and design movements', explained *Car Design News* (2003). The article continued:

> The studio is housed in The Rotunda, a former British Rail maintenance depot built in the 1960s which had fallen into disrepair and been unused since the 1980s. The site was selected specifically for its spacious interior which allowed Nissan to transform the building into a tailor-made urban design space.

In this most traditional of all 'industries', which gave birth to Henry Ford's famous dictum that 'you can have it any colour you want, as long as it's black', creative design, accessed via its embedded workforce, had become the new black.

Between 2002 and 2011 the Greater London Authority (GLA) produced five reports on employment and output in the Creative Industries in London, and the London Development Authority (LDA) produced *London: A Cultural Audit* (Freeman et al. 2008), a comparison of five global world cities on a wide range of cultural indicators.[1] A second edition in 2012, supported by the GLA, widened coverage to 12 cities, and rebranded the project as the *World Cities Culture Report*,[2] now headed for its third edition with over 20 participating cities. These studies found that London plays a highly distinctive role in the UK's Creative Economy. With its surrounds in the Greater South East, it accounted for nearly two-thirds of the UK's creative employment, half of this in London itself (Freeman 2009, 4).

Coining the term 'creative intensity' to designate the proportion of those working for creative firms who were engaged in creative occupations, the GLA found that this was systematically higher in London than elsewhere. According to the *2007 Update*, this proportion was 54 per cent compared to 45 per cent. Also, when examining all creative workers in the UK, the GLA found that the proportion of these who worked for creative firms was nearly twice as high in London as elsewhere in the UK.

Moreover, in the language of the Centre for Creative Industries and Innovations's Trident methodology, London's embedded creative workforce was also emerging as an important contributor to other sectors. Across all sectors in London the proportion of workers in creative occupations was 14 per cent. London, these results suggested, was a crucible in which the creative workforce of today was forging the Creative Economy of tomorrow. If so, the embedded workforce cannot be regarded as a mere supplement to the Creative Industries themselves. Not only is it a primary reason that these industries locate and grow in London, but is critical to the dynamics of a sector constantly expanding into new, previously uncreative, spheres. In this chapter, I describe the development of the idea of London's Creative Economy and study some of the reasons for its importance and emergence.

GOVERNANCE, INTELLIGENCE, POLICY AND RESEARCH

The perception that creativity and culture are keys to London's role as a global city has become an unstated backdrop to almost all GLA strategies. These include its Economic Development Plans and Cultural Strategies; the championship of London's culture as the lynchpin of its global status beginning with its first mayor, Ken Livingstone and its successful rebranding as a world centre of creativity, culminating in its selection as the site of the 2012 Olympic Games. Under London's second mayor, Boris Johnson (elected in 2008), impressive displays promoting London as a world centre of creativity greeted visitors to many world airports for most of 2012. The idea of London as a creative–innovative hub lived on in the 'High-Tech City' project of a corridor linking the Olympic site to the Shoreditch roundabout, a vibrant creative cluster on the City's north east fringe.

Yet disputes on what to do about the Creative Economy grew in proportion to agreement on its importance. In common with most capitals, London is a highly political environment where multiple interests jostle for attention. As soon as a new strategy emerges, the question most generally asked is 'What's in it for me?' Bashing the unpopular – which normally includes the unfamiliar, culture, and anything that undermines privilege – is not only a proven route to power but, in so far as the business of government concerns maintaining incumbency, a workable substitute for policy. Johnson's victory owed much to an attack campaign centring on allegations of corruption in the funding of a creative centre catering for Brixton's black community – charges that both a police investigation and a subsequent high-profile 'forensic audit' revealed to be unfounded. Creative London, the initial vehicle for Creative Industry policy, had been wound up in 2006 after the mayor's office assumed direct control over many key policies.

This disparity illustrates the central difficulty that this chapter aims to tackle: there was no workable theory of how the cultural or Creative Economy even functioned, let alone how to influence it. It epitomized Innovation Minister John Denham's 2008 remark that he had spent all his life trying to get his hands on the levers of power, only to find that they weren't connected to anything. The GLA's research sought to find the connections: to place decision-making on a sound basis by providing evidence for, and an explanation of, the relation between London and its Creative Industries.

Our starting point was the statistical approach of the British Department of Culture, Media and Sport (DCMS)'s *Mapping Document* (1998), which focused, narrowly according to some, on the specifically economic side of creativity, providing data for employment, firm counts, and output in the industries and occupations that the DCMS defined as creative. However, unlike the DCMS, the GLA research placed creative occupations – the jobs that people were doing – at the forefront of its studies of the enterprises that employed them.

The fundamental problem confronting policy-makers and advisers alike was that no authoritative body of knowledge existed to inform their judgements. There were sound reasons for the general policy orientation: it drew on the experience embedded in London's cultural scene, rich in arts management and investment skills; a new generation of creative entrepreneurs and developers emerging from the shadows of the post-Thatcher era; an active community of specialist consultancies such as the Burns Owens Partnership, which later managed the *Cultural Audit* (Freeman et al. 2008) and subsequently launched the *World Cities Report* in conjunction with the GLA; independent research centres such as Nesta,[3] a long-time champion of the elusive link that creativity might provide between art, science and innovation; an ongoing legacy of data and research methods from pioneers, such as Sara Selwood, cultural economists, the controversial proselytizer Richard Florida with his concept of the creative class, and the thoughtful visionary Charles Landry, founder of Comedia, who coined the term 'creative city' as far back as the 1980s.[4]

There was, however, no rigorous body of evidence-based theory to call on. Beyond simply giving all Creative Industries what they asked for, hiring specialists who had yet to codify their results, or consulting academics who were considerably more at ease when explaining our mistakes than when advising us what to do, there was no rational basis for such elementary decisions which industries, initiatives or clusters to support, nor how, or even whether, to do so.

The result was a paradox. The mayor's interventions transformed London's creative scene, defining London as a world creative hub and consolidating the decisive creative sectors that made up that scene. Yet the reasons for the transformation were poorly understood. Even Livingstone sympathizers such as Elliott and Atkinson (2007) dismissed the Creative Economy as a fantasized outgrowth of the overweening ambition and bloated finance of the Labour government of the Blair era.[5] In the absence of a transparent rational basis for decision-making, decisions came to depend on the capacity and personality of the key players, not on the actual strategy pursued. This situation arose not because of any lack of attention; the volume of writing, not to mention speaking, was as prolific then as it is now. The problem was, simply, that we were studying a new beast.

ON STUDYING NEW THINGS

Williams (1958, xiii) astutely notes:

> In the last decades of the eighteenth century, and in the first half of the nineteenth century, a number of words, which are now of capital importance, came for the first time into common English use, or, where they had already been generally used in the language, acquired new and important meanings . . . five words are the key points from which this map can be drawn. They are *industry, democracy, class, art and culture* [italics in original].

Nowadays, hitherto esoteric words such as 'innovate', 'digitize' and 'electronic' have emerged into common speech even as 'network' or 'cluster' – not to mention 'tweet' – acquire meanings they never had before. Historians may well record these as signalling social changes comparable to the Industrial Revolution. The rational observer of society has to be alive to the presence of the new.

The working hypothesis of the GLA research was that the Creative Industries, taken as a composite, constituted a new object despite the pre-existing meanings of both 'creation' and 'industry'. This hitherto unknown entity had to be studied in its own terms, free of static schemas or imported preconceptions.

This presented a unique challenge: where to begin? Simply to collect data, we needed some signpost of what to collect. I give the name 'pragmatic theoretical elaboration' to the resulting process, which adapted theory to data to theory in an iterative cycle of refinement. We began with the *Mapping Document* (DCMS 1998) because it was a working definition expressing international precedents established over some time by scholars, decision-makers and industry experts.[6]

We applied this to London and its boroughs, providing a test bed for the concept, hitherto unknown conclusions to test, and hitherto unasked questions to answer. Our conceptual framework, therefore, evolved in parallel with its real-world applications.

The third leg of this tripod was the method of doubt. Our conclusions were and remain highly novel. Each time one was drawn, it was articulated so that it could be tested by different means. In this the GLA was assisted by its critics, of whom, felicitously, there was no shortage. Every inch of ground was contested – by political sceptics, business interests, pundits and scholars. Criticism ranged from simple denial to alternative definitions so radically different from each other that almost nothing remained in common, but included more considered critiques from the arts world. We responded in three ways: empirically by interrogating each contested conclusion against the evidence; theoretically by refining, revising and, where necessary, scrapping our concepts; and practically by using the refined concepts to redefine the data.

In parallel with Hasan Bakhshi at Nesta and Peter Higgs at the Queensland University of Technology, the GLA developed a robust methodology, leading to the subsequent collaboration that produced *A Dynamic Mapping of the UK's Creative Industries* (Bakhshi, Freeman and Higgs 2013), which features the first rigorously founded definition of the Creative Economy, which has in turn been adopted by the DCMS for the purposes of producing the UK's official Creative Industries estimates.

A BENIGN PRODUCTIVITY REVOLUTION

Creativity: London's Core Business showed above all that we were looking at growth. Employment and gross value-added were rising faster than all but one comparator industry (business services) and, significantly, faster in London than elsewhere.

Unexpectedly, productivity appeared to be rising. Britain's lacklustre performance had for decades been attributed to uncompetitive practices – leading to the conventional wisdom that productivity could be increased only by cutting labour costs. But in the UK both employment and wages were rising, and output was rising even faster. The report coined the phrase 'benign productivity revolution' to describe this phenomenon. 'London's Creative Industries', the report found, 'are at the centre of a productivity revolution, expanding both jobs and wealth, with employment up by 5 per cent per year, output by 8.5 per cent and productivity by 4 per cent between 1995 and 2000' (Freeman 2002, 4). The report confirmed these industries as a key element of London's emerging new economy: with creative employment growing faster than anywhere except business services, it accounted for one in every five jobs.

These unusual patterns were repeated across nearly all the DCMS's disparate sectors, the first confirmation that we were dealing with a real economic object. A further reason to treat them as a coherent unity was that they occurred as 'clusters' of closely related industries such as advertising's Golden Square in the West End or West London's film and video clusters, which had formed organically in many parts of London and within which other Creative Industries co-located: advertisers, architects, designers, print companies, video studios, boutiques, rock venues and hangout joints nestled cheek by jowl.[7] Nor did their location simply shadow the financial sector, as suggested by the somewhat simplistic theory that they located close to high-spending sources of demand, making their clustering an accidental consequence of an external cause with no autonomous dynamic.

Core Business, backed up by the 2004, 2007 and 2009 updates, proved that the Creative Industries were no chimera. Yet the data told us neither why they grew, nor why they clustered. The absence of a causal model accounts for the many worldwide failures of scattergun cluster-building identified in an early LDA-commissioned report (see Evans 2009) – possibly including the LDA's own 'hub' strategies. Beyond mere evidence, the decision-makers needed to understand causes. When these were articulated, the significance of the creative workforce steadily rose to the fore.

DEFINING THE PRODUCT AND IDENTIFYING THE CONSUMER

Core Business advanced the first economic model of the Creative Industries, significantly refining the DCMS definition. 'This report', it said, 'expands on [the DCMS] definition by taking the decisive linking factor in Creative Industries to be intellectual and creative input, producing goods and services that are distinguished by brand, identity and difference' (Freeman 2002, 3).

Bridget Rosewell, the GLA's consultant chief economist, contributed a definition of these industries' distinctive product – 'brand, identity and difference'. This signposted the later understanding that a new connection was emerging between 'aesthetic' quality and consumer choice. The new industries were distinguished by their capacity to understand, anticipate, design and produce what a specific group of customers wanted – the antithesis of the mass-production model most strongly associated with Henry Ford.

DEFINING THE CREATIVE RESOURCE

Industrial policy, in any sphere, arguably becomes a science from the moment researchers identify the resources on which an industry depends. We had discovered that London itself supplied this resource to the Creative Industries, as shown both by their faster growth in the city and its surrounds, and their high concentration there. The *2007 Update* showed that 57 per cent of all UK creative employment was in London and the South East. However, to say that this resource was located in London, or even nurtured by London, begged the question. The problem was to define it.

The report included, in common with the beliefs of the time, many references to London's cultural diversity as a factor in these industries' successes. It bears the stamp of Florida's (2002) flagship hypothesis that 'diversity' is a primary cause of creativity. Yet diversity was vaguely defined, ranging from the number of products, through the range of industries that populated them, before settling on the indisputable variety of London's linguistic, ethnic and cultural make-up.

However, the facts did not square with the 'diversity is creative' thesis. *Play it Right* (GLA 2003), dealing with Asian employment in London's Creative Industries, challenged the wide perception that they were strongholds of diversity and ladders of opportunity. The 2004, 2007 and 2009 updates to *Core Business* established that the employment practices of most Creative Industries excluded the very cultural influences on which their commercial success was built. With the exception of industries such as fashion, arguably itself a gender ghetto, they were below London par for equality. The diversity of London's culture certainly played a role in making it a location of choice for both making and selling creative products. This diversity had yet to penetrate the workforce itself.

SLINGS, ARROWS AND NOBLE MINDS: THE POLITICAL CLIMATE CHANGES

The LDA's ambiguous status was a poisoned chalice: it imposed a hands-off regime on the mayor while handing him the rap for all its actions. When Creative London was wound up in 2006, establishing strategies became the hallmark of the Livingstone administration: recapturing London's fashion leadership, laying the foundations of a new stage for the film industry, converting London's festival scene from a series of marginal displays into a world showcase for London's talent, and consolidating the brand that secured the Olympics for London: a 'world in one city'.

Key research conclusions emerge from the mere fact of this success. The success confirmed the elusive synergy expressed in the concept of place – the combination of a space, and what happens in it. London's success depended not just on the individuals in its workforce, but also on the way they interacted in the places that London put at their disposal. We used the concept of 'the city as a creative factory' to capture this idea (Freeman 2002, 34).

Yet such conclusions, although they stood ready to be drawn, were rarely formulated and certainly neither absorbed nor promulgated by the GLA's management. The decisiveness of the mayor's office contrasted with the increasingly formulaic responses of his bureaucracy. The economics unit, wedded to archaic rational choice methods rooted in the *a priori* assumption that the market had to work, developed the criterion of 'market failure' into a profoundly conservative mantra. Creative Industry advocates faced the uphill task of proving that a policy might improve an industry that nobody understood. 'Leave it alone unless you can prove it's going wrong' became a straightforward case for doing nothing. Ironically, given the Schumpeterian underpinnings of this case, it erected an impenetrable barrier to innovation in the very area where openness to the new was the *sine qua non* of rational enquiry and effective action alike.

This nascent conservatism overlooked an essential piece of the puzzle, identified in an unassertive, but highly informative book on creative contracts by Caves (2002) and receiving increasing attention from writers on 'open innovation' (see, for example, Chesbrough 2003) and the economic functions of social networks (see, for example, Currid 2007). These all highlighted the critical role of non-market factors, such as the 'gatekeeper' functions of global cities in the vital role of social interaction in the creative production process.

The 'market failure' approach predisposed the outfield to drop this catch. Suffocating in this arid environment, the spirit of creative enquiry decamped. Graham Hitchen, Creative London's former head, started his regular 'Creative Breakfast', bringing together leading players from all over London's creative scene. Regular participants included Hasan Bakhshi, with his research on the economics of creativity, art and innovation; Tom Campbell, director of the LDA's much-reduced Creative Industry team and later a key member of the GLA's enterprising Culture Team, who habitually opened team meetings with a poetry reading; and a stream of creative entrepreneurs and political enthusiasts.

This was only one nexus in a dispersed network of practitioners and researchers. But it catalysed what was, in effect, a new governance structure for London's search to understand its new creative foundations. Participants had learned, and adapted, the networking methods described by Caves and Chesborough. This was an extraordinarily fertile period in London's thinking about both culture and creativity, for which no single individual can be assigned exclusive credit. In the industries' best tradition, it produced a whole much greater than the sum of its parts.

It yielded a series of research collaborations, some published as blogs by the Mission, Models, Money collective, each with a major impact on subsequent thinking.[8] It inspired and informed the GLA's further work; not least, it made possible Jude Woodward's brainchild, the path-breaking *Cultural Audit*.

The idea of the Creative Industries, widely perceived as a British export although international influences figured heavily in its origins, had taken root outside Britain. In emerging markets, not least China, policies centred on the Creative Economy were becoming a central plank of developmental strategy. The next step was not to drop the concept of Creative Industries but to make it adequate. The process consisted in addressing, one by one, the issues that arose both from our initial results, and from their reception.

QUESTIONS, QUESTIONS, QUESTIONS

The first problem, as the fallout settled from the 2000 downturn, was whether the Creative Industries really were growing. Were they just a flash in the pan or was there evidence of something more sustainable? We triangulated, bringing multiple time-series to bear, including two huge business databases yielding a wealth of information about geographical distribution: the Interdepartmental Business Register, a tax-based record of over 70 per cent of UK businesses, and a proprietary company database derived from Dun and Bradstreet data, diligently maintained by Trends Business Research.

The result was the first microgeographical database on London's creative sector, which was used as input to the 2007 Creative Industries update.

For the first time local planners could study Creative Industry clustering on the geographical scale on which it operated. Electoral ward, postcode, even street concentrations emerged from the blurry picture offered by survey data.

A second result was a long-term analysis of Creative Industry growth, demonstrating that its cyclic ups and downs overlaid a clear growth trend. This also suggested how the industries reacted to downturn, revealing a hitherto unnoticed lag of two years behind the regular business cycle. A proper model, and a possible guide to action, was in sight.

Yet a still more basic question was driven to the fore by the gathering storms of political confrontation: did the Creative Industries exist at all? The 'market failure' framework accompanied conventional anti-interventionist arguments such as Hayek's 'picking winners' critique to question the case for action of any kind. If an industrial sector was growing through an expansion of the market, why do anything to fix it?

Fundamental issues of definition and existence came to the fore, dominated by the charge of 'double-counting'. The LDA had constructed criteria for intervention by defining a set of arbitrary 'sectors', of which the creative sector was one. This typically formulaic gambit left a gaping political hole: the 'sectors' supplemented, rather than replaced, the existing traditional industrial classifications of manufacturing, business services, retail, finance and so on. But in consequence, if a special 'Creative Industry' incentive was given to an enterprise also finding itself in business services, it would get two bites at the cherry because it could also avail itself of 'business service' incentives.

The real task was to identify the actual reality of London's economy, to which the traditional sector classification was increasingly irrelevant. If the Creative Industries were the source of dynamism in the traditional sectors, the double-counting should actually have been reversed: subsidies to business services should have been cut, to concentrate on the core business of creation. Indeed, in manufacturing, where creative enterprises dominated by design were actually growing, and which the GLA had abandoned as a lost cause, this made total sense.

Even more politically sensitive was the relation of London's Creative Economy to its finance sector. If it was an offshoot of finance, then it made more sense to support finance, for creation would then be an automatic beneficiary. And even if finance, heaven forbid, encountered problems it could not solve, no special policy for creation could save it. There were grounds for such ideas. If discretionary spending was primarily associated with high incomes, then, even if morally repugnant on other grounds, the Creative Industries might well be best supported by harnessing London's vibrant and high-spending financial sector. But if there was a growing source of creative dynamism independent of both finance and high spending, then, to the contrary, as the mayor's policies in fact virtually proved, London could be freed of its finance habit by building up a new, dynamic and genuinely independent productive sector – creation, its core business. To choose between these courses, it was necessary to establish if the Creative Economy really existed. To decide that, it was necessary to define how it functioned. It had become indispensable to identify the resources on which it depended.

CREATIVITY, A HUMAN RESOURCE

London's Core Business identified the nature of the Creative Industries' special product, diversity and brand, and its source of demand, discretionary spending – but had not resolved what its special resource might be. The clue was the interaction between the occupations defined by the DCMS classification and the industries. It was possible to ask the simple question 'How many creative people do the Creative Industries employ?' The results were striking. *Dynamic Mapping* (Bakhshi, Freeman and Higgs 2013) showed that at the national level intensity in the Creative Industries is 25 times greater than in the rest of the economy – with intensities ranging from 30 to 80 per cent. Even more striking, as the 2007 GLA update showed, intensity was distinctively higher in London and the South East – and appeared to be growing, suggesting a dynamic process of emergence led by London.

This was the first empirical confirmation that the missing 'resource' of the Creative Industries was, in fact, its workforce. This idea ran counter to the received economic wisdom that labour is a substitute for capital, and also the trend established by Braverman (1974), which saw the 'deskilling' of labour as a long-term trend of capitalism. The Creative Industries seemed to buck both trends. They depended on a type of labour defined by the fact that it could not be mechanized: the indispensable input provided by this labour was precisely that which could not be replaced – its creativity.

This provided a further causal link between workforce and space by explaining why the Creative Industries might cluster. Clustering is not new to economics, but the scale of the clusters studied by writers such as Porter (1990) is generally large – groups of industries are often 50 to 100 miles apart. In London's Creative Economy, groups of industries located characteristically extremely close to each other, for example in London's Golden Square, the centre of its advertising industry, in the West End more generally, and in recognizable and even iconic formations, such as the Paddington Basin, which it will be recalled is what brought Nissan to London. Why should these industries be so close together? Pre-market selection gives part of the answer. It is the workforce itself that offers the full explanation: collaborative team, Caves's (2002) 'motley crew' principle and open innovation all belong to the realm of the productive process of creation. They are 'how creation happens'. And they require face-to-face interaction. 'Microspatial clustering', as we called it, is the expression of process whose primal means of production are the brain, the foot and the mouth.

CONCLUSION: SERVICE AND THE CITY

Due consideration to the city's embedded workforce allows us, I believe, to join up the two most important aspects of what the modern city achieves. As a space within which face-to-face interactions can be achieved, it organizes the collaborations and gatekeeping functions of creative production – and it slakes the social hunger for personal interactions – to be part of an audience, a crowd, a social gathering or a group – organizing them into the iconic moments that characterize commercial creativity and that, ironically and ecstatically, characterize the primal and eternal aspects of what makes us social beings: *event* and *place*. Neither of these two opposed and alienated terms makes the remotest sense without *humans*, situated by them in the time and space frames of modern life. These three words define the Creative Economy

Such pioneer geographers of communication as Marshall McLuhan and, to some extent, Harold Innis sketched a planet in which communication would obliterate settlement. If everyone can speak to everyone else, why does it matter where we live? Yet society has evolved in the opposite direction. The modern city has not been made an anachronism by communication: it has been redefined by it. Cities are where humans go to interact.

This development has to be set against the background of a proper understanding of the so-called digital revolution. In the age of which Williams wrote, technology was associated above all with the production of things. Yet today, by far the largest grouping of labour in advanced economies produces services – essentially, human interactions. Understanding, again failing to keep up with this new phenomenon, is dominated by the paradox of Baumol's 'cost disease' (Baumol and Bowen 1966; see also Heilbrun 2003), one of the earliest justifications for funding the arts. Baumol argued that productivity in services, by their very nature, cannot be augmented. An orchestra, for example, cannot increase its productivity by playing faster. Therefore the public had to fund the arts, because normal market mechanisms would not allow them to increase their revenues.

But even as Baumol was writing, electronic technology was already transforming the productivity of the service industries by simply removing the need for humans to be next to each other in order to interact. Broadcast and communications were removing barriers of distance; recording and reproduction technologies were steadily eradicating the barriers of time. And, finally, with digitization and the Internet, the last barrier of quantity has fallen. It is now possible to deliver services across any distance, in any quantity, and at any time – at a vanishing cost.

This redefines the value of the product, which was never purely quantitative and is now predominantly qualitative. An orchestra *can* improve its productivity – by playing better or reaching new audiences. This is indeed already known to economic theory, in the notion that the utility (whether social or individual) of an object defines its value in use. But the modern implications are clear only now that the service revolution has transformed the cost structure of service delivery. The use value of creative services and products lies not in their quantity, but in the breadth of human experience they cater for. Their primary means of production are no longer machines, but the talent and creativity of the humans who make them. This talent and creativity, in turn, is not only organized by interactions between these producers, but consumed by the crowd, by multiples of humans, by audiences. The city is what makes this possible. The embedded workforce is, then, what creates the city.

We can thus think of London's embedded workforce as performing two functions in parallel. As the researchers cited in the introduction to this volume point out, it acts on 'the economy as a whole' (Chapter 1, p. 6) – making the city what it is, a space that affords specialists and their associated support workers an environment in which to make creative products and services. Second, within that space, it provides a resource from which new Creative Industries, emerging from their materialist cocoon, draw the nutrition essential to invigorate the 'innovation-based growth' that is their hallmark.

NOTES

1. The five GLA papers are: *Creativity: London's Core Business* (Freeman 2002), *Play it Right: Asian Creative Industries in London* (GLA 2003), *London's Creative Sector: 2004 Update* (Freeman 2004), *London's Creative Sector: 2007 Update* (Freeman 2007), *London's Creative Workforce: 2009 Update* (Freeman 2009). I was a team member of the GLA.
2. http://www.worldcitiescultureforum.com/.

3. Formerly NESTA, the National Endowment for Science, Technology and the Arts, which changed names when it became a charitable body in 2012.
4. See, for example, Selwood (1994), Florida (2002), Landry (2006), Towse (2003).
5. Referring to Prime Minister Tony Blair.
6. These origins are discussed in *A Dynamic Mapping of the UK's Creative Industries* (Bakhshi, Freeman and Higgs 2013, 8). See also O'Connor (2007).
7. See, for example, Pratt (2013).
8. To give an example: *Not Rocket Science* (Bakhshi, Desai and Freeman 2010), was the driving intellectual force behind the Digital Research and Development Fund for the Arts, a £7 million fund in England led by Arts Council England, the Arts and Humanities Research Council and NESTA.

REFERENCES

To provide a permanent research resource, all the GLA and LDA reports referenced in this text are located at www.londonculturalresource.com. All papers published by the Mission, Money, Models collective are at www.missionmodelsmoney.org.uk.

Bakhshi, H., R. Desai and A. Freeman (2010), *Not Rocket Science: A Roadmap for Arts and Cultural R&D*, London: Mission, Money, Models.
Bakhshi, H., A. Freeman and P. Higgs (2013), *A Dynamic Mapping of the UK's Creative Industries*, London: Nesta.
Bakhshi, H., A. Freeman and G. Hitchen (2009), *Measuring Intrinsic Value – How to Stop Worrying and Love Economics*, London: Mission, Money, Models.
Baumol, W.J. and W.G. Bowen (1966), *Performing Arts, The Economic Dilemma: A Study of Problems Common to Theater, Opera, Music, and Dance*, New York: Twentieth Century Fund.
Braverman, H. (1974), *Labor and Monopoly Capital*, New York: Monthly Review Press.
Caves, R. (2002), *Creative Industries: Contracts between Art and Commerce*, Cambridge, MA: Harvard University Press.
Car Design News (2003), 'Nissan opens European design centre in London', at http://archive.cardesignnews.com/features/2003/030124nissan-london/ (accessed 17 September 2013).
Chesbrough, H.C. (2003), *Open Innovation: The New Imperative for Creating and Profiting from Technology*, Boston, MA: Harvard Business School Press.
Currid, W. (2007), *The Warhol Economy: How Fashion, Art and Music Drive New York City*, Princeton, NJ: Princeton University Press.
Department of Culture, Media and Sport (DCMS) (1998), *Creative Industries Mapping Document 1998*, London: DCMS, available at http://webarchive.nationalarchives.gov.uk/+/http://www.culture.gov.uk/reference_library/publications/4740.aspx (accessed 29 July 2013).
Elliott, L. and D. Atkinson (2007), *Fantasy Island: Waking up to the Incredible Economic, Political and Social Illusions of the Blair Legacy*, London: Constable.
Evans, G. (2009), 'Creative cities, creative spaces and urban policy', *Urban Studies*, **46** (5–6), 1003–40.

Florida, R. (2002), *The Rise of the Creative Class: And How it's Transforming Work, Leisure, Community and Everyday Life*, New York: Basic Books.

Freeman, A. (2002), *Creativity: London's Core Business*, London: Greater London Authority.

Freeman, A. (2004), *London's Creative Sector: 2004 Update*, London: Greater London Authority.

Freeman, A. (2007), *London's Creative Sector: 2007 Update*, London: Greater London Authority.

Freeman, A. (2009), *London's Creative Workforce: 2009 Update*, London: Greater London Authority.

Freeman, A., K. Oakley, R. Naylor and A. Pratt (2008), *London: A Cultural Audit*, London: London Development Agency, available at http://www.london culturalresource.com/sites/default/files/ResearchAndPolicyDocs/London%20 Cultural%20Audit.pdf (accessed 17 September 2013).

Greater London Authority (2003), *Play It Right: Asian Creative Industries in London*, London: GLA.

Heilbrun, J. (2003), 'Baumol's cost disease', in R. Towse (ed.), *A Handbook of Cultural Economics*, Cheltenham, UK and Northampton, MA, USA: Edward Elgar, pp. 67–75.

Landry, C. (2006), *The Art of City-Making*, Sterling: Earthscan.

O'Brien, D. (2010), *Measuring the Value of Culture*, London: Department of Culture, Media and Sport.

O'Connor, J. (2007), *The Cultural and Creative Industries: A Review of the Literature*, London: Arts Council England.

Porter, M.E. (1990), *The Competitive Advantage of Nations*, New York: The Free Press.

Pratt, A.C. (2013, in press), 'Clustering of the media industries in London', in R.G. Picard and C. Karlsson (eds), *Media Clusters*, Cheltenham, UK and Northampton, MA, USA: Edward Elgar.

Selwood, S. (1994), *Benefits of Public Art in Britain: Impact of Permanent Art in Public Places*, London: Policy Studies Institute.

Towse, R. (ed.) (2003), *A Handbook of Cultural Economics*, Cheltenham, UK and Northampton, MA, USA: Edward Elgar.

Williams, R. (1958), *Culture and Society*, Chatto and Windus.

PART II

Case studies of embedded creative employment

6. Embedded creatives in Australian healthcare – an update

Janet Pagan and Jess Rodgers

INTRODUCTION

Healthcare is a particularly interesting context within which to examine creative engagement in economic activity. It entails the provision of knowledge- and information-intensive goods and services in a complex web of many types of interacting public and private service providers, government and other funders, and various regulatory and supporting mechanisms. Healthcare is one of the largest and most rapidly expanding parts of the Australian economy. According to the Australian Institute of Health and Welfare (2013), Australian expenditure on healthcare was AU$140.2 billion in 2011–2012, that is 9.5 per cent of gross domestic product, up from 8.3 per cent a decade earlier. This expenditure is projected to increase significantly, reflecting pressures from an ageing population, along with increasing demand for high-quality health services, reliable information and access to new technologies (Secretariat Australia 2012; Segal and Bolton 2009). Additional cost pressures have arisen over the first decade of the 2000s as equity has assumed greater prominence in health policy, driven by community expectations that services and health outcomes should be of similar high quality for remote and/or Indigenous Australians to those provided to city dwellers. Additionally, greater attention is being paid to addressing mental health and some lifestyle issues with long-term ill health implications. Caught between these changes and the budget constraints imposed by their major government funders, healthcare providers are under considerable pressure to change while balancing the objectives of cost containment and healthcare quality. Innovation is seen as key to dealing with this squeeze (Angus 2002; Omachonu and Einspruch 2010). However, there is resistance to change, for reasons including the conservatism of time-poor doctors, deficiencies in the technological skills of health providers and their patients, and the inherent risks of introducing new products and processes to a system and institutions with complex operations.

The *Getting Creative in Healthcare* report (Pagan, Higgs and Cunningham 2008) examined the contribution of creative workers to Australian Healthcare, using case studies to explore the ways in which they contribute to the operation of the Australian healthcare system and the development and delivery of services that have proven healthcare benefits. The number of creative workers embedded in healthcare (employed in creative occupations within this sector) was also quantified through extraction of data from the 2001 and 2006 Australian Census. The proportion of embedded creatives within modern Australian healthcare was found to be just 0.5 per cent of the total healthcare workforce. This appears to be low compared with most other industries and it is in stark contrast with the 2 per cent observed in manufacturing, for example. It is a surprising result in view of the historically long association of creativity with healthcare and the widespread use of creative skills identified throughout the healthcare sector. *Getting Creative in Healthcare* found that creative contributions occur in other ways that are not captured in the available statistics, such as external Creative Services and Cultural Production contracted by the healthcare sector, and volunteers and creative skills deployed by medical and other non-creative specialists in healthcare.

In line with the thematic emphasis of this book on embedded creatives, this chapter uses data from the 2006 and 2011 Australian Census to provide a statistical update on the *Getting Creative in Healthcare* report, focusing on the employment of creatives in healthcare against the backdrop of changes within the healthcare industry that have occurred in the intervening period. Further analysis of earlier case studies is also undertaken to explore facets of the healthcare system shaping demand for creative skills that might provide possible explanations for the observed 'low' level of embedded creative skills in Australian healthcare. Additional perspectives have been added from literature to update areas of creative contributions that have emerged or grown since the report, and to reflect technology shifts.

METHODOLOGY

Data on employment within Australian healthcare were extracted from the 2006 and 2011 censuses using revised Australian Bureau of Statistics (ABS) industry (ABS 2008) and occupation (ABS 2006) statistical identifiers based on *Getting Creative in Healthcare*. The general definition for the collation of OECD health statistics was the basis for the industry statistics selected for the Australian healthcare sector, and included hospitals, nursing homes, medical and surgical equipment manufacturing, health services (such as physiotherapy, chiropractors, medical and ambulance services) and insurance. Because organizations in healthcare varied widely, they were grouped into three sectors of internally similar components, namely manufacturing, institutions and health services.[1] The creative occupations were divided into six segments: advertising and marketing; publishing; architecture, design and visual arts; music and performing arts; film, radio and TV; and software and digital content. In view of the classification revisions since the earlier report, only trends in the data for the periods 2001 to 2006 and 2006 to 2011 could be directly compared.

CREATIVES WITHIN THE HEALTHCARE SYSTEM

Creative employment is found in each health industry sub-sector, reflecting the widespread integration of creative skills in the services, processes and organizations involved in healthcare. Evidence for the healthcare impacts for healthcare operations involving creative skills is summarized in the *Getting Creative in Healthcare* report (Pagan, Higgs and Cunningham 2008). The main features of this include the pool of evidence demonstrating that direct creative services make significant contributions to healing (for example, Staricoff 2006; Peruzza and Kinsella 2010), as well as bringing a more human-centred focus to the other processes and buildings involved in the provision of healing services. Creative skills are central to the escalating rollout of information and communication technology (ICT), in dealing with the ever greater amounts of data generated in healthcare diagnosis and treatment processes and institutional operations (Angus 2002) and in the provision of mental health and distance services that are particularly important in the Australian context (Australian Institute of Health and Welfare 2012; Pagan, Higgs and Cunningham 2008). The case studies of *Getting Creative in Healthcare* also identified the involvement of a range of creative skills in training medical practitioners, in improving infrastructure efficiency and effectiveness, in planning and performing medical treatments, and in alleviating some of the most difficult and intractable medical conditions. Creative skills were used individually, in creative teams and in mixed creative and medical teams. In addition, the transient use of creative skills was found in the development of services and medical devices routinely used in medical treatments and organizational operations. With the prospect of intensifying technological inputs throughout healthcare, it would appear that creative workers have the potential to become more significant to healthcare in addressing the human–machine interface.

Employees in creative occupations embedded in Australian healthcare comprised about 0.5 per cent of the total healthcare workforce in 2006 and

2011, much the same as in 2001. Between 2006 and 2011, creative employment in healthcare grew from 3356 to 3993, or by 19 per cent. This was the same growth rate as the total healthcare workforce, but slower than over the previous five-year period. The mean income of embedded creatives was AU\$72 083 in 2006, 37 per cent above the average for the whole healthcare sector. However, the average remuneration for embedded creatives grew only 3 per cent between 2006 and 2011, slower than the overall healthcare industry's 5.6 per cent growth. It is notable that, despite the pressures of international competition, relatively high wages and the value of the Australian dollar over the period, the healthcare manufacturing sub-sector grew 9.6 per cent between 2006 and 2011 and creative employment within it grew twice as fast.

In 2011, embedded creative employment was distributed between the manufacturers of healthcare products (20 per cent), the institutions (41 per cent) and healthcare services (39 per cent). The concentration of embedded creatives within the healthcare industry sub-sectors provides an indication of the intensity of the use of creative skills. The proportion of creatives was six to ten times higher in the two sub-sectors – manufacturing and health insurance – than in healthcare overall. Among the larger healthcare sub-sectors, creative employment grew fastest in the health insurance, aged care residential, and general and specialist medical services between 2006 and 2011.

Turning to the types of creative skills segments within healthcare, software and digital content was the largest segment in 2011 (comprising 42 per cent of the total), followed by advertising and marketing (27 per cent), publishing (16 per cent), architecture, design and visual arts (10 per cent), music and performing arts (4 per cent), and film, radio and TV (1 per cent). The changes in employment of healthcare creatives are shown in Table 6.1. Between 2006 and 2011, employment of creatives grew fastest in the music and performing arts segment, albeit from a low base. The overall increase in embedded creative employment was driven by the 34 per cent growth of the largest segment, software and digital content.[2] A finer analysis of the distribution of embedded creative skills is presented in Table 6.2 and discussed below.

SOFTWARE AND DIGITAL CONTENT

Market analysis by Frost and Sullivan reports that Australia leads the Asia-Pacific region in the healthcare IT market (Australian Centre for Health Innovation 2013). According to the Census data there were 1694 people in software and digital content occupations embedded in health-

*Table 6.1   Employment: creative occupations by segment and in total
healthcare and percentage change over the periods 2001–2006
and 2006–2011*

Occupational segment	Number employed 2006	Number employed 2011	Employment growth 2001–06 (%)	Employment growth 2006–11 (%)
Advertising and Marketing	967	1 089	43.4	12.6
Software and Digital Content	1 265	1 694	*	33.9
Publishing	653	629	24.5	–3.7
Architecture, Design and Visual Arts	344	390	7.1	13.4
Music and Performing Arts	96	159	–45.0	65.6
Film, TV, Radio	31	32	3.1	3.2
Total embedded creatives	3 356	3 993	31.5	19.0
Total all healthcare	718 778	856 560	12.2	19.2

Note: *Not comparable between the two five-year periods due to different occupations selected within this segment.

care in 2011, a rise of 34 per cent from 2006. This was driven mostly by their increased employment within hospitals and insurance organizations. Some 35 per cent of these occupations in 2011 were software programmers, of whom 42 per cent were employed in hospitals and 16 per cent in insurance organizations. While people involved in web design and maintenance accounted for only 11 per cent of the total segment in 2006, employment in these occupations had grown 53 per cent by 2011. The number of people in ICT systems analysis occupations remained at 250 over the five years, but the employment in ICT business analysis doubled, reaching almost 200 by 2011. Several features of the health system are shaping the demand for software and digital content skills.

Creative skills are sourced externally as well as from those employed in creative occupations within the healthcare system. Many factors bear on the decision where to source skills, including firm size (Houseman 2001), market fluctuations (Abraham and Taylor 1996) and the pace of technological change (Bartel, Lach and Sicherman 2005). As large producers and consumers of data and information, healthcare organizations are potentially significant users of computer programs designed for the sector-specific operational and regulatory environment. However, this situation has not translated into high levels of employment for programmers embedded within the sector as there is a strong bias towards purchasing

Table 6.2   Creative occupations by segment in healthcare sub-sectors in 2006 and 2011

Creatives in healthcare industry sub-sectors	Number employed in 2006	Number employed in 2011
Software and Digital Content		
Manufacturers	231	264
Institutions	508	732
Services	526	698
Marketing and Advertising		
Manufacturers	307	383
Institutions	196	214
Services	464	492
Publishing Creatives		
Manufacturers	55	59
Institutions	404	428
Services	194	142
Music and Performing Arts		
Manufacturers	3	10
Institutions	46	86
Services	47	63
Film, TV and Radio		
Manufacturers	3	0
Institutions	12	11
Services	16	21
Architecture, Design and Visual Arts		
Architecture and Design		
Manufacturers	64	78
Institutions	149	175
Services	82	106
Visual Arts		
Manufacturers	7	3
Institutions	24	12
Services	18	16

proprietary software and using local skills to maintain the IT systems for several reasons. Reasons include the government-encouraged purchase of standardized (generally overseas-derived) programs for managing hospital operations and facilitating data and patient record exchange, to address the issues of the many sources of individual data spread across the health system and the need for ready access to them. Smaller organizations also appear to have concerns about using in-house website development and programming in view of the need to keep websites current with new functions and their flow-through to changes in client demands (Summers 2012).

Very large data sets are an increasing feature of healthcare operations and patient diagnoses. This trend is reflected in the demand for data mining skills. For example, insurance companies are interested in patient data and information on treatments from the myriad of medical and allied professionals. Medical research is working towards better diagnosis and treatments for brain dysfunction and degenerative diseases. The neurological scans involved produce data sets that are currently unmanageably large. Data mining is an area of active research in many Australian research organizations and, if this research turns out to have many applications, the current demand for these high-level IT-based analysis skills may translate into a more generalized demand for data mining skills, potentially resulting in more opportunities for embedded creatives.

With the need to increase the efficiency and the reach of healthcare services, web-based delivery has assumed greater importance; it has become accepted as an effective treatment modality for mental health disorders and for some telehealth applications. The 2006 Council of Australian Governments mental health reform package allocated AU$57 million for development of telephone counselling, self-help and web-based support programs, and this government funding may be partially reflected in the sharp increase in employment observed for web design and maintenance between 2006 and 2011. Case studies of web-based services (Pagan, Higgs and Cunningham 2008) demonstrated that a variety of creative skills are used in the construction and ongoing development of websites in the health system. For example, in addition to core web development skills, the Inspire Foundation utilizes digital games, photography, video and art as core parts of its web-based programs to encourage self-expression and social participation in young people at higher risk of mental health problems. Once the programs are developed, the organization's skill set demand shifts more towards health service delivery and thus some of the creative employment is transitory within a specific organization. While the bulk of the employment related to website development and maintenance was in healthcare services, the growth of this employment was mostly in hospitals. Many Australian hospital websites are static information providers (Cadogan 2013), although a few are starting to utilize multimedia content, such as videos, blogs and other social networking tools. In contrast, over 80 groups of Australian and New Zealand doctors, nurses and researchers are utilizing blogs for small group medical discussion purposes (Life in the Fast Lane 2013).

In addition to the above major areas of work for software and digital content creatives, the case studies (Pagan, Higgs and Cunningham 2008) provided some examples of ad hoc software produced to assist in 3D visualization for planning purposes, such as surgery. Some electronic games used in mental health services and diversionary therapies have been developed for, or by, health organizations. These software developments were one of a kind for defined medical purposes and, once completed, generally led to little, if any, ongoing employment for the creatives. As the case studies showed, while the final objective was generally specified by the medical or organizational need, the degree of independence of creatives involved in the innovation projects varied widely. At one extreme, the medical practitioner exerted tight control throughout the development of True Life Anatomy software. In contrast, while the broad end goal was set for the development of the health and lifestyle educational tool MARVIN (Messaging Architecture for the Retrieval of Versatile Information and News), there were several spontaneous and chaotic elements, including direct community input throughout its creation.

A growing area of research and uptake in healthcare delivery and education has centred on mobile platforms, either as applications (apps) developed specifically for this platform, or utilizing a combination of PC and mobile platforms (see, for example, Baranowski et al. 2008; Primack et al. 2012; Klasnja and Pratt 2012). There are numerous Australian-developed examples. ditto™ is a stand-alone hand-held video game designed to distract children from pain and anxiety during medical procedures (Skiba 2008). It was designed in collaboration with the Royal Children's Hospital Paediatric Burns and Trauma Service in Brisbane, Queensland (Queenslandersign 2011) and is now being used in children's hospitals internationally (Diversionary Therapy Technologies 2012, 2013). Nursim is a web-based clinical diagnosis training tool that takes nurses and other health professionals through the steps required to learn about a patient, make a diagnosis and take appropriate action (Howarth 2012). The Australian Emergency Medicine Application (AusEM; see *CNet* 2011) was designed by SDP Health in collaboration with the Accident and Emergency Department of the Gold Coast Hospital, Queensland (Australian IMG: International Medical Graduates of Australia 2011). AusEM takes the user through the Australian guidelines and protocols for emergency medicine (Australian IMG 2011). It assists in the steps of the patient consultation and takes into account big-picture considerations, such as administration and public health concerns. AusEM can be used offline, which makes it ideal in rural areas. These examples give some insight into recent developments at the intersection of health, technology and creative skills, however there is insufficient data available to quantify the creative employment involved in these types of innovations or identify its sources.

Healthcare's regulatory environment may be affecting the speed of development and/or adoption of such software. For example, medical apps require approval in Australia from the Therapeutic Goods Administration (TGA), whereas health apps, which relate to the general health and well-being of the individual, do not. There are fewer medical than health apps in use (Sutton and Fraser 2013). While educational tools may be used on an experimental basis within organizations, their adoption more broadly hinges on approval by the various professional medical organizations. The legal and medical consequences of errors in this field mean that software to assist in diagnosis, treatment and nursing is subject to intense scrutiny.

ADVERTISING AND MARKETING SEGMENT

The 2011 Census revealed some 1090 embedded creatives in the advertising and marketing segment of healthcare. The employment consisted mostly of marketing specialists and managers, and it was most intense among the healthcare manufacturers, where these creatives constituted almost 2 per cent of the total workforce. A contrasting and conspicuous feature of this creative segment was the low number of advertising specialists, even among the most commercial organizations, the manufacturers. The regulatory system appears to be a significant determinant of this result – the Australian regulatory environment restricts advertising of pharmaceuticals and surgical and medical equipment essentially to medical service providers (Gilbody, Wilson and Watt 2005). Some cultural perspectives also come into play and enhance this impact. The Australasian Medical Publishing Company cautiously treats even informational advertising of medical drugs and appliances in its journals, in line with the general industry concern that effectiveness should be the primary guide in the choice of treatment (Pagan, Higgs and Cunningham 2008).

Elsewhere in this book, public relations professionals are included in the segment, so they are also addressed here. Analysis of Census data revealed 904 public relations managers and professionals in 2011, up by 40 per cent since the 2006 Census. More than half of them were employed in hospitals and residential care facilities. While these professionals may have a role in strategic development within organizations (Patrick and Gauthier 2001; Grunig and Grunig 2000), Australian surveys have found that their roles are primarily information providers (Watson and Simmons 2004).

PUBLISHING SEGMENT

Creative employment in the publishing segment, which had been essentially static between 2001 and 2006, fell by some 4 per cent to 629 in 2011. Employment for both the embedded producers of content (the various types of writers, editors etc.) and information organizers (librarians, archivists etc.) declined, and this was driven primarily by the drop within the health services sub-sector (27 per cent). Counter to this trend, employment of these creative skills in the manufacturing sub-sector rose. It is not clear whether the decline in the number of content producers was driven by factors such as outsourcing of publishing services, and whether the information organizers fell victim to labour substitution effects from a combination of the greater sophistication of searching tools and health-care worker skills.

FILM, RADIO AND TV SEGMENT

The film, radio and TV segment comprised just 1 per cent of the total embedded healthcare occupations. There are several structural factors that might contribute to this outcome. For example, film and video are widely used as tools within healthcare, but mostly in routine tasks undertaken by medical technical staff. There are only a few instances of in-house radio services within the large hospitals, although some organizations use video production for medical education purposes (Pagan, Higgs and Cunningham 2008). While public health campaigns might seem to be a potential source of major funding for employment of creatives in this and the advertising and marketing segment, the health issues being addressed are not specific to individual health institutions, manufacturers or health services. Instead, governments have turned to advertising companies to source the expertise for major community-wide campaigns, such as 'Slip, Slop, Slap' (a sunburn and skin cancer prevention campaign).

ARCHITECTURE AND DESIGN

Of the 359 architecture and design creatives identified as embedded in the healthcare sector in the 2011 Census, just over 30 were architects. While there was little change in the total number of architects employed between 2001 and 2011, there was considerable movement in the concentration of such personnel within the healthcare industry and, by 2011, some 70 per cent of them were concentrated in the healthcare institutions. Research is increasingly recognizing the importance of design and space for positive health and well-being outcomes (see, for examples, Adams et al. 2010; Jackson 2003; Wood et al. 2013). Designing medical buildings such as hospitals, medical centres and pathology laboratories involves many complex considerations, including the requirements of good healthcare, efficient operating environments and patient welfare (Devlein and Arneil 2003; Ulrich 2006). While the high requirement for sector-specific knowledge might suggest some institutional tendency to rely on in-house expertise, the investment in building new or renovating old facilities is relatively expensive and infrequent. As indicated in a case study of the new Royal Children's Hospital in Melbourne (Pagan, Higgs and Cunningham 2008), major work is undertaken by specialist architectural firms in close consultation with various managers within the relevant institution to identify the needs for operational purposes, personnel work patterns, and patient and community movements within the building. In general, the labour requirement in major projects would be unmanageably lumpy for individual institutions, although large ones have a small ongoing requirement for architectural expertise in managing the complex of buildings on hospital campuses.

MUSIC AND PERFORMING ARTS

The core cultural groups – musicians and the performing and visual artists – amounted to just 3 per cent of the embedded creatives. Most were actors employed in the healthcare institutions. Hospitals and nursing homes would seemingly offer the prospect of longer-term employment than such professionals typically experience (Throsby and Hollister 2003); however, a number of factors combine to make their situations tenuous. Despite the long association of cultural activities and healthcare, it has proven difficult to provide conclusive demonstrations of health benefits from cultural activities, other than through music (Cochrane 2013). Even when indicated, the benefits tend to be long term and often diffuse – not a strong situation when cost savings are being sought. In addition, the healthcare system derives significant benefit from the unpaid services of cultural practitioners, such as actors and musicians, who are universally uncounted and whose healing skills vary.

Nevertheless, there are a few influential advocates, particularly doctors, whose personal interest in the arts leads them to foster their use. For example, clown doctoring was brought from the US to Australia through the friendship of a general practitioner, Dr Peter Spitzer, and the actor Jean-Paul Bell. They founded the Humour Foundation, a charitable organization that provides some training and the funding for over 50 clown doctors working in Australian hospitals (Clown Doctors 2010; Bell 2013). While the feel-good factor of laughter is a general human experience, scientific studies have struggled to demonstrate therapeutic benefits other than suggestive evidence of impacts on the immune system (Strean 2009).

The complementary health therapists are not classified as creative workers, although their roles of both healer and cultural creative and their use of Cultural Production would support their inclusion.[3] Some 760 complementary health therapists were identified in the 2011 Census, of whom 516 were embedded in healthcare. Art and music therapists work in a team under the leadership of doctors responsible for the diagnosis and determination of the overall patient treatment program. These creative professionals often find a place in healthcare dealing with the most intractable and difficult healthcare problems where the patients are extremely disabled and only small alleviations are possible. Music therapists have music training usually at the undergraduate level, followed some years later by postgraduate training in therapy. They tend to experience employment in part-time fragments across several institutions, such as hospitals and schools. The funding arrangements for their services may result in reduced demand since Medicare currently does not provide rebates for either form of creative therapy; however, some private insurance funds provide support for a restricted number of sessions each year (Better Health Victoria 2013).[4] Interestingly, the average salary of these professionals even when working part time was about 10 per cent higher in 2006 than music creatives not in therapeutic occupations.[5]

CONCLUSIONS

By including the music and art allied therapists and public relations managers and professionals, we estimate that embedded creatives in Australian healthcare comprised up to 0.6 per cent of the total healthcare workforce in 2011. While the number of embedded creatives grew at the same rate as the overall healthcare workforce between 2006 and 2011, 67 per cent of the increase was due to the employment of software and digital content creatives in the institutions and services sub-sectors. This strong growth reflected the various digitization processes taking place broadly across healthcare.

This chapter demonstrated some of the contributions of creative workers in the Australian healthcare industry. Four segments saw a significant increase in employment between census periods. Software and digital content creatives contribute widely in information management, and the development of websites, software and apps. Advertising and marketing creatives are mostly concentrated in healthcare manufacturing and PR professionals contribute to the strategic development of, and information provision for, institutions. Architects and designers are significant to the creation of spaces in institutions. Music and performing artists contribute to patient care and treatment in institutions and external services.

The increasing employment of embedded creatives over the first decade of the 2000s demonstrates implicit recognition by the industry that creative skills are important and integral to all aspects of medicine. In a time of evidence-based medical treatments the *sine qua non* of their direct engagement in healthcare is that what they do 'works'. However, the demand for these skills was found to be affected by several factors, which varied with the type of creative skills and the circumstances of their use. Overall, industry structures are significant factors that generally limit the potential for embedded employment. For example, the big and intermittent nature of some projects requiring advertising, marketing, architects and their associated creatives leads towards outsourcing arrangements for their skills, leaving much of the ongoing and routine work to be performed in-house. The need for advertising and marketing and software and digital content skills (both embedded and outsourced) is partly constricted by the regulatory framework, while government policies have reduced demand for some software and digital content skills. In contrast, the examples of allied health therapists and clown doctors point to a balance between funding arrangements, budget priorities, the existence of gatekeepers and the evidence of healthcare benefits.

NOTES

1. 'Institutions' refers to hospitals and residential aged care.
2. Employment in this segment includes the following ANZSCO occupations: ICT business development manager, multimedia designer, web designer, ICT business and systems analysts, ICT business analyst, systems analyst, multimedia specialists and web developers, multimedia specialist, web developer, software and applications programmers, analyst programmer, developer programmer, software and applications programmers not otherwise classified. Software and digital content occupations are the second-most numerous and third-fastest-growing embedded creative occupations. They make up one-quarter of embedded creatives.
3. Complementary health therapists nec 252299.
4. Medicare is Australia's public health system.
5. Calculated from data on the website: www.myfuture.edu.au/The%20Facts/Work%20 and%20Employment/Occupations (accessed 31 January 2013).

REFERENCES

Abraham, K. and S. Taylor (1996), 'Firms' use of outside contractors: theory and evidence', *Journal of Labor Economics*, **14**, 394–424.

Adams, A., D. Theodore, E. Goldenberg, C. McClaren and P. McKeever (2010), 'Kids in the atrium: comparing architectural intentions and children's experiences in a paediatric hospital lobby', *Social Science & Medicine*, **70** (5), 658–67.

Angus, J. (2002), *A Review of Evaluation in Community-based Arts in Health*, London: Health Development Agency, available at http://www.nice.org.uk/nicemedia/documents/artforhealth.pdf (accessed 6 March 2013).

Australian Bureau of Statistics (2006), *1220.0 – ANZSCO – Australian and New Zealand Standard Classification of Occupations*, Catalogue, ABS.

Australian Bureau of Statistics (2008), *Australian and New Zealand Standard Industrial Classification (ANZSIC)*, 2006 (Revision 1.0), available at http://www.abs.gov.au/ausstats/abs@.nsf/mf/1292.0 (accessed 20 November 2012).

Australian Centre for Health Innovation (2013), 'Australia leads in eHealth', available at http://www.healthinnovation.com.au/index.php/insights/entry/new-report-australia-leads-in-ehealth (accessed 19 June 2013).

Australian Institute of Health and Welfare (2013), *Health Expenditure Australia 2012–2012*, Canberra.

Australian IMG: International Medical Graduates of Australia (2011), 'Australian Emergency Medicine app by SDP Health', available at http://www.australian-img.com/?p=454 (accessed 18 June 2013).

Baranowski, T., R. Buday, D.I. Thompson and J. Baranowski (2008), 'Playing for real: video games and stories for health related behaviour change', *American Journal of Preventative Medicine*, **34** (1), 74–82.

Bartel, A., S. Lach and N. Sicherman (2005), 'Outsourcing and technological change', Working Paper 11158, National Bureau of Economic Research.

Bell J.-P. (2013), *Onya Soapbox: Talent: Jean-Paul Bell*, available at http://www.onyasoapbox.com/talent/bio/jp_bell.htm (accessed 28 January 2013).

Better Health Victoria (2013), *Allied Health*, available at http://www.betterhealth.vic.gov.au/bhcv2/bhcarticles.nsf/pages/Allied_health (accessed 2 December 2013).

Cadogan, M. (2013), *ANZ MedBloggers Health, Science, Nursing, Midwifery and Medical Blogs from Australia and New Zealand*, http://lifeinthefastlane.com/resources/anz-medical-blogs/ (accessed 28 January 2013).

Clown Doctors (2010), *Clowning Around* [newsletter] (Autumn/Winter).

CNet: Download.com (2011) 'AusEm', CBS Interactive Inc. available at http://download.cnet.com/AusEM/3000-2129_4-75444307.html (accessed 17 June 2013).

Cochrane (2013), Database, available at http://summaries.cochrane.org/search/site (accessed 17 June 2013).

Devlein, A. and A. Arneil (2003), 'Healthcare environments and patient outcomes', *Environment and Behaviour*, **35** (2), 665–94.

Diversionary Therapy Technologies (2012), 'ditto™ device lowers anxiety in patients at Birmingham Children's Hospital', available at http://www.kristen-fischer.com/docs/DTTrelease.pdf (accessed 16 June 2013).

Diversionary Therapy Technologies (2013), 'Shriners hospitals in Galveston using ditto™ lite – innovative multi-cultural tool for children', available at http://www.

prnewswire.com/news-releases/shriners-hospitals-in-galveston-using-ditto-lite–innovative-multi-cultural-tool-for-children-201346921.html (accessed 16 June 2013).

Gilbody, S., P. Wilson and I. Watt (2005), 'Benefits and harms of direct to consumer advertising: a systematic review', *Quality and Safety in Health Care*, **14** (4), 246–50.

Grunig, J.E. and L.A. Grunig (2000), 'Public relations in strategic management and strategic management of public relations: theory and evidence from the IABC Excellence project', *Journalism Studies*, **1** (2), 303–21.

Houseman, S. (2001), 'Why employers use flexible staffing arrangements: evidence from an establishment survey', *Industrial and Labor Relations Review*, **55** (1), 149–70.

Howarth, B. (2012), 'Health in the third dimension', *The Age*, 16 May, available at http://www.theage.com.au/it-pro/government-it/health-in-the-third-dimension-20120516-1ypwf.html (accessed 17 June 2013).

Jackson, L.E. (2003), 'The relationship of urban design to human health and condition', *Landscape and Urban Planning*, **64** (4), 191–200.

Klasnja, P. and W. Pratt (2012), 'Healthcare in the pocket: mapping the space of mobile-phone interventions', *Journal of Biomedical Informatics*, **45** (1), 184–98.

Life in the Fast Lane (2013), available at www.lifeinthefastlane.com (accessed 1 February 2013).

Omachonu, V. and N. Einspruch (2010), 'Innovation in healthcare delivery systems: a conceptual framework', *The Innovation Journal: The Public Sector Innovation Journal*, **15** (1), 2–20.

Pagan, J., P. Higgs and S. Cunningham (2008), *Getting Creative in Healthcare: The Contribution of Creative Activities to Australian Healthcare*, Brisbane: Australian Research Council Centre of Excellence for Creative Industries and Innovation.

Patrick, K. and C. Gauthier (2001), 'Toward a professional responsibility theory of public relations ethics', *Journal of Mass Media Ethics*, **16** (2/3), 193–212.

Peruzza, N. and E. Kinsella (2010), 'Creative arts occupations in therapeutic practice – a review of the literature', *British Journal of Occupational Therapy*, **73** (6), 261–8.

Primack, B.A., M.V. Carroll, M. McNamara, M.L. Klem, B. King, M. Rich, C.W. Chan and S. Nayak (2012), 'Role of video games in improving health-related outcomes: a systematic review', *American Journal of Preventative Medicine*, **42** (6), 630–38.

Queenslandersign (2011) 'ditto™ device', 15 June, available at http://www.queenslandersign.com.au/index.php/dittotm-device-diversionary-therapy-technologies/ (accessed 17 June 2013).

Secretariat Australia Pty Ltd March (2012), *National and Global Perspectives on Health and Medical Research*, Strategic review of health and medical research in Australia.

Segal, L. and T. Bolton (2009), 'Issues facing the future healthcare workforce: the importance of demand modelling', *Australian and New Zealand Health Policy*, **6** (12), n.p.

Skiba, D.J. (2008), 'Games for health', *Nursing Education Perspectives*, **29** (4), 230–32.

Staricoff, R. (2006), 'Arts in health – the value of evaluation', *The Journal of the Royal Society for the Promotion of Health*, **126** (3), 116–20.

Strean, W. (2009), 'Laughter prescription', *Canadian Family Physician*, **55** (10), 965–7.

Summers, J. (2012), 'Ehealth service delivery – issues and challenges of a digital age ... this is not what we did social work for', presented at Centres Against Sexual Assault Workforce Development Workshop, 'Engaging with Cyberspace', Melbourne (September).

Sutton, M. and M. Fraser (2013), 'The rise of smartphone health and medical apps', *Australian Life Scientist*, 31 January, Westwick Farrow PTY LTD, available at http://lifescientist.com.au/content/biotechnology/article/the-rise-of-smartphone-health-and-medical-apps-1072193834 (accessed 19 June 2013).

Throsby, D. and V. Hollister (2003), *Don't Give Up Your Day Job – An Economic Study of Professional Artists in Australia*, Sydney: Australia Council.

Ulrich, R. (2006), 'Evidence-based health-care architecture', *Lancet*, **368**, S38–S39.

Watson, T. and P. Simmons (2004), 'Public relations evaluation – a survey of Australian practitioners', presented at ANZCA04, Sydney (July).

Wood, V.J., S.E. Curtis, W. Gesler, I.H. Spencer, H.J. Close, J. Mason and J.G. Reilly (2013), 'Creating "therapeutic landscapes" for mental health carers in inpatient setting: a dynamic perspective of permeability and inclusivity', *Social Science & Medicine*, **91**, 122–9.

7. Embedded creatives in the Australian manufacturing industry[1]

Jess Rodgers

INTRODUCTION

According to 2011 Australian Census figures, embedded creative employees (creative employees not working in the core Creative Industries) make up 2 per cent (or a total of 17 635) of manufacturing industry employees.[2] The average for all industries is 1.6 per cent. In the 2011–2012 financial year the manufacturing industry formed 7.3 per cent of Australia's gross domestic product (GDP), contributing approximately AU$106.5 billion to the economy (Department of Industry, Innovation, Science, Research and Tertiary Education 2013). Manufacturing is central to innovation, accounting for over one-quarter of all business expenditure in R&D in 2010–2011, representing around AU$4.8 billion invested in R&D (ibid.). Facing challenges such as sustainability concerns, ever-increasing offshore production and the global financial crisis, the Australian manufacturing industry needs to remain relevant and competitive to succeed. Innovation is one way to do this. Given the contribution of the manufacturing industry to the Australian economy, and the above-average portion of embedded creatives in manufacturing, it is important to consider what exactly embedded creatives add to the industry. This chapter, inspired by the *Getting Creative in Healthcare* report (Pagan, Higgs and Cunningham 2008), examines the contribution of embedded creatives to innovation in the manufacturing industry via case studies and supplemental data.

There is little qualitative research into embedded creatives (Vinodrai 2005; Kirby 2007; Pagan, Higgs and Cunningham 2008; Donald 2009; Bryson and Rusten 2011; Laaksonen and Gardner 2012). Some qualitative research external to the Creative Industries field looks at this topic (Getz, Andersson and Larson 2007; Male, Bower and Aritua 2007; Jacobs and Hackett 2008), but – given the differences in disciplinarity and definitions – it is difficult to apply this research to the Creative Industries. This chapter aims to address this dearth.

In Laaksonen and Gardner's *Creative Intersections* report (2012), 104 survey respondents from 'arts and culture' reported on their experience working across sectors (ibid., 1). Some of the ways that respondents contributed to other fields included: 'creative thinking, innovation, new solutions, instruments for networking, interdisciplinary research, alternative perspectives and working methods, and fresh insights', and 'creating dialogue and understanding between different disciplines and the public' (ibid., 20). Laaksonen and Gardner's study also reported on the challenges of collaboration. One common challenge is summarized thus: 'result and measure-driven sectors were accused of simply taking advantage of the arts and culture as a platform for dissemination or awareness-raising rather than as a source of new methods, skills and solutions' (ibid., 19). Creative inputs were used in the delivery or communication of programs or products, rather than being utilized from inception. These are just some of the contributions and challenges of arts and cultural producers collaborating with other fields, as described by Laaksonen and Gardner.

In this chapter, interview data inform case studies that demonstrate exactly what embedded creatives do, how they contribute to innovation and what challenges they face. This is further explored with additional examples from other interviewees. These discussions provide a snapshot of embedded creatives in manufacturing. This research, demonstrating some of the roles of key innovators in a crucial industry, is important to Australia's economic development. This research also informs the education of Creative Industries students who will go on to contribute to a variety of industries.

METHOD

Various definitions of manufacturing are used in this study. The Census statistics are based on self-reported occupations. Census occupations are sorted based on these descriptions. On this, Hearn and Bridgstock (2014) state:

> embedded creatives would not be categorized as such if they were not doing essentially the same work as those in creative firms. For example, a journalist outside the publishing industry must have described their work in such a way to be categorised as a journalist per se.

The GDP figures come from the 2006 Australian and New Zealand Standard Industrial Classification (ANZSIC) classification of manufacturing (Australian Bureau of Statistics 2012, 2008). The interviewees were sourced from any company that describes itself as manufacturing anything, as per the company's website 'about' section or similar information.

This chapter uses a dual approach to consider the capability and value-add of embedded creatives in the Australia's manufacturing industry. First, census data were examined for creative occupations within the manufacturing industry. However, these data do not say exactly what these workers do and how they contribute to innovation. These questions were explored during interviews conducted with embedded creatives.

Interviews were sought with people employed in the manufacturing industry, in Australia, working in one of the following positions: graphic designer; marketing specialist; industrial designer; developer programmer; fashion designer; ICT business analyst; architects, designers, planners and surveyors; arts professionals, and visual arts and crafts professional not elsewhere classified. These were selected from the Australian and New Zealand Standard Classification of Occupations (ANZSCO) creative occupations. These positions were chosen because they represent a spread of occupations and those more commonly employed in the manufacturing industry, as demonstrated by 2011 Australian Census figures. More detailed figures support this. Table 7.1 shows how many people were employed in the manufacturing industry in each of these occupations, in 2011, and what percentage of the corresponding segment each occupation forms.

Table 7.1   Occupations sought for interview

ANZSCO creative occupation	Number of employees	% of segment	Segment
Graphic Designer	3608	45	Architecture and Design
Marketing Specialist	4148	86	Advertising and Marketing
Industrial Designer	1463	18	Architecture and Design
Developer Programmer	988	35	Software and Digital Content
Fashion Designer	1141	14	Architecture and Design
ICT Business Analyst	503	18	Software and Digital Content
Architects, Designers, Planners and Surveyors	673	8.5	Architecture and Design
Arts Professionals	65	38.5	Music and Performing Arts
Visual Arts and Crafts Professional nec	610	51	Visual Arts

*Table 7.2   Occupations of interviewees and goods their companies
manufacture*

Company	Interviewee role	Product/s company manufactures
1	Senior Industrial Designer	Weighing equipment and technology
2	Communications Coordinator	Energy-saving fans and energy-efficient blowers
3	Marketing Communications Manager	Commercial and urban lighting
4	Design Manager	Lighting
5	Digital Designer	Automotive and transport seating
5	Automotive Designer	Automotive and transport seating
6	Sales and Marketing Manager	Automotive seating
7	Marketing Communications Coordinator	Blinds and shutters
8	Architectural Representative	Access and security systems in domestic and commercial buildings
9	Marketing Manager	Fabric architecture

Interviewees were recruited via LinkedIn and participated in a semi-structured interview. Ethics protocols made recruiting challenging. Only those who responded to the invitation via LinkedIn, or got in touch after hearing about the research from someone else who had received an invitation, were able to be interviewed. This meant that a reduced spread of occupations was included in the results. Table 7.2 shows the position titles of interviewees and the type of product their company manufactures. This study is limited due to the small number of interviewees and the few occupations of embedded creatives they represent. Despite this, those interviewed are somewhat representative of the statistical majority of Architecture and design (45 per cent of embedded creatives in manufacturing) and advertising and marketing (27 per cent) employees. Quantitative data from the 2011 Australian Census strengthen the case by supplementing the picture of embedded creatives in the manufacturing industry.

Companies are not named, to protect commercial confidence. This also assisted in recruiting. It was decided that people were more likely to talk about their roles and their company's output if the company's intellectual property was not compromised. The interviews focused on the roles and contributions to their company of people employed in creative occupations, their role in innovation, and the impacts of the creative contributions on the final good, service or activity in manufacturing. This helps to uncover what embedded creatives in manufacturing do and how they contribute to innovation.

The data were analysed thematically, using Carol Grbich's (2012) approach, which reduces the transcripts into meaningful groupings, allowing the participants to 'speak for themselves' through the data. The findings are presented here as individual company-interviewee case studies (Yin 2009) with a further section that provides a higher-level synthesis of the thematic results. Some company details are provided to contextualize the interviewee responses and to demonstrate the significance of these companies, and thus their embedded creatives, to the industry.

EMBEDDED CREATIVES IN THE MANUFACTURING INDUSTRY

Across all sectors, the most embedded creatives are in advertising and marketing roles (33 per cent). This is followed by software and digital content with 25 per cent. The remaining positions follow: architecture and design (22 per cent), publishing (9 per cent), music and performing arts (5 per cent), visual arts (4 per cent), and film, TV and radio (2 per cent). A study of Seek.com (Australia's biggest employment advertising website) advertisements supplements these data. From a sample of 281 ads, there were 107 PR/marketing ads; 79 per cent of these were for embedded positions. Of the 174 design ads, 35 per cent were for embedded positions. Web designer was the most common embedded position for the design ads, followed by industrial designer. Advertising and PR manager was the main position for the PR/marketing ads. The dominant industries for design positions were financial services, e-commerce and manufacturing. For PR/marketing positions, financial services was the main industry. Retail, fast moving consumer goods and IT followed. Overall, the financial services sector had the most embedded positions, followed by manufacturing, e-commerce and government. This contextualizes the data about creative workers in manufacturing among other figures about embedded creatives.

In December 2012 manufacturing constituted 8.5 per cent of Australian employment (Department of Industry, Innovation, Science, Research and Tertiary Education 2013). Creative employees made up 2.6 per cent of manufacturing industry employees. These creatives are mostly embedded, forming 74 per cent (17635) of manufacturing industry creative employees. The majority of these undertook architecture and design work (45 per cent). Advertising and marketing totalled 27 per cent of employees. The remainder of the employees were as follows: software and digital content – 16 per cent;

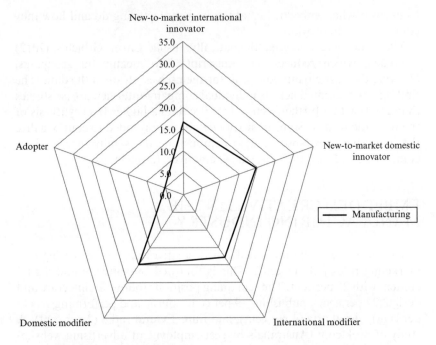

Source: Arundel and O'Brien (2007, 61).

Figure 7.1   How Australian manufacturing innovates

visual arts – 7 per cent; publishing – 2.5 per cent; film, TV and radio – 1.5 per cent, and music and performing arts – 1 per cent. Every segment, bar advertising and marketing, decreased between 2006 and 2011. In this period, advertising and marketing employment increased by 7 per cent.

Arundel and O'Brien (2009, 61) show how Australian manufacturing innovates. Figure 7.1 illustrates that Australian manufacturers primarily innovate through modifying domestic products and introducing new products to the domestic market (ibid., 15, 61). The UK Design Council's report, *The Value of Design* (2007), provides a useful context for the significance of design to business and manufacturing. For every £100 a business spends on design, turnover increases by £225 (ibid., 8). Design is highly utilized, with 80 per cent of UK manufacturers surveyed using design in their business (UK average 68 per cent) (ibid., 43). This is more than any other sector. Investment in design by manufacturers was also found to be significantly increasing: 44 per cent of manufacturers (more than any other sector) invest more than they did in 2004 (ibid., 46). Design adds value, and is valued, in the UK Manufacturing sector. In Manufacturing, design is mostly applied to external facing functions, such as branding and new product development (ibid., 44). This chapter captures some of the ways that this value-adding is done in Australia.

CASE STUDIES

Company 1 – Smart Weighing

This company develops smart weighing – digital weighing equipment. The equipment consists of embedded computer systems that work with load cells (load cells are the basic units that detect weights). The main customers are original equipment manufacturers (OEMs). Company 1 designs and manufactures instruments that are then sold as other brands. Other customers include installers who, for example, build weighbridges or processing plants. The main, and only, office in Australia undertakes manufacturing and R&D.

Company 1 employs three types of creative workers: Industrial Designers, Software Developers and Marketing Staff. The Industrial Designer and the Software Developers have a considerable influence on the shape of products. They either design new products or repurpose or modify existing products. The Industrial Designer also has multimedia and graphics qualifications. He is in charge of product design, detail design and concept design – everything except electronics or software. He also undertakes graphic design when required, such as rebranding of graphics panels and label design on smart weighing products. The Software Developers create the software that runs in the embedded systems. They also produce custom applications.

One example of recent innovation is a set of scales being developed for marine trawlers. These scales need to account for the fact that a trawler goes over waves, so that the weight of things varies. The Industrial Designer (Respondent 1) stated,

> R1: One of our competitors who buys stuff from us was trying to develop a solution and basically couldn't. They came to us in the end to, well they actually came to us for custom software, but in the end it became a lot more than that. So we've assisted, I guess, in coming up with a solution for them and having done that we're now developing our own in the same line.

The frame is now being modified to fit another load cell.

Future innovation in the industry, generally, includes a move towards digital converters. An analogue-to-digital converter is more prone to damage and interference. This affects calibration and accuracy. The digital converters are situated closer to the actual load cells inside the scales, increasing lifespan and accuracy.

The involvement of creatives in Company 1 is fairly critical to enhancing the wider benefits of the organization's activities. An example of this is the Industrial Designer:

> R1: One of the differentiating things between [our company] and our competitors is that our products are designed, they're not typical products in this industry. [The typical products are] in square stainless steel boxes with a minimal amount of design involved. Obviously there's electronics design in them but . . . a lot of them . . . were designed a long time ago and haven't really been developed very much since. There's not a lot of that sort of thing happening in Australia . . .
>
> I guess, that's one of the unique things about [our company] . . . its products tend to be a lot more attractive than most of the others in the industry.
>
> The industry as a whole is very conservative, so one of the things I have to be careful of is not making the designs too modern.

This exemplifies the differentiation that this embedded creative provides for his company.

Company 2 – Fans and Pumps

Company 2 is a wholly owned subsidiary of a company whose head office is in Europe. Most of its products are produced in Europe, but some are produced in Australia. It manufactures fans and motors for air movement – fans for ventilation, heating, air conditioning and car ventilation. Some products are produced exclusively for the Australian market, which has different needs from the European market.

The main customers for Company 2 are air conditioning, ventilation or car OEMs. The company modifies existing products for Australian OEM requirements. This is an increasing part of the value-add because it differentiates the business from Chinese manufacturers. This allows OEMs to obtain quality products specifically suited to their needs, rather than having to use an off-the-shelf product. Company 2 also sells, for example, replacement fridge motors to wholesalers and undertakes a great deal of testing for customers.

In terms of creative staff, Company 2 employs two design staff and a Communications Coordinator. There is a Design Engineer whose degree is in Design. The other design employee tweaks existing products, from Europe, based on equipment manufacturer requirements. One of the design employees also assists with packaging design, that is, boxes for motors and pumps. Company 2 outsources some marketing work to a creative production agency; however, more and more of this is undertaken in house. The design of advertisements is always outsourced, along with a catalogue published every one to two years. Flyers are designed both by the Communications Coordinator and by the creative agency, depending on how complicated the job is and how much time the Communications Coordinator has. Three years ago there were no creatives in the company. Now there are three.

The Communications Coordinator is in charge of marketing, communications, PR and events. She organizes marketing material and participation in trade shows and conferences. She designs flyers and produces short YouTube videos. These marketing materials are targeted at end customers. The Communications Coordinator is also in charge of internal communications, such as the website, press releases and media bookings.

The interviewee (Respondent 2) spoke about her current marketing innovations.

> R2: I'm looking after our social media presence . . . it's still very much just trying stuff out . . .

> We have Facebook and we have a YouTube channel, which is actually very good. LinkedIn just to have a business presence in the business community I guess . . . I think [Facebook is] effective for our employees and especially to connect with employees across the world.

> Interviewer: So what kind of things do you . . . do you post stuff on there?

> R2: Well at the moment I do lots for a fundraiser that we're doing. We are participating in the Bay Bike Ride and we support Engineers without Borders. And that's just sort of publicity . . . Just a bit sort of behind the scenes. If we have a barbecue I upload a photo of . . . Yeah just to give the business I guess a bit more of a human profile yeah.

> Interviewer: Uhum and so do you think if you're using that kind of thing as a social marketing, humanising process, do you think that that really what you are doing is targeting your employees rather than . . . ?

> R2: Yeah.

> I: Yeah. And are there any other kind of, sort of ways that you're using, that you think you're innovating you think or you might innovate in your role in the future?

> R2: Yeah well the videos are quite innovative I think because they . . .

> I: Can you describe a little bit what's in them?

R2: At the moment I'm working on one that's targeted at fridges. So they buy the product and then they have problems with it and you say okay well maybe you know you need to wire the fan like this. Or we've made this and this change and it's good because of that and the cabling goes in here and you do this and whatever. Or we have product related videos that are targeted at wholesale customers. So you have a product that people buy and put in the wholesaler, and the wholesaler can show that video on site. But they can also just refer to the video, you also have training videos. So either our customers show to their employees or other subsidiaries show it to their employees.

So far, feedback on these videos has been positive, including that from colleagues in the European office. The channel has had (as of December 2012) nearly 10000 hits since March 2011. This channel was the Managing Director's idea, and the Communications Coordinator undertakes the filming and editing.

Company 3 – Lighting Solutions

Company 3 is a large lighting design, manufacture and supply business. It provides commercial lighting, street lights, building lights and neon signs. The main markets are energy authorities and councils, architects, interior and lighting designers, and specifiers. The company also provides lighting for projectors, concerts, smaller gigs and nightclubs.

This company employs a number of creative workers: Marketers, Graphic Designers, PR employees, Application Designers and Lighting Designers. Graphic Designers and Web Developers are sometimes out-sourced. The Marketing and Communications Manager leads a team of Graphic Designers, Applications Designers and Marketers, and organizes web development and design, and trade shows. He may also undertake photography, graphic design and web coding. The Lighting Designers form part of the LDE team (lighting, design, engineering) and develop light visualization. They use 3D software to give the customer an impression of what the installed product will look like. The Graphic Designer designs packaging and promotional outputs, such as catalogues. The Applications Designers develop web and mobile applications for marketing purposes, such as lighting calculators, energy-saving calculators and online catalogues. The Marketers assist in administering the logistics of trade shows and expos, design and create datasheets and catalogue pages, administer content that is to go onto the web, liaise with sales team members about their needs, and design adverts for print and online media.

The Marketing Manager (Respondent 3) is doing some innovative things with QR (quick response) codes:

> R3: I introduced QR codes into the system, we use QR codes for things like, for example, if a guy is stuck seventy-five metres up on a lighting tower, every single product has a QR code on it . . . if he scans it with his iPhone, it will have installation instructions on there and a troubleshooting guide. So stuff like that is very important for people and the more we put it out the better reaction we've had because people have gone, 'wow this is really cool, I don't have to sit here and sift through multiple websites or carry around folders of instructions, it's all there on the physical product'.

Traditionally, marketing has been very conservative. Fax streaming was the norm in the company until recently. The Marketing Manager took up his position by making the switch to emailing catalogues and other information to wholesalers. He has implemented social media to communicate with business partners. Discussions with business partners also generated the development of QR codes and website and mobile applications (apps).

> R3: We launched a new website a month and a half ago [interview conducted November 2012] and that's now integrated with apps. So we're doing a lot of apps for things like lighting calculators, energy-saving calculators, online catalogues, which are accessible via mobile devices, they see that as innovative.

The head of the LDE team and the Marketing Manager are currently developing an augmented reality booth to take their pre-visualization software up a notch.[3] It will be a projection-based booth that replicates what any environment will look like with any kind of lighting. The booth is called City of LEON (Lighting Education ONline). This will enable the company to present potential customers, such as city councils, with an experience of lighting design. The booth will use Xbox's Kinect with a PC to track a person's movement. The environment will change based on the movement of the viewer, such as by creating shadows and glare where appropriate.

EMBEDDED CREATIVE VALUE-ADD

This section briefly explores the various ways that the embedded creatives interviewed add value to their organizations.

The creatives at Company 4 influence the nature of the product, its delivery and how the customers are reached. The designers influence the nature of the product – the shape it takes, its effect, its power usage and output, and its appearance. The Design Manager at Company 4 (Respondent 4) detailed the role of designers at his company:

R4: From my point of view our job in the creative part of the process is incredibly important. I mean I'm not trying to put it above the rest but it is important together with all the rest of the positions and all the rest of the job[s] . . . but the difference is that we are the stage that makes things happen. Okay it could be anything of deal, contract, financial, staff etc. etc. dealing at this stage. But all that is theory until it reaches us. When it reaches us that theory, that financial, that idea, that really becomes a reality. We convert all that into something that is tangible, is physical, you can touch and feel, smell.

The involvement of the creatives – Industrial Designers – in Company 6 influences the nature of the product, in terms of the design – from the look and feel of the product to how it functions.

Company 3's marketing department influences the delivery of the product and how customers are reached. They add the sizzle and tell the story of the product. The Sales and Marketing Manager of Company 6 influences the delivery of the product in terms of the way the customers are reached. He developed systems where the retailers, and those who purchase the products from retailers, can find with ease the information they require about the product. At Company 8 there has recently been a shift in the way products are developed. A change in management has meant that Marketing now comes up with ideas and takes them to R&D to make them happen. R&D has a more technical perspective. They develop based on industry standards and design products that can be retrofitted, easily installed and easy to operate. Marketing seems to have the opposite approach. They will do what is easiest for them and what meets their targets, without considering how easy a product is to install or use. With Marketing taking the lead, the marketing staff influence the nature of the product, in addition to the way it is delivered and how the customers are reached.

These examples demonstrate that embedded creatives in Manufacturing influence products and their dissemination. In both these ways, as the earlier case studies have shown, embedded creatives are vital to innovation. This makes them critical to the Manufacturing industry.

CHALLENGES

Throughout the interviews, the various challenges of being a creative worker in Manufacturing became apparent. The main challenges were financial restrictions and a lack of company support for creative workers and innovation. Other concerns included the move of manufacturing offshore, the lack of government support for the industry and difficulties working with customers and outsourced creatives. Due to space restrictions, discussion here focuses on financial and company support for creative endeavours.

The Marketing Communications Manager for Company 3 found that marketing budgets in Manufacturing are very tight. Any creative endeavour within the manufacturing environment is done on a small budget and with other restrictions. Everyone loves new and exciting things, but it comes down to profitability. The creative workers are the first to go if things get tough. The Marketing Communications Manager believes that manufacturing companies do not appreciate creative workers as much as they should. The Design Manager for Company 4 feels restricted in terms of his design potential:

> R4: Innovation is something strange and something that I deal with on a daily basis but at the same time I feel limited . . . I wish I could do more. But I work for this company; I got to do what I got to do . . .

> I wish we could have a more versatile way of developing things a bit more organic in regards to shape . . . You're always working kind of the same variation from the same thing. Rather than creating new ones and that sometimes feels you know a bit restrictive and that is probably why you know I feel the way I feel with regards to development. I want, I would like to do something more but perhaps if we were to involve the company in something else we will need to invest in new machinery, new technology and things like that and sometimes we're not prepared to do that. Or not ready to do that.

> Always, everything turns into a financial [consideration] unfortunately. I mean this company is owned by shareholders. What they want is a profit and we need to deliver that. Okay they don't care if the product is sophisticated; they care if the product sells well. And that is at all levels, that gets passed on all the way down. We've got our values, we've got our targets, we've got our technology.

Company 5's Digital Designer noted that manufacturing companies do not know the best way to get the most from their creative staff, due to financial and other restrictions, including time. In his work for a previous automotive company, design decisions would sometimes be diverted to Management or Accounting. If a part cost 50 cents extra, it might be left out, despite the fact that the end customer might be happy to pay the additional A$20 for better quality. At Company 7 the Marketing and Communications Coordinator felt that the Designer was restricted in his innovation due to costs. In order for him to be innovative with fabrics, more money would have to be spent. This would increase the costs of an already expensive product. The Marketing and Communications Coordinator often makes innovative design suggestions to the boss, but her ideas are rejected. Product innovation is not a company priority and marketing innovation is restricted by finances.

The Marketing Manager for Company 9 thinks the creative perspective is really missing from the company.

R9: Our product, our smaller product that we sell to residential and small businesses hasn't changed in something like 25 years because it works I guess. But there's been no stylistic change either because the engineers at the top don't see style and change as necessary, they just ignore market desire for that. That's a product issue. As far as delivery, the same thing with how it's being done, why bother and why change?

I: Do you feel that creative workers bring a different perspective of ways of doing things that the other employees don't?

R9: Most definitely. I think it's really missing in our organisation. Our senior management team is all men over 45 that are engineers, they're the carbon copy of each other, what's the point of having more than one of you? So a mix is very important in the industry and those types of people definitely are more willing to take a risk and think more outside the box, which is something we don't do well I think.

I: So we definitely think finance and the senior management [are] not listening to younger ideas and voices?

R9: Yeah that's possibly holding the company back, I'd say so, yeah . . . that conservative nature of engineers, in general, I think is something that really squashes a lot of creativity for the business.

I: What additionality do the creatives bring to the innovation in the company?

R9: I think just an understanding of our clients. Yes. Like a fresh perspective on even just the way the business is run, but that often gets squashed, I think. It's not allowed to sort of grow.

I: Is there an age gap between the people we're labelling as creative workers and the other employees?

R9: Yes. Generally it's a pretty young office but yeah senior management is over 50 and [Colleague 1] and [Colleague 2] I think are both under 30. So there is a bit of that, yeah age and experience not working for us.

These various factors make it hard for the creatives at Company 9 to influence change.

CONCLUSION

This chapter illustrates who the embedded creatives in the Manufacturing industry are, what sorts of organizations they work in, what they do, how they contribute to innovation and what challenges they face. As in

Laaksonen and Gardner's (2012) study of interdisciplinary creatives, the embedded creatives interviewed bring a variety of value-add propositions to their companies, including translation, reaching customers and differentiation. However, the interviewees often feel that their creative input is not valued by their companies. The use of creative skills for dissemination purposes and ignoring other ideas from embedded creatives was also captured by Laakosen and Gardner (2012, 19). Following from this, the presence of high numbers of Advertising and Marketing occupations across embeddeds (also supported by data from the Seek.com study), and the 7 per cent increase of this segment in the Manufacturing industry, perhaps indicate that industries undervalue design and put their energy and funds into promoting current products, rather than designing new ones. Arundel and O'Brien's innovation diagram (Figure 7.1) somewhat supports this, demonstrating that innovation in Australian manufacturing focuses on modification or new domestic products. The companies featured in this chapter largely modified or developed products solely for the Australian market. This gives rise to the suggestion that the contributions of the embedded creatives interviewed, and the challenges that they face, are not atypical.

The interviews suggest that embedded creatives have the skills and knowledge to innovate, and move beyond incremental innovation, but the firms do not create an accommodating environment. The creatives accommodate the client. One way firms can move beyond this level of innovation and harness the talent of embedded creatives is by listening to their ideas and allowing for greater creative freedom. The firms need to foster dynamic capabilities (Teece, Pisano and Shuen 1997; Teece 2007). The embedded creatives would also benefit from applying this concept. Dynamic capabilities can be defined as: 'the capacity (1) to sense and shape opportunities and threats, (2) to seize opportunities, and (3) to maintain competitiveness through enhancing, combining, protecting, and, when necessary, reconfiguring the business enterprise's intangible and tangible assets' (Teece 2007, 1319). Embedded creatives need to become intrapreneurs (Hearn and Bridgstock 2014). Organizations and structures need to support creative workers. Regulatory environments and the way industry is set up should encourage intrapreneurs and risk taking. Creating and allowing space for process innovation is one way to do this. Strengthened interdisciplinary communication is another avenue for development. Training can support embedded creatives by teaching intrapreneurship and interdisciplinary communication. Supplemented by further research, the additions that embedded creatives bring to manufacturing, and the challenges they face, provide a starting point for influencing policy, educating industry, and educating future creative workers about embedded and interdisciplinary conditions and how they can contribute to innovation.

NOTES

1. Thanks to Janet Pagan for sharing planning documents from the *Getting Creative in Healthcare Report*, and to Michelle Hall for conducting some of the interviews featured in this chapter.
2. The Census figures cited in this chapter come from a custom data set developed for the CCI by Peter Higgs.
3. This information is published with the express permission of the interviewee.

REFERENCES

Arundel, A. and K. O'Brien (2009), *Innovation Metrics for Australia*, Canberra, Australia: Department of Innovation, Industry, Science and Research.

Australian Bureau of Statistics (2008), *Australian and New Zealand Standard Industrial Classification (ANZSIC)*, 2006 (Revision 1.0), available at http://www.abs.gov.au/ausstats/abs@.nsf/mf/1292.0 (accessed 20 November 2012).

Australian Bureau of Statistics (2012), 'Manufacturing', *Year Book Australia, 2012*, available at http://www.abs.gov.au/ausstats/abs@.nsf/Lookup/by%20Subject/1301.0~2012~Main%20Features~Manufacturing%20industry~147 (accessed 29 January 2013).

Bryson, J.R. and G. Rusten (eds) (2011), *Design Economies and the Changing World Economy: Innovation, Production and Competitiveness*, Oxford and New York: Routledge.

Department of Industry, Innovation, Science, Research and Tertiary Education (2013), 'Manufacturing industry', available at http://www.innovation.gov.au/Industry/Manufacturing/Pages/default.aspx (accessed 9 January 2013).

Design Council (2007), *The Value of Design*, available at http://www.design council.org.uk/Documents/Documents/Publications/Research/TheValueOfDesignFact finder_Design_Council.pdf (accessed 29 April 2013).

Donald, S.H. (2009), 'Education, class and adaptation in China's world city', *Chinese Journal of Communication*, **2** (1), 25–35.

Getz, D., T. Andersson and M. Larson (2007), 'Festival stakeholder roles: concepts and case studies', *Event Management*, **10** (2), 103–22.

Grbich, C. (2012), *Qualitative Data Analysis: An Introduction*, London: Sage Publications.

Hearn, G. and R. Bridgstock (2014), 'The curious case of the embedded creative: cultural occupations outside the creative industries', in S. Cummings and C. Bilton (eds), *Handbook of Management and Creativity*, Cheltenham, UK and Northampton, MA, USA: Edward Elgar Publishing.

Jacobs, J. and J. Hackett (2008), 'Experiential design drives an established brand to a youthful market', *Design Management Review*, **19** (2), 47–52.

Kirby, B. (2007), 'Country practice: a case study of regional public relations practice', *PRism*, **5** (1/2), 1–11.

Laaksonen, A. and S. Gardner (2012), *Creative Intersections: Partnerships Between the Arts, Culture and Other Sectors*, Sydney, New South Wales: International Federation of Arts Councils and Culture Agencies.

Male, S., D.A. Bower and B. Aritua (2007), 'Design management: changing roles of the professions', *Management, Procurement and Law*, **160**, 75–82.

Pagan, J., P. Higgs and S. Cunningham (2008), *Getting Creative in Healthcare: The Contribution of Creative Activities to Australian Healthcare*, Brisbane: Queensland University of Technology.

Teece, D.J. (2007), 'Explicating dynamic capabilities: the nature and microfoundations of (sustainable) enterprise performance', *Strategic Management Journal*, **28** (13), 1319–50.

Teece, D.J., G. Pisano and A. Shuen (1997), 'Dynamic capabilities and strategic management', *Strategic Management Journal*, **18** (7), 509–33.

Vinodrai, T. (2005), *Locating Design Work: Innovation, Institutions and Local Labour Market Dynamics* (thesis), Toronto, Canada: University of Toronto.

Yin, R.K. (2009), *Case Study Research: Design and Methods*, Thousand Oaks, CA: Sage Publications.

8. Embedded digital creatives

Ben Goldsmith

INTRODUCTION

Widespread and thoroughgoing participation in the digital economy – 'the global network of economic and social activities that are enabled by information and communications technologies' (Department of Broadband, Communications and the Digital Economy 2013) – is widely acknowledged to be one of the keys to future productivity, competitiveness and social well-being. The direct contribution of the Internet to the Australian economy was AU$50 billion in 2010 (with an additional AU$80 billion in productivity increases for business and benefits to households) (Deloitte Access Economics 2011, 1). The equivalent UK figure was £100 billion in 2009 (ibid., 8). In recent years, digital economy policy in countries such as Australia, the UK and the US, has focused on technological issues around the construction and availability of high-speed fixed and mobile broadband, access to broadband services including e-government services, and the affordability of broadband connectivity. These are clearly important, but such a concentration has had the effect of softening policy focus on issues around digital content and on the circumstances of, and challenges facing, digital content producers and service providers. A recent OECD Digital Economy paper acknowledged that infrastructure development and access prices are priority areas, but it also noted that they are 'simply tools' to achieve larger social and economic goals (OECD/ISOC/UNESCO 2013, 5). The role of digital content cannot be ignored. The Digital Economy Paper reported 'a strong correlation between local content, infrastructure development and access prices', noting that 'these three elements are connected and feed into each other in a virtuous circle' (ibid., 7).[1] The paper concludes that 'More local content helps encourage more Internet development, which in turn, helps promote more local content' (ibid., 61), and recommends that 'Policy makers should take the necessary steps to foster an innovative environment for content creation', since this will both reinforce infrastructure development and help to lower access prices (ibid., 9).

With this recommendation in mind, attention must be paid to the creators or facilitators of digital content, or 'digital creatives'.[2] The rapid development of digital technologies and the digitization of content have opened up opportunities for non-professional creators either working alone or co-creating with professionals; therefore it is important to acknowledge the contribution that 'produsers' (Bruns 2008) are making, but my focus here is on those who both have creative training and who work principally or exclusively in creative occupations.

Digital creatives are spread widely across the economy, and are growing rapidly in number. New industries, such as mobile applications (apps) development, are creating new occupations and services, and transforming some older ones. Digital creatives are driving innovation and economic growth in these industries and service sectors. Digital technologies and processes are becoming increasingly important in virtually all spheres of creative work, across the economy. And yet there is no broad agreement either in Australia or worldwide about the constitution of the digital creative grouping, and only limited understanding of both the role of creatives in the digital economy and innovation, and the issues and challenges they face. Who are they? Where are they working? Where are their numbers growing? The answers to these questions will help to inform the development of policy and the fostering of an environment that promotes digital content and creativity.

This chapter analyses the ways in which digital creatives have featured or been defined or understood in a range of official reports and studies from several countries. The limitations of these studies led me to propose a preliminary typology of digital creative occupations in Australia. This exercise not only generates new insights into the size of the digital creative workforce, but will also help to assess the economic and social contributions that both specialist and embedded digital creatives make. In turn, these findings can assist policymakers and scholars to understand and plan for the needs and potential of this increasingly important grouping.

The second section of this chapter charts the growth in digital creative employment in Australia. Among the most striking findings from analysis of 2006 and 2011 Australian Census data is the high growth in both specialist digital 'Cultural Production' and 'Creative Services' occupations, to use categories from the Australian Research Council's Centre for Creative Industries and Innovation Trident Mark II (see Cunningham 2013, 133–8; Cunningham, Chapter 2 in this volume). There is, by contrast, considerably slower growth in embedded occupations. But, before describing this growth in more detail, it is necessary to outline who digital creatives are and how they have been understood.

DEFINING DIGITAL CREATIVES

There is no uniform, shared understanding at national levels, let alone internationally, of what constitutes a digital creative occupation. Creative occupations and industries are classified in different ways, while designations of job titles by industry associations, within firms, and by writers about the Creative Industries (CI) also show considerable variance. In February 2013 the Australian digital industry association AIMIA released the first *Digital Industry Salary Report*, covering 66 job titles, ranging from executive and management positions, to sales, marketing and business support (AIMIA 2013). Most job titles can be directly matched to a six-digit occupation code in the Australian and New Zealand Standard Classification of Occupations (ANZSCO) (Australian Bureau of Statistics 2009), but some (such as UX [user experience] director and experience architect) cannot. The rapid change and emergence of new occupations, products and services as a result of digitization and media convergence have meant that official classifications, which have slower update cycles, have struggled to keep pace. This finding, in part, provided the impetus behind new efforts to map and define the CI from around the turn of the twenty-first century.

First Iteration of Creative Industries Mapping Studies

Initial surveys, beginning with the UK Department of Culture, Media and Sport (DCMS)'s 1998 *Creative Industries Mapping Study*, were limited in their analyses of digital creatives. This 'first iteration' (Cunningham and Higgs 2008) of studies, which also included the *Australian Creative Industries Cluster Study Stage One Report* (Department of Communications, Information Technology and the Arts 2002), focused on industry-specific employment data rather than the economy-wide employment of creatives. Basing analysis on industrial classifications and gathering data on specialist firms within each segment alone produces misleading findings, since focus is limited to specialist creatives and misses the many creative workers embedded in industries and firms outside the core (Pratt 2004). This was particularly the case in design and interactive media in the 1998 UK study. As a consequence, these studies underestimated employment numbers, the economic impact of creative activities generally and of digital creative activities in particular.

The original 1998 mapping exercise used different data sources for each segment. To complicate the picture further, the UK Standard Occupational Classification was updated between the first mapping exercise in 1998 and the second in 2001. Methodological differences between these two studies had a significant impact on employment figures. Digital creative occupations were limited to the 'software and computer services' and 'interactive leisure software' segments. The 1998 study reported the Office of National Statistics' finding that 272 000 people were working in 'computer services'. This included software and was the largest by employment of any of the segments. By 2001 the 1998 figure had been revised up to 420 000. The equivalent figure for 2001 was 555 000 (out of a total CI workforce of 1.322 million), and included the 'interactive leisure software' industry (meaning, principally, computer games development), in which a further 21 000 were employed in 2001 (27 000 in 1998).

Second Iteration of Creative Industries Mapping Studies

The 'second iteration' of mapping methodology (Cunningham and Higgs 2008), beginning with the 2003 Baseline Study of Hong Kong's CI and the DCMS CI *Economic Estimates Statistical Bulletin* series from 2003, included occupational data to explore creative employment across the whole economy. The Hong Kong study divided the 'content/creative production' workforce into two broad groups: 'occupation' and 'associate profession'. Among 11 sectors, the study identified two major digital CI: digital entertainment (animation, digital effects and games), and software and computing. The digital entertainment industry was difficult to define, since

> Theoretically, entertainment such as film, animation, games, music composition, publishing and media services could nearly all be digitalized. However, local conditions for growth vary from one sub-segment to another and therefore a list of all these potentials is too equivocal. (Centre for Cultural Policy Research 2003, 94)

The study also found that 'Many of [the digital entertainment industry companies] are engaged with cross-sector activities', indicating potentially high numbers of embedded digital creatives and specialist creative service providers (ibid.). However, the study did not analyse these groups, despite 'industry sources reveal[ing] more number [sic] of designers, software engineers or multi-media workers who are working in establishments outside the scope of our mapping' (ibid., 48).

Coincident with the Hong Kong study, the Australian government's *CI Cluster Study* examined aspects of digital content production, from industry mapping (Department of Communications, Information Technology and the Arts 2002), to cluster dynamics and firm-level analysis (Cutler and Co. 2002) and outputs (Pattinson Consulting 2003). The report, *From Cottages to Corporations: Building a Global Industry from Australian*

Creativity (Higgs and Kennedy 2003), attempted to measure creative digital employment, turnover and export potential across a broad range of sectors, and identified 12 sectors of the Australian 'Creative Digital Industry'.[3] Like the Hong Kong study, this report relied on several data sources, with different definitions and methodologies. Drawing principally on industry sector data from the 2001 Census, total employment in the 12 sectors (albeit with several gaps) was calculated as 211 638, of which 98 798 were 'Creative Digital Industry Relevant', or specialist digital creatives. But like the Hong Kong study, this report was unable to measure the number of embedded digital creatives.

Following on from the *Cluster Study*, the Australian government launched the *Digital Content Industry Action Agenda* in February 2004. The following year, the Centre for International Economics report, *Australian Digital Content Industry Futures*, made a useful distinction between 'core' and 'embedded' production, with the former comprising digital content created by 'firms and individuals in the Creative Industries', and the latter comprising digital content created within the 'professional service industries rather than the Creative Industries' (Centre for International Economics 2005, 6). The report estimated the industry's total output (AU$18 billion) and employment (289 000, of whom 54 per cent were embedded). 'Embedded digital content production activities' included 'scientific research', 'surveying services' and 'consulting engineering services', among others. However, the practice of using industry rather than (or in addition to) occupation data limits this study's utility for assessments of the creative workforce, just as Pratt (2004) and others noted for the DCMS studies. The Strategic Industry Leaders Group acknowledged this in their discussion of the Centre for International Economics' findings on the property and business services, and cultural and recreational services sectors:

> Because much of the digital content activity in these sectors will be undertaken within larger companies which are not mainly digital content businesses, these figures are likely to significantly underestimate the extent of digital content activity in all sectors. (Department of Communications, Information Technology and the Arts 2005, 24)

Third Iteration: The Creative Trident and Australian Digital Creative Employment

The third iteration of CI mapping, comprising the Australian Research Council Centre of Excellence for Creative Industries and Innovation's (CCI) Creative Trident and a parallel French study on cultural employment in Europe (Ministry of Culture, France 2005), turned the focus on to occupational data. The Trident defined creative employment as: those in creative occupations in the CI (core or specialist), those in creative occupations outside the CI (embedded), and those in non-creative roles within the CI (support).

Higgs, Cunningham and Pagan (2007) used the Trident methodology to estimate that, in August 2001 (at the time, the most recent available census data), employment in the Australian software development and interactive content segment accounted for 31 per cent of total CI employment. This was, by some margin, the largest of the six CI segments, accounting for 40 per cent of total employment earnings, with employees enjoying mean average incomes approximately 30 per cent higher than average. Twenty-eight per cent, or just over 38 000, were embedded in other industries, surprisingly below the overall CI average (31 per cent). However, recognizing that the software development and interactive content segment did not capture the entire digital creative workforce, Higgs, Cunningham and Pagan (2007, 22) identified a 'creative digital grouping':

> those activities involved in the production, creation and publishing of experiential and informational media that are currently being (or soon will be) produced or delivered or experienced in digital form. Inherent in the definition are the 'software' based applications and services that enable or assist in these production, management, publishing and consumption activities.

> Many of these activities are traditional 'analogue' segments and sectors, such as film and television that are moving rapidly into partial, or complete, digital production and delivery chains. Other activities are the 'born digital' sectors that have recently emerged such as broadband and mobile content where there is no analogue media to manage or process through the value chain. Other activities, such as libraries, provide a critical preservation, access and re-use role not only of 'born digital' media but also of physical media and even three dimensional artefacts that are in the process of being digitised so that they can be preserved, discovered, accessed and experienced in different ways in digital form.

Occupations in each of the six CI segments were included.[4] Most of the excluded (that is, non-digital) occupations were in architecture, design and visual arts (ibid., 31).[5] Taking this creative digital group as a whole, the researchers calculated that, in Australia in 2001, 109 457 people were employed in creative digital occupations within the core digital Creative Industries, with an additional 120 546 embedded in other industries, such as banking, government and manufacturing. Digital creatives accounted for over half of the total creative workforce. Embedded digital creatives alone accounted for more than 25 per cent. Further underlining the significance of the embedded digital creative workforce is the fact that, of the overall total of embedded creatives (137 017), almost 90 per cent (120 546) were embedded digital creatives (ibid., 32).

These figures are, however, slightly misleading because they include occupations in which some – but not all – workers are using digital technologies and processes. For example, the ANZSCO code 212312 (director – film, television, radio or stage) includes some workers who will routinely, if not exclusively, use digital technologies and processes in the course of their work, and thus can legitimately be described as digital creatives. Television directors cannot work exclusively with 'analogue' production and delivery technologies and processes, and neither can the majority of film directors. Stage directors, on the other hand, may use digital technologies and processes, but their work is not digitally dependent in the same way as that of their counterparts.

Since analysis of Australian census data from 1996 to 2006 showed that growth in employment was not uniform across the CI, in 2011 the CCI team revised the Creative Trident, dividing the CI into two sub-groups. 'Cultural Production' comprises three of the original CI segments: music and performing arts; film, television and radio, and writing, publishing and print media – plus the visual arts. 'Creative Services' comprises advertising and marketing, software and digital content, and architecture and design. While both specialists and embedded workers in Creative Services had roughly doubled over the decade 1996–2006, Cultural Production occupations had experienced virtually no employment growth. As illustrated above, and as will be shown in detail in the second section of this chapter, digital creatives can be found in both Cultural Production and Creative Services sub-groups.

Recent UK Changes, and the 'Creative Intensity' Test

UK estimates of digital creative employment have been further complicated by definitional changes in 2011. 'Computer consultancy activities' and 'business and domestic software development' were removed from the software/electronic publishing sector 'as the industries these captured were more related to business software than to creative software' (DCMS 2011, 9). Two software occupation codes (IT strategy and planning professionals, and ICT managers) were removed from the 2011 *CI Economic Estimates*. In addition, the previous 'software, computer games and electronic publishing' category was split into 'software/electronic publishing' and 'digital and entertainment media' in order to represent the computer games sector (the latter category) separately from other software development. Drawing from the *Labour Market Statistics Bulletin* (February

2011), the DCMS estimated total employment in these combined segments in 2010 as 36 384. However, of this number, only 2888 were 'creative employees' or 'creative self-employed' in the CI. The remainder (33 497) were 'support employees' or 'support self-employed', with 22 290 or almost 67 per cent in the software/electronic publishing sector. Of the 2888 employed in the CI, the vast majority (1973, or 68 per cent) were working in digital and entertainment media. Unlike the other CI segments, no figures were provided for embedded creatives ('employees/self-employed doing creative jobs in other industries') in the 'software/electronic publishing' and 'digital and entertainment media' sectors. Total core creative employment was 476 835, meaning that these two sectors accounted for only 0.6 per cent of the total (DCMS 2011, 28). This is a far cry from the 555 000 'computer services' workers recorded in the 2001 DCMS mapping study.

Digital creative employment in the UK is very low, if restricted to these sectors. And yet, aside from the significant absence of what could be expected to be the large numbers of embedded digital creatives – in particular in the software sector – these figures do not account for 'born digital' occupations (that is, those that have been created as a direct result of digitization) classified in other segments, such as web and multimedia design (Higgs, Cunningham and Bakhshi 2008, 23).

In the light of this dramatic restructuring of creative employment statistics, the British charity Nesta, drawing on the early work of the European Leadership Group on Culture (or LEG) and on the work of Alan Freeman initially for a report on London's creative sector (Greater London Authority 2004), developed a 'Creative Intensity' methodology to respond to issues raised by the DCMS classifications and figures (Bakhshi, Freeman and Higgs 2012). A creative occupation is defined as 'a role within the creative process that brings cognitive skills to bear to bring about differentiation to yield either novel, or significantly enhanced products whose final form is not fully specified in advance' (ibid., 23). The report then proposes five criteria: novelty in the process of production; the absence of a mechanical substitute for human activity; constant variation in function; novel or creative outcome; and interpretation rather than simple transformation of a service or product (ibid.). Occupations need to meet at least four of these criteria in order to qualify as creative.

The application of the criteria (or 'creative grid') to all occupations produced a significantly higher creative employment figure for the UK than the DCMS's 2011 *Creative Industries Economic Estimates*.[6] The report found that 'a large (and growing) software-related segment of the CI' excluded by the DCMS should be classed as creative because the occupations therein met at least four of Bakhshi et al.'s five criteria (ibid., 3).

Their omission resulted in the DCMS understating UK creative employment by almost one million, most of which were digital creative jobs and over half of which were embedded.

A TYPOLOGY OF DIGITAL CREATIVES

Useful though they are, these findings still do not answer the questions: what are digital creative occupations? And if, as noted above, some occupation codes contain both digital and analogue creatives, how can totals be calculated? I propose a tri-level distinction between: 'Born Digital' creative occupations, such as software developers, whose work essentially did not exist before the digital age; 'Digital Migrants', such as television presenters, whose occupations existed pre-digitization but whose creative work is now entirely reliant on digital technologies or processes; and 'Semi-Digital' creative occupations in which digital technologies and processes may or may not be used, such as advertising and marketing professionals. The Semi-Digital creative category includes many (pre-digital) creative occupations that have been transformed by the adoption or extension of digital technologies or services, and others that will eventually become Digital Migrants. I have further broken down these categories based on the Trident II division between Cultural Production and Creative Services.

Applying the 'Creative Grid' to the six digit ANZSCO codes within the Australian version of the CI, my typology looks as in Tables 8.1–8.3.

While parts of occupations in the Semi-Digital creative group can be classified as either Digital Migrants (for example, television director, within director [film, television, radio or stage]) or Born Digital (web site/ blog editor, within newspaper or periodical editor), the available census data details the figures only to six-digit code level, meaning that it is not possible to segment and accurately calculate part of an occupation code as digital creative. Table 8.4 details the occupations in each of the three groups, and the relevant data from the 2006 and 2011 Australian censuses for specialist and embedded creatives.

Among the Born Digital cohort, the developer programmer code, which includes applications developer, was numerically largest in both specialist and embedded categories in both 2006 and 2011. The largest cumulative annual growth rates (CAGR), however, were among ICT business analyst specialists (16.8 per cent), business development manager specialists (14.9 per cent) and web developer specialists (13.7 per cent). Despite growth in Born Digital specialists (5.1 per cent), embedded (1.9 per cent) and overall (3.3 per cent), two codes (analyst programmer and system analyst) experienced falls over the period.

Table 8.1   Born Digital creatives

Cultural Production occupations	Creative Services occupations
	225212 ICT Business Development Manager
	232413 Multimedia Designer
	232414 Web Designer
	261100 ICT Business and Systems Analyst nfd (not further defined)
	261111 ICT Business Analyst
	261112 Systems Analyst
	261200 Multimedia Specialists and Web Developers nec (not elsewhere classified)
	261211 Multimedia Specialist
	261212 Web Developer
	261300 Software and Applications Programmer nfd (not further defined)
	261311 Analyst Programmer
	261312 Developer Programmer
	261313 Software Engineer
	261399 Software and Applications Programmer nec

Note: All occupations in the Born Digital category are in Creative Services.

Table 8.2   Digital Migrants

Cultural Production occupations	Creative Services occupations
212113 Radio Presenter	211311 Photographer
212114 Television Presenter	232000 Architects, Designers, Planners and Surveyors nfd
212313 Director of Photography	232111 Architect
212314 Film and Video Editor	232411 Graphic Designer
212315 Program Director (Television or Radio)	232611 Urban and Regional Planner
212317 Technical Director (Technical Producer)	
212318 Video Producer	
212414 Radio Journalist	
212415 Technical Writer	
212416 Television Journalist	

Table 8.3   Semi-Digital creatives

Cultural Production occupations	Creative Services occupations
139911 Arts Administrator or Manager	131111 Advertising and Public Relations Manager
211111 Actor	131114 Public Relations Manager
211299 Music Professional nec (music researcher)	212411 Copywriter
211211 Composer	225100 Advertising and Marketing Professionals nfd
211499 Visual Arts and Crafts Professionals NEC (Multimedia Artist, New Media Artist)	225111 Advertising Specialist
212111 Artistic Director	225113 Marketing Specialist
212112 Media Producer (excluding video)	225311 Public Relations Professional
212211 Author	232100 Architects and Landscape Architects nfd
212212 Book or Script Editor	232112 Landscape Architect
212311 Art Director (Film, Television or Stage)	232300 Fashion, Industrial and Jewellery Designers nfd
212312 Director (Film, Television, Radio or Stage)	232311 Fashion Designer
212399 Film, Television, Radio and Stage Directors NEC	232312 Industrial Designer
212412 Newspaper or Periodical Editor	232412 Illustrator
212413 Print Journalist	232511 Interior Designer
212499 Journalists and other writers nec	233916 Naval Architect
224211 Archivist	
224212 Gallery or Museum Curator	
224611 Librarian	
599912 Production Assistant (Film, Television, Radio or Stage)	

Among Digital Migrants, graphic designer was numerically the largest code by a significant margin in all categories, in both 2006 and 2011. In terms of CAGR, directors of photography experienced the highest specialist growth (7 per cent, although embedded fell –6.2 per cent), with urban and regional planners recording the highest embedded growth (6.4 per cent). The total numbers of both radio presenters and radio journalists fell over the period, although there was a small rise in specialist radio presenters. The number of embedded architects fell slightly, but this was more than compensated by a rise in the number of specialists. There were

Table 8.4   Total digital creatives

	2006			2011		
	Specialists	Embedded	All employed	Specialists	Embedded	All employed
Born Digital	33872	46701	80573	43576	51345	94921
Digital Migrants	40162	28165	68327	53671	32366	86037
Semi-Digital creatives	40019	61419	101438	47594	69332	116926
All creative occupations	123841	147333	271174	148984	161072	310056
Total workforce			9104179			10057145

Note: 'All Creative occupations' includes occupations not in any of the three categories above.

also falls in the numbers of embedded television presenters (−7.9 per cent), photographers (−2.3 per cent), and program directors (television or radio) (−4.4 per cent). The combined Digital Migrants CAGRs were: specialist 6 per cent; embedded 2.8 per cent, and overall 4.7 per cent.

In the Semi-Digital grouping, marketing specialist was the largest code numerically in both censuses, and the largest embedded code in both 2006 and 2011. The largest specialist code numerically was print journalist in 2006 and media producer (excluding video) in 2011. In terms of CAGR, among specialists the largest growth was in the 'placeholder' category advertising and marketing professionals not further defined (24 per cent). The actual number of people in this code is small, and the large rise is probably due to the growing number of new job titles that do not fit current ABS categories. This is likely to change by the next census. Director (film, television, radio or stage) also recorded a high level of specialist growth (16.9 per cent), although again the actual number of people in this code is very small. Other significant specialist growth rises were recorded in marketing specialist (11.6 per cent), fashion designer (11 per cent), journalist and other writers not elsewhere classified (9.5 per cent), book or script editor (7.7 per cent) and copywriter (7.7 per cent). The highest embedded growth rates were among book or script editor (15 per cent), artistic director (10 per cent) and copywriter (6.7 per cent). There was strong growth in the embedded advertising and marketing professionals not further defined code (9.9 per cent), although the same caveat as above regarding the size of the sample applies. For the Semi-Digital grouping as a whole, the CAGRs were: specialist 3.5 per cent, embedded 2.5 per cent, and overall 2.9 per cent. All the CAGRs for each of the groups compare favourably with both the equivalent rate for all creative occupations (2.7 per cent), and for the entire Australian workforce (2 per cent).

If the total digital creative workforce comprises Born Digital occupations + Digital Migrants + a proportion of Semi-Digital creatives, then calculating an exact total raises two difficulties. The first is the appropriateness and inclusiveness of the typology. The second is the calculation of the digital proportion of the Semi-Digital creative group. Notwithstanding these difficulties, we can estimate workforce size. We can then compare this with the remainder of the CI, and begin to observe some changes over time to the digital creative workforce as a whole, to particular occupations and to embedded digital creatives in particular.

First, excluding the Semi-Digital group entirely, Born Digital and Digital Migrant occupations, both specialist and embedded, comprised 54.9 per cent of the total creative workforce in 2006. By 2011 that figure had risen to 58.4 per cent. Second, in 2006, Born Digital and Digital Migrant embedded creatives made up 50.1 per cent of the total embedded creative workforce. In 2011 that figure had risen to 52 per cent.

If we take a conservative estimate – say 10 per cent – of the proportion of Semi-Digital creatives whose creative process is either newly dependent on digital technologies and techniques, or has been made possible by such means, and add that to the Born Digital and Digital Migrants totals, we can estimate that the digital creative workforce comprised 58.7 per cent of the total creative workforce in 2006, and 62.1 per cent in 2011. If we assume that the proportion is as high as 50 per cent of Semi-Digital creatives, then the digital creative workforce comprised 73.6 per cent of the total creative workforce in 2006, and 77.2 per cent in 2011. If, in an extreme scenario, all Semi-Digital creatives are digital creatives, then the digital creative workforce would have comprised 92.3 per cent of the total creative workforce in 2006, and 96.1 per cent in 2011. In the latter scenario, digital creatives would have made up 2.7 per cent of the total Australian workforce in 2006, and 3 per cent in 2011.

Of course, this latter scenario is impossible. It is, however, not only possible but highly likely that in the future many of the occupations that are currently in the Semi-Digital category will move into the Digital Migrant category as digital technologies and processes become intrinsic to more fields of creative work. It is also likely that new Born Digital occupations will emerge as new industries evolve, just as the apps industry has emerged over the last five years or so. The point is that the digital creative workforce is both a substantial and growing part of the digital economy.

Not unexpectedly, digital Creative Services occupations show both higher total numbers and higher growth rates than digital Cultural Production in both specialist and embedded categories. What is striking here is the growth rate and numerical increases in specialist occupations in both digital Cultural Production and digital Creative Services. Born Digital and Digital Migrant Creative Services specialists experienced the highest growth, indicative of the much higher growth in Creative Services in general versus Cultural Production occupations. In all specialist scenarios (that is, where 10 per cent, 50 per cent or 100 per cent of the Semi-Digital cohort are counted), the cumulative annual growth rate is considerably higher than the equivalent figure for the workforce as a whole, which grew at a rate of 2 per cent per year between 2006 to 2011.

While there is growth (albeit small in several cases) in four out of the six embedded scenarios, the rates of growth and numerical increases are below the growth in specialist digital creative occupations. In all embedded digital Cultural Production scenarios, growth is either significantly below the equivalent figure for the workforce as a whole, or there are very small declines. But the presence of growth in the digital creative services occupations is significant in itself. As Cunningham has argued, 'the growth of the embedded workforce and of Creative Services is an indicator of innovation insofar as this demonstrates a specific call on these particular attributes and skills where they have not been needed before' (2013, 121).

CONCLUSION

Digital technologies and processes are increasingly important to social, cultural and economic life. Digital creatives – both specialists and embedded, Cultural Producers and Creative Service providers – are at the heart of the action, just as they are at the heart of digital innovation. And yet this grouping is infrequently collectively defined, and consequently its dynamics, needs and potential are rarely considered. In the first half of the first decade of this century in Australia, the federal government commissioned a three-stage *CI Cluster Study* and a range of reports that were intended to outline and advance the *Digital Content Industry Action Agenda*. While certain elements and ideas were taken up, in large part the focus on digital content and its creators softened as the imperatives of infrastructure building and technology development took precedence. This chapter represents an attempt to bring the focus back on to digital content. It has proposed a new typology of digital creatives, and presented initial findings on the size and growth of employment of this grouping in Australia. This exercise not only provides an estimate of the size of the digital creative workforce, but also will be useful in considering the contributions that both specialist and embedded digital creatives make across the economy. These findings may assist policymakers and scholars to understand and plan for the needs and potential of this increasingly important part of the workforce.

NOTES

1. 'Local content' here means 'relevant content in the speaker's own language' (OECD/ ISOC/UNESCO 2013, 15).
2. I define digital creatives as those employed in creative occupations either within (specialists) or outside (embedded) the core CI whose work is reliant upon digital technologies and processes.
3. Screen/film pre-production, production and post-production; free-to-air and subscription television pre-production, production and post-production; broadband content development; interactive and digital television applications and content development; online and interactive games; internet based marketing, design and advertising; internet based digital content publishing and distribution; experimental digital media; online education content development; mobile content development and publishing; content creation and manipulation software; and learning, rights and content management and other related software applications (Higgs and Kennedy 2004, 30).
4. The six segments are: Advertising and Marketing; Architecture, Design and Visual Arts; Film, TV and Radio; Music and Performing Arts; Publishing; and Software and Digital Content.
5. The full list of excluded occupations and their six-digit occupational codes are as follows: 498381 Apprentice Jeweller, 212100 Architects And Landscape Architects, 312100 Building, Architectural And Surveying Associate Professionals, 253315 Industrial Designer, 253317 Interior Designer, 498300 Jewellers And Related Tradespersons, 212921 Naval Architect, 253113 Sculptor, 212111 Architect, 312113 Architectural Associate, 253311 Fashion Designer, 399911 Interior Decorator, 498311 Jeweller, 212113 Landscape Architect, 253111 Painter (Visual Arts), 252311 Urban And Regional Planner.
6. While it is not my principal purpose here to critically interrogate the grid, it should be pointed out that, although this is an extremely useful intervention, and will probably result in revision of the UK figures, it is not without its own problems. The criteria are not exclusive to occupations within the CI; that is, while the grid was devised as a test of jobs within the segments previously defined as part of the CI, if it is applied across the entire range, then a number of other occupations would appear to qualify. For example, life scientists such as biochemists, judges or parliamentarians could conceivably pass the 'four out of five' test.

REFERENCES

AIMIA (2013), *AIMIA Digital Industry Salary Report 2012*, http://www.aimia. com.au/home/business-resources/research–surveys/aimia-digital-industry-salary-report–2012 (accessed 22 March 2013).
Australian Bureau of Statistics (2009), *Australian and New Zealand Standard Classification of Occupations* (Revision 1.0), 25 June, available at http://www. abs.gov.au/AUSSTATS/abs@.nsf/Lookup/1220.0Main + Features1First%20 Edition,%20Revision%201?OpenDocument (accessed 22 March 2013).

Bakhshi, H., A. Freeman and P. Higgs (2012), *A Dynamic Mapping of the UK's Creative Industries*, London: Nesta.

Bruns, A. (2008), *Blogs, Wikipedia, Second Life and Beyond: From Production to Produsage*, New York: Peter Lang.

Centre for Cultural Policy Research, Hong Kong (2003), *Baseline Study of Hong Kong's CI*, Central Policy Unit, HK Special Administrative Region Government.

Centre for International Economics (2005), *Australian Digital Content Industry Futures*, report prepared for the Department of Communications, Information Technology and the Arts, Melbourne.

Cunningham, S. (2013), *Hidden Innovation: Policy, Industry and the Creative Sector*, St Lucia, Queensland: University of Queensland Press and Lexington Books, an imprint of Rowman & Littlefield.

Cunningham, S. and P. Higgs (2008), 'CI Mapping: where have we come from and where are we going?', *Creative Industries Journal*, **1** (1), 7–30.

Cutler and Co. (2002), *Producing Digital Content*, report for the Department of Communications, Information Technology and the Arts, Melbourne.

Deloitte Access Economics (2011), *The Connected Continent: How the Internet is Transforming the Australian Economy*, report for Google Australia, August.

Department of Broadband, Communications and the Digital Economy (2013), 'What is the Digital Economy?', available at http://www.dbcde.gov.au/digital_economy/what_is_the_digital_economy (accessed 16 July 2013).

Department of Communications, Information Technology and the Arts (2002), *Creative Industries Cluster Study Stage One Report*, Canberra: Department of Communications, Information Technology and the Arts and NOIE.

Department of Communications, Information Technology and the Arts (2005), *Unlocking the Potential: Digital Content Industry Action Agenda*, Strategic Industry Leaders Group report to the Australian Government, Canberra, November.

Department of Culture, Media and Sport (DCMS) (1998), *Creative Industries Mapping Document 1998*, London, DCMS, available at http://webarchive.nationalarchives.gov.uk/+/http://www.culture.gov.uk/reference_library/publications/4740.aspx (accessed 29 July 2013).

Department of Culture, Media and Sport (DCMS) (2011), *Creative Industries Economic Estimates*, London: DCMS, December, available at https://www.gov.uk/government/publications/creative-industries-economic-estimates-december-2011 (accessed 22 March 2013).

Greater London Authority (2004), *London's Creative Sector: 2004 Update*, London: Greater London Authority.

Higgs, P. and T.A. Kennedy (2003), *From Cottages to Corporations: Building a Global Industry from Australian Creativity*, report on Access to Overseas Markets for Australia's Creative Digital Industry, Department of Communications, Information Technology and the Arts.

Higgs, P., S. Cunningham and H. Bakhshi (2008), *Beyond the Creative Industries: Mapping the Creative Economy in the United Kingdom*, London: NESTA, Technical Report, February.

Higgs, P., S. Cunningham and J. Pagan (2007), 'Australia's Creative Economy: basic evidence on size, growth, income and employment', unpublished, available at http://eprints.qut.edu.au/8241/ (accessed 22 March 2013).

Ministry of Culture, France (2005), *L'emploi culturel dans l'Union européenne en 2002: Données de cadrage et indicateurs*, Paris: L'Observatoire de l'emploi Culturel, Département des études, de la prospective et des statistiques.

OECD/ISCO/UNESCO (2013), 'The relationship between local content, Internet development and access prices', OECD Digital Economy Papers, no. 217, Paris: OECD.

Pattinson Consulting (2003), *The Measurement of Creative Digital Content*, report for the Department of Communications, Information Technology and the Arts, June.

Pratt, A.C. (2004), 'The cultural economy: a call for spatialized "production of culture" perspectives', *International Journal of Cultural Studies*, 7 (1), 117–28.

9. Embedded digital creative workers and Creative Services in banking

Ben Goldsmith

INTRODUCTION

This chapter explores the roles and functions of both embedded digital creative workers and Creative Services firms in an industry beyond the core Creative Industries: banking. The chapter focuses on the design and development of applications (apps) and mobile websites for smartphones and tablet computers, with examples drawn principally from the Australian banking sector. While it might be assumed that utility and practicality are more important and more highly valued in apps development for financial services institutions than innovation and aesthetic design, this chapter illustrates the growing importance placed on creative work in this sector.

The finance industries, and in particular banking, are information-intensive businesses. They have typically been early adopters of information technology (IT) (Bons et al. 2012, 198), and major employers of IT and software professionals. According to figures from the 2006 and 2011 Australian censuses, the highest proportion of embedded creative workers (that is, workers in creative occupations employed outside the core Creative Industries), measured as a percentage of the total industry workforce, was employed in the finance and insurance services industries, of which banking forms a part. In addition, in both censuses, across all divisions, these industries employed the largest total number of software and digital content workers. The largest proportion of embedded creative workers in the finance and insurance sector in both 2006 and 2011 was in software and digital content occupations, followed by those in advertising and public relations occupations. It is, however, insufficient to consider only embedded workers when seeking insight into the role of creative workers in the banking industry. In addition to their employees in creative occupations, and in common with many other companies, banks employ the services of specialist Creative Industries firms on a range of projects. In censuses, these specialist firms and their employees are not counted in the embedded creative cohort; rather, they appear in employment figures for the core Creative Industries. Given the difficulties in disaggregating firms providing specialist creative services only to particular non-Creative Industry sectors, census data are insufficient on their own to provide a full picture. Additional insights can be generated through case studies, and this will be the approach adopted here.

BANKING, SMARTPHONES AND THE MOBILE INTERNET

In a 2012 survey of the importance that Australians place on the Internet in daily life, the Australian Communications and Media Authority (ACMA) found that respondents viewed the Internet as more important for banking and paying bills than for any other surveyed activity (ACMA 2012, 121). This finding was true for Australians living in metropolitan and regional areas, and for all age groups (ibid., 122–3). It was supported by the third survey of the Australian component of the World Internet Project, conducted in 2011 (Ewing and Thomas 2012). This survey found that, whereas in 2007 two-thirds of users banked online, by 2009 this had increased to three-quarters and by 2011 to four-fifths. The proportion of Internet users banking online, at least weekly, increased from 54.2 per cent in 2007, to 61.8 per cent in 2009, and to 65.5 per cent in 2011 (ibid., 51). The number of bank customers accessing information or services via mobile devices is set to increase further, as smartphone, tablet computer and mobile Internet use grows.

At the end of 2012, almost 17.4 million subscribers to an Internet service provider in Australia accessed the Internet via a mobile handset (Australian Bureau of Statistics 2013). In May 2012, 49 per cent of the adult Australian population (8.67 million people) was estimated to be using a smartphone, compared with 25 per cent (4.25 million people) in June 2011, an increase of 104 per cent in less than a year. In addition, approximately 25 per cent of the adult population used a tablet computer to access the Internet in the six months to May 2012 (ACMA 2013, 22–3). Mobile data traffic has been estimated to grow at twice the rate of fixed IP traffic in Australia over the next several years, from an average of 8.8 petabytes per month in 2011 to 119.3 petabytes per month by 2016 (Cisco Systems 2013). All these developments collectively increase the pressure on customer-facing institutions, such as banks, to adapt or reinvent their online offerings for the mobile Internet.

Optimizing websites and building apps for mobile devices requires designers and developers to confront a different set of challenges than in traditional web design. Device fragmentation is perhaps the most pressing issue. In its annual *Technology, Media and Telecommunications Predictions* in 2012, Deloitte Australia noted

> To reach more than 90 per cent of all app users, a developer may need to create versions for five different operating systems (plus HTML5), five major languages, three different processor speeds, and four different screen sizes. In other words, 360 variants of a single app may need to be created in order to fully cover the global market. (2012, 42)

This number will have increased in the intervening period, which has seen the launch of the iPad Mini as well as countless other tablets and smartphones. Fragmentation is especially an issue for organizations developing for the Android operating system. In contrast with the 'closed' operating systems created for mobile devices by Apple (iOS) and Microsoft (Windows Mobile, Windows Phone and Windows 8), in which independent modification is tightly controlled and actively discouraged, Android is an 'open' system (as in 'open source'). This means that, in addition to the versions produced by Google (Gingerbread, Ice Cream Sandwich, Jelly Bean etc.), developers of Android apps must also contend with multiple versions that have been modified or customized by carriers and device makers. The challenge for developers is further complicated by the variety of brands running Android, many of which contain different hardware and software features. In May 2012 the operators of OpenSignal, an app that collates data on signal strength readings and Wi-Fi access points around the world, reported that over the previous six months their app had been downloaded to almost 4000 distinct Android devices, representing almost 600 distinct brands, with multiple different screen resolutions or aspect ratios (*Android Fragmentation Visualised* 2012).

In addition to these technological challenges, traditional banking institutions are also coming under competitive pressure from new digital and mobile-first players. Independent online personal financial management platforms and tools, such as Yodlee, Mint and the Australian start-up Pocketbook, are creating image-rich, intuitive apps and services that provide users with new insights into their finances. In May 2013 the French bank BNP Paribas launched Europe's first 'stand alone digital mobile bank', Hello Bank!, in Germany and Belgium (Daneshkhu 2013). Other similar services, such as Simple, GoBank and Moven, have existed for some time, although they are confined to the American market at this stage. Moven is the brainchild of Brett King, and the range of disruptive factors wrought by digitization and the growth of the mobile Internet is described in more detail in his book – *Bank 3.0: Why Banking is No Longer Somewhere You Go, But Something You Do* (2012).

In its *State of Mobile Banking 2012* report, Forrester Research asserts that 'Mobile banking is the biggest innovation, or cluster of innovations, in retail banking in years, arguably in a century' (Ensor, Montez and Wannemacher 2012, 2). In another international survey of 70 financial institutions, 45 per cent of banks declared that the development of their mobile offerings was a priority for 2013, rising to 63 per cent considering it a priority over the following three years (Misys and Finextra 2012, 3). Mobile banking is growing in parallel with the growth in smartphone use. In the US, a 2013 survey for the Federal Reserve Board found that, while 28 per cent of all mobile phone owners had used mobile banking in the previous 12 months (an increase of 7 per cent from the previous year), the equivalent figure for smartphone users was 48 per cent. The survey also noted that mobile is 'a potential platform for expanding financial access and inclusion' given the 'relatively high prevalence of mobile phone and smart phone use among younger generations, minorities, and those with low levels of income – groups that are prone to be unbanked or under-banked' (Browdie 2013). The World Bank, meanwhile, has highlighted the potential for 'mobile money' (of which mobile banking is a part) to 'become a general platform that transforms entire economies, as it is adopted across commerce, health care, agriculture and other sectors', especially in the developing world (World Bank 2012, 61).

In Australia, Roy Morgan Research's Digital Universe study released in August 2012 reported that banking on smartphones had increased by 333 per cent between January 2011 and April 2012 (Levine and Braun 2012). In a report for the Australian Mobile Telecommunications Association released in February 2013, Deloitte Access Economics reported that 38 per cent of Australians were using mobile banking in June 2012, compared with 67 per cent using online banking services. The equivalent figures for 2011 were 28 per cent and 68 per cent (Deloitte Access Economics 2013, 22). In late 2012, one of Australia's 'big four' banks, ANZ, reported that customer log-ins to the bank's mobile apps had exceeded Internet banking for the first time, while another of the big four, Westpac, reported 1.7 million active users of its mobile services in 2012, and more than 5.5 million log-ins per month by April 2013 (Bennet 2013, 19).

EMBEDDED CREATIVE WORKERS AND CREATIVE SERVICES IN THE AUSTRALIAN BANKING SECTOR

Many banks offer certain kinds of functionality, such as balance checking and transaction overviews either via mobile apps or mobile optimized websites (Ensor, Montez and Wannemacher 2012, 5). If balance checking or transaction listings were the only functions necessary, then it might be argued that apps development for banks requires no creative input or expertise in its design or build. And yet while some mobile banking services do simply (and superficially) repurpose existing online banking services for mobile, this is decreasingly the case as retail customers become accustomed to personal banking via mobile devices. In Australia, 62 per cent of finance and insurance businesses surveyed for the 2013 *Optus Future of Business Report* were using the mobile channel to interact with customers, compared with the average for all surveyed companies of 46 per cent (Optus 2013, 4, 11).

There are clear signs that bank apps are evolving and changing in response to technological and market developments, as smartphone and tablet capability increases and as competition in the sector increases. The growing popularity of in-app payments in mobile gaming and other apps, and the spread of technologies such as quick response (QR) codes and near field communications (NFC), which allow users to make purchases via a mobile device, are increasing expectations for mobile banking applications in terms of functionality and ease of use. As mobile Internet availability and use increase, users expect to be able to conduct transactions and engage with their financial institution via an app or mobile-enabled website, just as they do with many retailers and other organizations. But while functionality and convenience are clearly important, so too are aesthetics and user engagement, and this is where the work of digital creatives comes into its own. The most successful apps across all categories tend to be those that prioritize these elements. The recognition of the importance of these factors is feeding into the banking sector, evident in the growing calls for user experience expertise both within internal apps development teams and from external consultants and suppliers of apps development services. Additionally, the 'customer centred design' (CCD) philosophy in banking is further evidence that financial institutions are recognizing the importance of users' expectations and views in the development of both on- and offline banking experiences. And there is a kind of virtuous circle here: CCD is in part driving the growth in the number and variety of banking apps. As bank apps become more commonplace, they are becoming increasingly complex in their functionality, which in turn requires enhanced design thinking and creative input into software development.[1]

Increasingly, banks are developing apps that utilize the attributes of smartphones and tablets, including cameras (used to deposit cheques virtually) and global positioning system locators (to suggest nearby branches or other services). But, as described above, this increasingly requires banks to negotiate a technological minefield of multiple operating systems and devices, each requiring either dedicated apps or websites optimized for different screen sizes and resolutions. As a result, mobile offerings can be extremely expensive; in October 2012 the ANZ Banking Group announced that it would spend AU$1.5 billion over five years on new technology services including mobile apps (Ramli and Smith 2012). Australia's other three big banking groups had either already spent, or had committed to spending, over AU$4 billion on technology systems upgrades. These developments require digital banking specialists to work closely with customer experience teams (typically designers and advertising and marketing professionals) and apps development teams. Many banks engage external teams or agencies for the less financially sensitive development work, although 'insourcing', or the hiring of specialist teams for internal development, is not uncommon. This is consistent with the findings of the May 2013 *Clarius Skills Indicator*, a quarterly analysis of the availability of skilled labour across the Australian workforce by an Australian employment services provider. This report found that financial institutions and insurance companies were 'displaying the most positive … appetites' among Australian firms for hiring IT workers (Clarius Group 2013, 10).

The applications and services that enable mobile finance, mobile banking and mobile payments can deploy the talents of a variety of digital creative workers in a variety of ways, from the design and development of innovative models and interfaces, to creating entirely new systems, to animating icons, actions and services and developing graphical interfaces. Like many apps, the most successful banking apps tend to have intuitive interfaces, are image-based and graphically rich. And as customers access banking services via devices with different operating systems, screen sizes and resolutions, banks increasingly need to utilize responsive and adaptive design techniques for their websites to ensure optimal viewing and user experience. As the size of mobile phone screens increases, as tablet computer use grows, and as data transfer speeds become faster, poorly designed and unimpressive-looking apps and mobile sites will stand out, further necessitating the application of creativity and creative thinking to the tasks of app and mobile website development. That is, the role of digital creative workers and firms in the banking sector seems only set to increase.

In terms of the total number of employees, the Australian finance and insurance services sector is exceeded by only four other industry sectors: public administration and safety; manufacturing; education and training; and professional, scientific and technical services. When the focus is narrowed to the percentage of the workforce in each sector who are embedded creative workers, finance and insurance services, of which banking forms part, ranks first with 4.1 per cent of employees being embedded creatives in 2006, and 3.7 per cent in 2011 (see Figure 9.1).

As noted above, however, simply calculating the proportion of embedded creative workers does not give a full picture of the extent of creative

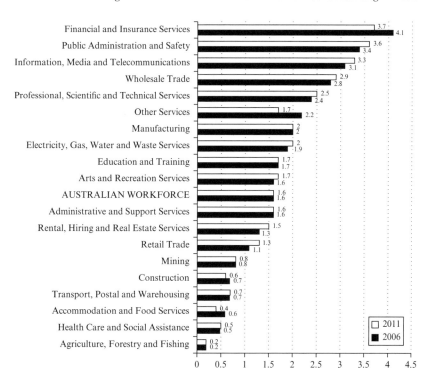

Figure 9.1   Percentage of embedded creatives within total workforce, by industry, 2006 and 2011. CCI analysis of census data

work in these industries. Creative Industries firms, such as advertising and marketing agencies, design companies, apps development studios and user experience consultants, which provide services to banking and other non-Creative Industries sectors, are counted as core or specialist creative workers in census data. Firms such as these, along with embedded creative workers, have played crucially important roles in the development of mobile websites and applications for a wide range of banks.

Banks typically adopt one of three distinct models of apps development: entirely in-house development; a hybrid model, which is led internally and involves one or more external partners throughout the product development cycle; and a predominantly outsourcing model, in which design and development are undertaken externally but overseen by an in-house project manager. As a result of banks' particular security requirements, the fully outsourced model is rare, and generally confined to non-sensitive applications such as branch and automatic teller machine (ATM) locators. The hybrid and in-house models are most common.

The first model, in-house development, is exemplified by the ANZ Bank's much-lauded goMoney app for the iPhone, launched in August 2010, with a version for smartphones running the Android operating system released in September 2012 (Lui 2012). The app was developed by the bank's innovation team that had been set up in 2009 under former ANZ Chief Information Officer Peter Dalton. Another example is BankWest's LocateMyColleague app, which was developed by three of the bank's software developers during the one day a week that staff are able to work on their own new ideas (Waters 2012). The app was designed to assist workers at the bank's corporate headquarters in Perth to find a desk after the bank introduced 'hot desking', whereby staff are not tied to a particular work station (Corrigan 2012).

In May 2012 another of Australia's big four banks, the Westpac Group, announced that new mobile applications development for the group would be handled in-house (Timson 2012). On one hand, this bucked a recent trend in the Australian banking industry of cutting locally based IT jobs and outsourcing work overseas. On the other, this was actually a continuation of a strategy for internal apps development that had been apparent within the Westpac Group since the merger with the St George Group in December 2008. Up to this point, the Westpac Group had employed a mixed-model approach to apps development, with some built entirely in-house by the 50-strong Mobile Applications Development (MAD) team, and some built on the hybrid model, under which some aspects of design and development are outsourced. The Westpac Group's current approach is exemplified in the statement by St George's Head of Mobile Travis Tyler, that 'Mobile is the front door to the bank' (Foo 2013).

Responsibility for apps development within the Westpac Group is divided between the Customer Experience (CX) team, and the Mobile Applications Development team. The CX team currently numbers between 15 and 20, although at its peak this internal design agency employed 35 people. Several former employees now run equivalent CCD teams at other Australian banking institutions. Over its life the Westpac CX team has partnered with external firms on a regular basis, both in order to cover internal capacity or capability gaps, and in order to gain perspectives and insights into current best practice from outside the banking sector. The CX team maintains a list of over 100 external firms that can provide specialist inputs at different stages of the design and product development cycle. The team typically engages between 30 and 40 of these firms each year. Most of the CX team have design backgrounds. The CX team also includes a four-person research group, led by a design anthropologist. The CX team espouses a CCD philosophy, and runs training workshops based on this approach within the Westpac Group. The CX team has also adopted 'gamification' in its approach to training, with several games developed in house to assist the training process. The MAD team is principally composed of software developers. The size of the team fluctuates, depending on project demands. Together and separately these two teams have developed a range of iOS, Android, BlackBerry, Windows Phone 7 and Windows 8 apps both for internal use and for the use of the bank's retail and corporate customers. The MAD team created the Tabula iPad app for use by the group's board members following the decision to stop issuing hard-copy documents before board meetings (Timson 2012).

Customer-facing apps include the innovative Westpac Banking for iPad app, developed by the CX team, and released in July 2012. This app is a prime example of the prioritization of design aesthetics and a particular version of user- or customer-centred design over functionality. The app is innovative in its use of gestural controls – swiping across the screen rather than the point-and-click familiar in the desktop environment ('tap-for-click' in the mobile environment, in which tapping the touchscreen replaces the mouse-click function). However, in its efforts to emphasize design over functionality, the Westpac CX team created an app that actually has less functionality than both the app it replaced and the bank's mobile website. Bank customers found that they were limited in what the app allowed them to do: they could check account balances and transfer funds between their accounts, but could make outgoing transactions only if a biller had previously been registered via Internet banking. Despite these limitations, Westpac reported in a quarterly earnings announcement in March 2013 that, since its launch, the iPad app had been downloaded 227000 times, with users recording 4.7 million sessions, and almost AU$2 billion in payments processed. Westpac chose not to develop a parallel Android app immediately, in part because of the proliferation of devices running various versions of the Android operating system with a variety of screen resolutions, in marked contrast with Apple's more limited and controlled ecosystem. A version of the original app was, however, adapted and used as the showpiece for the launch of Microsoft's new Windows 8 operating system in Australia in October 2012. Westpac was the only bank with an app available when the new operating system was introduced.[2]

The third model of bank apps development, predominantly outsourced, is exemplified by Australia's largest bank, Commonwealth Bank of Australia (CBA), which has employed the Sydney-based digital agency, Vivant, since 2010. Vivant has created the award-winning CommBank Kaching mobile payment application, the CommBank iPhone and Android apps, and the CommBank Property Guide app, which uses augmented reality to map property data, sales history and listings information onto a real-world view of a property. Vivant was formed in 2008, has its headquarters in Sydney, and has offices in London and the Isle of Man. The agency employs 25 people, including seven mobile and software developers, a creative director and senior creative, four user experience architects or consultants, a data scientist and three marketers. As well as its work with the CBA, Vivant has built a mobile marketing platform, Henry, a mobile venue-booking system, and a 'social good' platform, Jaro, which aims to raise AU$1 billion for charities through an online game.

CONCLUSION

The models of bank apps development described above clearly indicate the importance and centrality of creative work in this sector. Any suggestion that bank apps are not creative, or that those working on them within or for banks are neither embedded digital creative workers nor creative service providers, can be further countered in part with reference to theoretical work on knowledge labour. Mosco and McKercher (2008, 26) divide knowledge workers into 'content' and 'technical' categories:

> The content category encompasses artists, entertainers, teachers, journalists, musicians, and others who might be called cultural workers. The technical category covers software designers, biomedical engineers, audiovisual technicians, and those whose creative contribution is the constitution of code, the design of technologies, and the production of signals. The labor of this category makes possible the labor of cultural and other producers of what is typically viewed as content.

As Mosco and McKercher note, 'content' and 'technical' workers 'are increasingly part of the same workplace and the same work process' (ibid., 27). This is clearly the case in the banking examples described above. It also obliquely reinforces one of the findings of the Nesta report *A Dynamic Mapping of the UK's Creative Industries*, that 'a distinctive feature of the creative industries . . . is their tendency to use labour from software occupations – and more broadly from ICT occupations – in combination with other forms of creative labour' (Bakhshi, Freeman and Higgs 2012, 17). The point is that whether or not 'technical' workers, such as software engineers and systems analysts, are themselves regarded as creative (or rather digital creative) workers – and I would argue that they should be – their labour and input are intrinsic to the work of other (digital) creatives, such as web designers, apps developers or user experience designers. When thinking about what constitutes a digital creative occupation, this close connection between 'content' and 'technical' work must be taken into account since digital creative workers – and in particular embedded digital creative workers – are an important and growing part of the workforce, and critical to future innovation, as I argue in 'Embedded digital creative workers' (Chapter 8 in this volume).

In the particular case of mobile applications development in banking, digital creative workers seem set to become only more important. The IT company Ericsson estimated that in February 2013 there were over 6.3 billion mobile phone subscriptions in the world, of which between 15 and 20 per cent were for smartphones (Ericsson 2013, 2–3). Alongside efforts like that of Australian mobile app platform biNu to bring a smartphone-like experience to the 80–85 per cent of global mobile phone subscribers using feature phones (which have much more limited functionality), the smartphone market itself is predicted to continue to grow rapidly to over 80 per cent of all phone sales by 2017 (Moses 2012; Cocotas 2013; Meeker and Wu 2012). These predictions suggest that mobile apps – whether native to particular operating systems, hybrids of native and web-based apps, or entirely web-based – will continue to be important parts of the mobile ecosystem for many years to come. Given the high reported interest in mobile banking among smartphone users noted above, along with the predicted growth in mobile payments systems (Della Penna 2013), it seems likely that bank apps and mobile services will continue to evolve. Indeed, in its *State of Mobile Banking 2012* report, Forrester Research asserted that 'Mobile banking is the foundation for mobile payments' (Ensor, Montez and Wannemacher 2012, 22). Through their work on mobile apps and mobile-optimized websites, digital creative workers, be they embedded or creative service providers, designers or software developers, will drive the evolution of mobile banking, and the future of mobile payments.

NOTES

1. Corporate customers are also beginning to expect similar services, but because of the greater complexity in corporate banking than in retail banking, institutions will not simply be able to port mobile apps or services from their retail business to their corporate business. Rather, '[r]elevant mobile functionality must be identified, designed and securely delivered from scratch to meet the corporates' needs' (Misys and Finextra 2012, 5).
2. Ian Muir, Customer Experience Manager, Westpac, interview with the author, 6 November 2012.

REFERENCES

Android Fragmentation Visualised (2012), August, available at http://opensignal.com/reports/fragmentation.php (accessed 24 April 2013).

Australian Bureau of Statistics (2013), *8153.0 – Internet Activity, Australia, December 2012*, 9 April.

Australian Communications and Media Authority (ACMA) (2012), *Communications Report 2011–12*, Canberra: ACMA.

Australian Communications and Media Authority (ACMA) (2013), 'Smartphones and tablets: take-up and use in Australia', *Communications Report 2011–12 Series*, Report 3, Canberra: ACMA.

Bakhshi, H., A. Freeman and P. Higgs (2012), *A Dynamic Mapping of the UK's Creative Industries*, London: Nesta.

Bennet, M. (2013), 'Westpac sees marriage of branch and digital banking', *The Australian*, 5 April, p. 19.

Bons, R.W.H, R. Alt, H.G. Lee and B. Weber (2012), 'Banking in the Internet and mobile era', *Electron Markets*, **22**, 197–202.

Browdie, B. (2013), 'Mobile banking usage rises, but so do security concerns: survey', *American Banker*, 2 April, available at www.americanbanker.com/issues/178_63/mobile-banking-usage-rises-but-so-do-security-concerns-survey-1057989-1.html (accessed 22 May 2013).

Cisco Systems (2013), *VNI Forecast Highlights*, available at http://www.cisco.com/web/solutions/sp/vni/vni_forecast_highlights/index.html (accessed 23 May 2013).

Clarius Group (2013), *Clarius Skills Indicator*, May, available at http://clarius.com.au/media/clarius/Clarius%20Skills%20Indicator%20-%20May%202013.pdf (accessed 27 May 2013).

Cocotas, A. (2013), 'Smartphone market forecast: how price-sensitive global consumers will shape the next growth wave', *Business Insider Australia*, 1 March, available at http://au.businessinsider.com/smartphone-sales-wil-reach-16-billion-2013-2 (accessed 28 May 2013).

Corrigan, B. (2012), 'How BankWest tracks staff who hotdesk', *Australian Financial Review*, 21 August, available at http://www.afr.com/p/technology/how_bankwest_tracks_staff_who_hotdesk_Sqgx2dm53XWS9QyScKr3CJ (accessed 24 May 2013).

Daneshkhu, S. (2013), 'BNP Paribas eyes mobile and online banking', *Financial Times*, 12 May, available at http://www.ft.com/cms/s/0/c01e6284-bb0e-11e2-b289-00144feab7de.html (accessed 22 May 2013).

Della Penna, M. (2013), 'How mobile payments will transform the shopping experience', *readwrite.com*, 12 February, available at http://readwrite.com/2013/02/12/how-mobile-payments-will-transform-the-shopping-experience (accessed 28 May 2013).

Deloitte Access Economics (2013), *Mobile Nation: The Economics and Social Impacts of Mobile Technology*, report for the Australian Mobile Telecommunications Association.

Deloitte Australia (2012), *Technology, Media and Telecommunications Predictions 2012*, Deloitte Australia.

Ensor, B., T. Montez and P. Wannemacher (2012), *The State of Mobile Banking 2012*, Cambridge, MA: Forrester Research, 13 August.

Ericsson (2013), *Ericsson Mobility Report: Interim Update*, February, available at http://www.ericsson.com/res/docs/2013/ericsson-mobility-report-february-2013.pdf (accessed 28 May 2013).

Ewing, S. and J. Thomas (2012), *CCI Digital Futures 2012: The Internet in Australia*, Melbourne: ARC Centre of Excellence for Creative Industries and Innovation.

Foo, F. (2013), 'St George banks on real-time balances', *The Australian*, 29 January, p. 15.

King, B. (2012), *Bank 3.0: Why Banking is No Longer Somewhere You Go, But Something You Do*, Hoboken, NJ: John Wiley.

Levine, M. and A. Braun (2012), 'Digital touchpoints affecting the connected consumer', Roy Morgan Research White Paper, 21 August.

Lui, S. (2012), 'ANZ goMoney goes Android', *ZDNet*, 5 September, available at http://www.zdnet.com/au/anz-gomoney-goes-android-7000003730/ (accessed 17 October 2012).

Meeker, M. and L. Wu (2012), *2012 Internet Trends*, Kleiner Perkins Caufield Byers, December, available at http://www.kpcb.com/insights/2012-internet-trends-update (accessed 28 May 2013).

Misys and Finextra (2012), *Global Transaction Banking Survey 2012*, Misys and Finextra.

Mosco, V. and C. McKercher (2008), *The Laboring of Communication: Will Knowledge Workers of the World Unite?*, Lanham, MD: Lexington Books.

Moses, A. (2012), 'Smart money in dumb phones', *Sydney Morning Herald*, 16 August, available at http://www.smh.com.au/it-pro/business-it/smart-money-in-dumb-phones-20120816-24a70.html (accessed 23 July 2013).

Optus (2013), *Optus Future of Business Report 2013*, Sydney: Optus, available at http://www.optus.com.au/business/Business+insights/Knowledge+share (accessed 27 May 2013).

Ramli, D. and P. Smith (2012), 'ANZ banks on $1.5bn spending spree to win next gen customers', *Australian Financial Review*, 4 October, available at http://afr.com/p/technology/anz_banks_customers_bn_spending_eYkptmPAJe6vTjDNvw3VaI (accessed 22 March 2013).

Timson, L. (2012), 'Westpac to develop technology in-house', *Sydney Morning Herald*, 28 May, available at http://www.smh.com.au/it-pro/business-it/westpac-to-develop-technology-inhouse-20120527-1zd0j.html (accessed 22 March 2013).

Waters, C. (2012), 'Hot desking gone haywire: Bankwest has to develop an app to locate missing staff', *Smart Company*, 21 August, available at http://www.smartcompany.com.au/financial-services-and-insurance/051334-hot-desking-gone-haywire-bankwest-has-to-develop-an-app-to-locate-missing-staff.html (accessed 22 March 2013).

World Bank (2012), Maximizing Mobile: 2012 Information and Communications for Development, Washington, DC: The World Bank.

10. Looking inside the portfolio to understand the work of creative workers: a study of creatives in Perth[1]

Dawn Bennett, Jane Coffey, Scott Fitzgerald, Peter Petocz and Al Rainnie

INTRODUCTION

The research reported in this chapter forms part of a larger study that is investigating the work practices, orientations, career trajectories and skill requirements of individual creative workers in Perth, Western Australia (WA). The overarching purpose of the research is to generate a more detailed picture of the characteristics and dynamics of the work and careers of creative workers. This chapter focuses on creative workers' time, motivation and identity, investigating whether and why they might incorporate a range of activities from the creative to the mundane, and the extent to which these activities correspond with the Creative Trident employment modes of specialist, support and embedded work. Specialist refers to creative workers and occupations inside the Creative Industries, such as an actor in a television program or a software developer in a software company. Support refers to non-creative occupations within the Creative Industries, such as administration, management or accountancy. Embedded refers to creative workers and occupations in non-Creative Industries, such as a designer in manufacturing or a PR professional in healthcare. This chapter also considers the inclusion of non-creative work, which falls outside the Trident.

We begin by positioning our work within the context of Perth, which is an isolated capital city. As Stratton (2008, 614) has argued, this isolation is central to Perth's cultural identity: 'one of the most important tropes of Perth's culture is the centrality of the claim to isolation'. Isolation is also central to the specificities of creative work in Perth and across the state of Western Australia. Indeed, as Bennett (2010, 139) has suggested: 'the

WA creative sector is characterized by sparse, sometimes problematic communications between a multiplicity of networks such as venues and regulatory bodies, regional and metropolitan arts, and the metropolitan and geographically dispersed regions'. These characteristics are crucial to understanding the complexities of creative work in Perth, which can only be fully revealed when analysed at the individual level.

After establishing the context of the research, we present findings, focusing on the activities of individual creative workers. We then discuss how these findings might complement the Creative Trident model. Finally, in light of this critique, we argue that there are significant implications for the ways in which the terms 'creative work' and 'creative worker' are used.

BACKGROUND

Resonating with international policy developments that emphasized the importance of a new 'cultural' economy, in 2002 the WA government articulated a policy focus on Creative Industries and the Creative Economy: 'Creativity – the ability to create meaningful new forms – is now the decisive source of competitive advantage' (Gallop 2002, section 5). The policy direction was underscored with references to Creative Industry consultants, such as Charles Leadbetter and Richard Florida, and the WA Planning Commission employed creative consultant Charles Landry to write a report on how and why Perth should become a creative city. Employing numerous international examples, Landry's initial report urged Perth city planners to rethink their development strategies in the context of global competition based on creativity.

The job of developing locally researched and economically framed strategies fell, in part, to a Creative Industries Policy Taskforce (CIPT), which was established to 'evaluate global examples of the creative industries and to then determine if these models would be applicable to Western Australia' (Brabazon 2012, 173). The Taskforce's final report (July 2004) was never released to the public, as a result of which 'older models of culture and commerce were perpetuated' in departmental policy (ibid.). One direct outcome, however, was that the Taskforce collaborated with Perth City Council to commission a report titled *Perth's Creative Industries* (Morris et al. 2007).

Morris et al. drew on the expertise and frameworks of the Australian Research Council Centre of Excellence for Creative Industries and Innovation (CCI) to conduct geographical mapping and qualitative analysis of Metropolitan Perth's Creative Industry (CI) segments. The mapping employed the Creative Trident model, which was developed by the CCI in

2005 (Higgs, Cunningham and Bakhshi 2008, 4). The report highlighted many of the issues that had been, according to Brabazon (2012), identified in the unreleased Taskforce report. These included significant shortcomings in business capability, including financial capacity and the ability of micro-industries or sole traders to generate intellectual property. The report also emphasized the city's isolation from industry decision-makers and investors, and the weak connections between creative workers as a function of Perth's physical dispersal.

The *Perth's Creative Industries* (Morris et al. 2007) report showed that Perth's CI contributed AU\$4.6 billion to the local economy in 2006 and employed almost 40 000 people (data largely based on Australian Bureau of Statistics 2001 Census data and 2006 Australian Tax Office data). The report also found that total CI employment in Perth, in 2001, was equally divided between specialist and embedded creatives and support workers. Combined, these Trident segments represented approximately 5.2 per cent of total employment in Perth by 2006.

While international policy consultants such as Florida, Landry, Leadbetter and John Howkins provided potential creative city/economy models during visits to Perth between 2005 and 2008, *Perth's Creative Industries* provided far more specific information about labour markets in the city's CI, including the activities of embedded creatives. Among other things, it highlighted the need for further research, which would both heighten the understanding of Perth's creative workforce and enable the comparison of creative practice at the individual level and in different locations, including different cities. The survey detailed here was designed to meet the first of these two aims.

THE CREATIVE WORKFORCE INITIATIVE (CWI) SURVEY

The survey was piloted in Perth and with collaborating scholars in Vancouver before it was administered in Perth between 2010 and 2012. Using respondent-driven sampling, participants were recruited through CI networks. In addition, and bearing in mind that this is an unknown population, calls for participants were made through industry press, local media, industry associations and elsewhere. To reduce bias in what was essentially a chain-referral approach, sampling involved multiple 'seeds' (initial sources) selected to align with Perth's CI sectors. The survey was distributed in both hard copy and by email. It elicited 182 responses from a broad spectrum of creative occupations and employment types. Participants were aged from 18 to 80, with 60 per cent being female and 40 per cent being male.

Survey questions required closed and open-ended responses, and repeated items for the purposes of triangulation, validity and reliability. The survey incorporated a number of key filters to enable comparative analysis with other data collections: for example, the average number of hours per week spent on creative practice. The survey was designed in five discrete sections. Section 1 amassed data about the location of, and engagement with, creative work. It also asked about motivation and identity. Section 2 gathered data about the characteristics of work, including main occupation, income, time and access to benefits. Section 3 addressed the distribution of committed time. This was followed in Section 4 with questions about formal and informal learning. Section 5 recorded demographic information, including cultural background and patterns of relocation. Finally, respondents were invited to write about their creative work. Responses are being followed up as interviews to develop detailed career profiles. The focus of this chapter is Section 3, 'Time'. In addition to considering the distribution of free and committed time, this section also asked about the relationships between creative and non-creative roles.

Analysis, which is ongoing, necessitated multiple approaches. Textual data were transcribed, coded and analysed for emergent themes with the assistance of NVivo analysis software. Quasi-quantification was applied where relevant, and two researchers independently conducted initial coding, after which this was compared and refinements applied. Quantitative and quasi-quantified data were entered into SPSS. The next phase of research (2013–14) involves further profile interviews from which we will be able to interrogate the data using a unit-by-variable matrix. These data will enable us to triangulate empirical knowledge derived from the quantitative analysis.

Rather than provide forced occupational categories, the survey asked participants how they would define their creative practice. The 145 respondents who answered this question reported 61 diverse creative occupations and listed up to seven consecutive roles (a median of three roles was recorded). The largest representation was from visual artists (13 per cent), followed by writers (11 per cent) and musicians (8 per cent). All six Trident segments were represented: advertising and marketing; architecture, visual arts and design; film, TV and radio; music and performing arts; publishing; and software and digital content. As Heckathorn and Jeffri have argued (2001, 307), identifying a representative sample of creative workers is 'a sociologist's challenge, an economist's nightmare and an administrator's reality'. We do not claim that the survey is representative of the creative workforce in Perth; rather, the findings provide a very detailed snapshot of individual creative work portfolios across numerous sectors. The numbers are not yet sufficient to enable detailed analysis of work at the classification level.

While the self-identification of creative practice is more problematic in terms of analysis, an issue to which we return later, it provided respondents the opportunity to define their practice outside the confines of existing arbitrary and arguably bland classifications. The responses provide much-needed detail about the combinations of activities and roles within an individual creative worker's practice.

RESULTS AND DISCUSSION

Our discussion will focus on questions that addressed participants' work, time and energy (Section 3, 'Time'). These questions in particular drew on Bennett's (2007) Creative Practice Framework, which is concerned with the range of activities (creative to mundane) of individual creative workers. The Framework provides a logical basis for analysis of the characteristics of work at the individual level; thus survey respondents were invited to present a complete profile including paid and unpaid work, committed and non-committed time, and creative and non-creative roles. Respondents also described the relationships between their creative and non-creative roles.

Question 24 of the survey asked respondents to report their allocation of time using two tables, one for creative roles and one for non-creative roles. The two separate tables were included to encourage respondents to report all their roles. It was also hoped that the self-reporting of certain activities (such as administration) as either creative or non-creative work would contribute to our understanding of professional identity. Once they had completed the tables, respondents were asked (Question 25) to define the relationships (if any) between their creative and non-creative roles. The responses to these two questions, together with qualitative data drawn from other survey data and profiles, enabled us to generate three distinct sets of data:

1. the percentage of respondents for whom all work could be categorized by one of the Trident employment modes (specialist, support and embedded), or by non-creative work outside of the Trident;
2. the combination of roles undertaken by those whose work is not represented by a single Trident employment mode; and
3. the relationships between reported roles.

We present and discuss these sets of data in the following section.

EMBEDDEDNESS AS AN ASPECT OF PORTFOLIO WORK

The first target set of data concerned the percentage of respondents for whom all work could be categorized by a single Trident employment mode (specialist, support or embedded), or as non-creative. The set was generated by coding all Q24 data as specialist, embedded, support or non-creative. Qualitative data enabled us to locate each reported role within or outside of the Creative Industries. Q24 responses were coded according to Trident employment mode. Shown in the first column in Figure 10.1, the work of only 12.6 per cent (23) aligned with a single mode: 10.4 per cent (19) as specialist creatives, 1.6 per cent (3) as support workers, and 0.5 per cent (1) as embedded creatives. The work of 3.8 per cent (7) of respondents was coded non-creative, with 4.4 per cent (8) represented as invalid. The remaining 144 cases (79.1 per cent) were not represented by any of these categories. The Creative Trident is based on census data, which allocates individuals to a single occupation code on the basis of their main occupation. The main occupation of survey respondents is shown in the second column in Figure 10.1. Based on main occupation alone, 41.2 per cent (75) of respondents would be categorized as specialist creatives, 14.8 per cent (27) as support workers and 3.3 per cent (6) as embedded creatives.

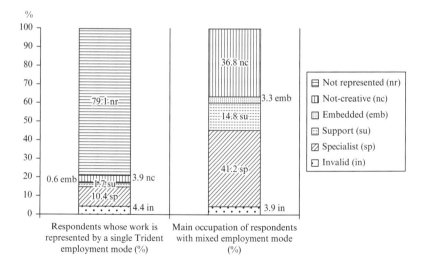

Note: Due to rounding, figures do not add up to exactly 100 per cent.

Figure 10.1   Representation (n = 182) by Trident modes and main occupation (%)

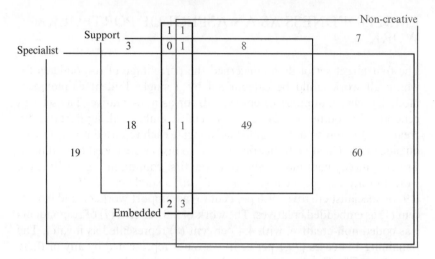

*Figure 10.2   Intersections of multiple simultaneous creative and non-
creative roles (count)*

A further 36.8 per cent (67) would be categorized as non-creative workers.
Data from seven respondents (3.8 per cent) could not be coded and are
shown as invalid.

Q24 data also enabled us to identify the main occupation of all respondents. Shown in the second column in Figure 10.1 is the information from
the 176 respondents who reported the number of hours they spent in each
paid role. Based on their main source of income, using this approach, 42.6
per cent (75) of respondents would be categorized as specialist creatives;
15.3 per cent (27) as support workers; and 3.4 per cent (6) as embedded
creatives. A further 38 per cent (67) would be categorized as non-creative
workers. Data from six respondents (3.4 per cent) could not be coded and
are shown as invalid.[2]

Figure 10.1 illustrates categorization according to main occupation.
Given the prevalence of portfolios of work, however, the picture is
incomplete. To understand the intersections of work across the Trident
employment modes we needed to include all activities reported within each
individual's portfolio of work, which may include multiple simultaneous
roles. For each of the creative workers who responded to Q24 ($n = 174$),
Figure 10.2 presents a more complete depiction, illustrating the complex
intersections of specialist, support, embedded and non-creative roles. For
example, 60 respondents reported specialist and non-creative work, while
18 reported specialist and support work. Of interest, the intersections
reveal no significant differences between the average number of hours in

each role, between sexes, or between employed/self-employed, contractual or casual work. This suggests a prevalence of complex and changeable patterns of work throughout the artistic or creative lifecycle and across creative disciplines and genres.

The chapters in this volume explore the phenomenon of the embedded creative on the basis that creative workers embedded in other industries have, for the most part, remained invisible. The complexities illustrated above suggest why this might be the case. To understand more about the nature and role of embedded work, our third target set of data concerned the relationships between reported roles, both within and outside the Creative Industries. This required us to consider again all the roles that contributed to each individual portfolio of work.

Portfolio careers encompass multiple concurrent, consecutive or over-lapping roles that combine to create a portfolio of work. In an ideal scenario the portfolio is proactively assembled to suit the needs of the individual (Handy 1989). At the extreme end of portfolio careers, however, are those described as 'protean'. Named after the mythological sea-god Proteus, who would change form to avoid danger, protean careers are particularly prevalent in the Creative Industries where the avoidance of danger is often a reactive manoeuvre. Hall (1976), who first coined the term protean careers, made the distinction between traditional work orientations and those in which decisions are at least partly driven by an individual's core values. This raises the questions of how and why specialist, support, embedded and non-creative work are combined at the individual level.

An obvious determinant is income, which is influenced by the availability of work. Cunningham (2013) notes that the real growth in Cultural Production (visual arts; music and the performing arts; Film, radio and Television; publishing) workers over the past decade has been in employment within Creative Services sectors (architecture and design; advertising and marketing; software and digital content), where Cultural Production employment increased by 3.1 per cent (136). Incomes for these creative workers are 18.2 per cent higher than for Cultural Production workers in Cultural Production segments (based on 2011 Census figures). This suggests that they do not generally exhibit the creative labour profiles that, in the main, characterize Cultural Production workers in Cultural Production segments.

Our study similarly reports that low income is normal for Cultural Production workers in the Cultural Production segments. Moreover, closer analysis reveals that most respondents (including musicians, performers and actors) within the Cultural Production category earned only a proportion of their income from their specialist work. In fact, only 10 per cent of these respondents earned above the national average income purely through their specialist work. Overall, most of the respondents' earnings from non-creative work were markedly higher than their earnings from creative work, regardless of their age or creative occupation.

While the inclusion of multiple roles indicates protean characteristics, it is possible to determine whether multiple roles are reactive or proactive only by asking that question at the individual level. Cunningham (2013, 147–8) surmises that Cultural Production creatives can manage precarious artistic practice by moving over the course of their careers from the specialist occupations into the broader Creative Industries, or beyond the Creative Industries into non-creative roles, such as teaching. This suggests a linear progression and level of control akin to Handy's (1989) notion of proactive portfolios, which were not evident among the sample reported here.

Cunningham (2013, 147) also proposes a complementary strategy: offsetting low or inconsistent income streams by balancing a range of concurrent labour conditions, engaging in 'precarious artistic practice while holding down more secure employment, or by pursuing both "self-generated" and "client-driven" projects within the one specialist firm or sole-trading operation'. These strategies were evident in the responses from Perth's creative workers: for example, a graphic designer who held multiple roles both within and without the Creative Industries and whose graphic design work could fluctuate between specialist and embedded work according to the employer or client for whom she was working. What is more, the use of these strategies and the complexity of work within the Trident modes do not appear to align with age, sex or the maturity of creative practice. In short, the findings do not indicate a linear progression from specialist occupations to the broader Creative Industries.

SHAPING THE PORTFOLIO

As discussed, shaping a portfolio involves putting together multiple roles. Our third set of data concerned the relationships between specialist, support, embedded and non-creative roles. These data may indicate whether multiple roles contribute to proactively assembled portfolios or reactive, protean manoeuvres. The relationships were explored by asking survey respondents to consider the relationship between their creative and non-creative roles and their creative practice.[3] Responses reveal complex relationships, including the scope for innovative interplay of multiple roles. They also reveal disparate conceptions of professional identity.

In terms of relationships, some respondents were keen to report that their creative and non-creative roles were unrelated: 'No relationship. I keep them very separate as a deliberate decision.' Other respondents explained that the relationship was far from a deliberate decision: for example, for one dance artist, 'dance work only happens when my physical health permits'. Similarly, one visual artist explained: 'I can't afford to be an artist.'

Many respondents described the relationship in terms of the transfer of skills and knowledge from one setting to another: for instance, one respondent had developed a role as a travel writer (embedded) while maintaining a teaching role (non-creative) and writing non-fiction works (specialist): 'My writing practice directly informs my teaching. Teaching has allowed for some travel opportunities that have informed my writing.' The transfer of skills to embedded roles was a feature for a number of respondents who included work within health settings, including this arts therapist: 'I teach art activities in my non-arts role as a recovery worker, so I draw on my creative skills in this job.'

Overall, non-creative roles were positioned as integral to an individual creative practice for multiple reasons that were reactive or proactive, temporary or permanent. These included: supplementing inadequate income from creative work (most often positioned as a temporary inclusion); ensuring that creative work did not have to please a dominant market in order to generate more sales (a permanent inclusion); providing intrinsic enjoyment (permanent); ensuring that creative work did not have to be the sole focus of one's time and energy (permanent); and developing new networks.

Several responses illustrated the inconsistency with which creative workers identify their activities as being creative or non-creative. Many of the participants included, as components of their creative practice, roles as specialist arts managers and administrators, and as teachers: for example 18 per cent included teaching as a component of their portfolio of creative work. This is logical given that teaching is a natural and prominent use of artistic skills. Conversely, 6 per cent categorized teaching as a non-creative role (aligning with the Trident coding), and as temporary, 'fall-back' work. Other respondents included only their specialist roles in their creative portfolio. For some respondents, though, everything was creative:

> I consider pretty much all the stuff I do to be arts practice, but some may disagree: e.g. an iPhone app development based on one of my published tarot decks. Managing the app may not be constant 'arts practice', but then even when I was a traditional painter a lot of my time was taken up organising exhibitions, printing and such. I personally consider all of the activity associated with my art to be part of my arts practice, even if it's just the usual blah that any self-employed business owner has to do. Commercializing my IP as much as possible helps support me to do the work.

To understand this we need to consider the issue of personal and professional identity (salient identity), which is fundamental to motivation and the construction of a positive sense of self.

The activity of work is central to how people identify themselves. Low incomes are well known as a characteristic of creative work, yet as Bourdieu (1993, 165) notes, 'where artists lack money, they possess "cultural capital" and the credibility that the title "professional" provides'. The term professional is crucial here, because the distinction between professional and hobbyist is often in the narrative. As Bain (2005, 29) explains, 'in this market-savvy entrepreneurial role, artists are encouraged to exaggerate and exploit their individuality and to feed into popular myths to reinforce their occupational authenticity'. Individual narratives may extend beyond measures, such as time, to consider product, occupational and social prestige and the position of creative work relative to other activities.

It is unsurprising, then, that the data from Q24, which amassed information on the allocation of time across multiple roles, are in contrast with those from Q1 in which respondents defined their creative practice in terms of their professional identity. Q1 data categorized 82.9 per cent (151) of respondents as specialist creatives, 7.7 per cent (14) as support workers, 4.9 per cent (9) as embedded creatives, and 1.1 per cent (2) as workers in non-creative roles. Six responses were invalid. Shown in Figure 10.3, the disparity between the two data sets reveals the difficulties of self-reporting on which many large-scale data collections depend (Higgs

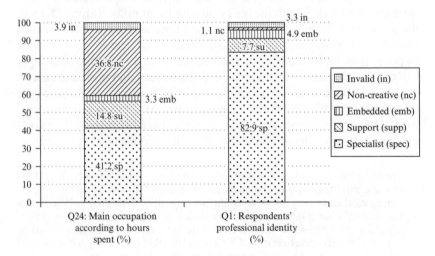

Figure 10.3   Respondents' main occupation and identity (n = 182) (%)

and Cunningham 2008) and the value of survey research that includes additional questions for the purposes of triangulation.

A key concern of our work is the ability to identify clearly the point at which creative and personal purpose meets economic purpose, thus shaping individual preferences and motivations. This is clearly aligned with identity. Following Bain (2005), over one-third of respondents reported that they adjusted their identity according to setting. Self-identification as a creative worker or dual professional bore little resemblance to the allocation of time to creative or non-creative roles, to the categorization of activities as creative or non-creative roles, or even to the income derived from each source. All this suggests that the points at which personal, creative and economic points meet may be fluid and opaque.

IS PERTH DIFFERENT?

While it will be possible to measure difference only once similar studies are completed in other cities, some aspects of Perth's location and size inevitably influence the nature of creative work. Perth, for example, is closer to South East Asia than to the Eastern seaboard of Australia, and the wide spatial distribution of creative activity makes intrastate, interstate and international activity prohibitively expensive. Western Australia also has the highest metropolitan primacy in Australia, with almost twice the rate of cultural occupations in Perth as in the balance of the state (Gibson, Murphy and Freestone 2002, 180).[4] Out-migration of creative talent is a common feature, aligned with 'push factors such as limited local opportunities and geographic isolation, and pull factors including experience, identity, networks, and the draw of more established industries or geographic clusters of activity' (Bennett 2010, 125).

Previous research, including the Taskforce report discussed earlier, has focused on value derived principally from intellectual property. What the reports do not attempt to capture is the full extent of a creative workforce within the larger metropolitan cultural ecology. This ecology, which includes a significant proportion of volunteers and paid workers within the not-for-profit and community sectors, evidences other important notions of value (Gollmitzer and Murray 2008; Hearn, Roodhouse and Blakey 2007) and is worthy of serious consideration.

Alongside evidencing multiple notions of value, ecology research may create a deeper understanding of creative work that is currently 'hidden' because of part-time, unpaid and/or portfolio work, and because of the fragmented nature of many CI networks. In WA, the Department of Culture and the Arts has responded with a project that aims to develop a cultural ecology map (CEM) charting the network of value relationships and exchanges between artists, organizations and consumers of culture, and assessing how changes to one part of the ecosystem influence others. The CEM pilot focused on Perth's dance sector and noted the short-term, project-based nature of production (Pracsys 2011). Participating dance artists frequently reported multiple roles within and outside the Creative Industries. Moreover, many older and more established dance artists reported voluntary roles within and outside dance organizations, thus contributing to the wider cultural ecology in ways beyond their paid roles.

The themes evident from these early findings align with dance sector research in other cities, and to an extent it is likely that any differences are largely scalar; however, it is possible that ecology research will contribute to a deeper, sector-specific analysis of the characteristics and dynamics of creative workers' portfolios, including the relationships between each creative or non-creative activity.

CONCLUSIONS

The survey reported here found that taxable income was markedly higher than income derived from creative work, that complex and changeable patterns of work persist throughout the artistic lifecycle, and that professional identity has a considerable impact on self-reporting. While the distinctiveness of Perth is noted, these characteristics are likely to be indicative of creative work elsewhere.

Markusen (2010) drew on Becker (1982) to emphasize that creative work involves a series of relationships that cross the divides separating commercial, non-profit, public and informal community sectors. We argue that it also crosses the divides of specialist, support, embedded and non-creative work. Our study suggests that the scope for innovation and enriched creative practice exists in the relationships between this work across and outside the Creative Industries. This goes beyond the ability to be more innovative or less market oriented by offsetting the precariousness of specialist Cultural Production work with the certainty of embedded or non-creative work. And it indicates the need for 'personal identification with meaningful work' (Bridgstock 2005, 45) as a psychological measure of success and career satisfaction.

As Higgs, Cunningham and Bakhshi (2008, 34–5) have acknowledged, it is not possible for the Creative Trident model to capture these complexities when categorizing individual workers within a single employment mode: its efforts are inhibited by a weak metrics culture and data sets that have insufficient resolution for finer analysis to be undertaken. In-depth surveys, such as the one reported here, can work as a complement to the Trident model by helping to understand what might lie beneath the larger data sets.

It would be simplistic to assume that the combination of specialist, support, embedded and non-creative work is primarily a strategy of offsetting individualized risk. The complex intersections of these activities, together with the reliance on self-identification as a creative worker or dual professional, have significant implications for the ways in which 'creative work' and 'creative worker' are understood across different contexts. The picture emerging from our data suggests that embedded work is for many creative workers only one element of a more complex portfolio of work. Indeed, whilst the dominant narrative is to speak of embedded workers, it is far more accurate to speak of embedded work as a component of a creative worker's portfolio.

NOTES

1. The authors wish to acknowledge seed funding from the Committee for Perth. We would also like to thank Professor Catherine Murray (Simon Fraser University) and Professor Ann Markusen (University of Minnesota) for their insight, support and expertise in the development of the CWI survey instrument.
2. Due to rounding, figures do not add up exactly to 100 per cent.
3. As this question required respondents to self-define what they determined as creative and non-creative work, answers may not exactly align with Trident categories.
4. Gibson, Murphy and Freestone (2002) classify the following segments as 'cultural occupations': authors and related professionals, designers and illustrators, musicians and related professions, photographers, visual arts and crafts professionals, and librarians, archivists and other library staff.

REFERENCES

Bain, A. (2005), 'Constructing an artistic identity', *Work, Employment and Society*, **19** (1), 25–45.

Becker, H.S. (1982), *Art Worlds*, Berkeley, CA: University of California Press.

Bennett, D. (2007), 'Creative artists or cultural practitioners? Holistic practice in Australia's cultural industries', *Journal of Australian Studies*, **90**, 133–51.

Bennett, D. (2010), 'Creative migration: a Western Australian case study of creative artists', *Australian Geographer*, **41** (1), 117–28.

Bourdieu, P. (1993), *The Field of Cultural Production: Essays on Art and Literature*, Cambridge: Polity Press.

Brabazon, T. (2012), 'A wide open road? The strange story of creative industries in Western Australia', *Creative Industries Journal*, **4** (2), 171–93.

Bridgstock, R. (2005), 'Australian artists, starving and well-nourished: what can we learn from the prototypical protean career?', *Australian Journal of Career Development*, **14** (3), 40–48.

Cunningham, S. (2013), *Hidden Innovation: Policy, Industry and the Creative Sector*, St Lucia, Queensland: University of Queensland Press and Lexington Books, an imprint of Rowman & Littlefield.

Gallop, G. (2002), 'Culture, creativity and the future of Western Australia', presented at the Callaway Lecture Series, University of Western Australia, Perth, June.

Gibson, C., P. Murphy and R. Freestone (2002), 'Employment and socio-spatial relations in Australia's cultural economy', *Australian Geographer*, **33** (2), 173–89.

Gollmitzer, M. and C. Murray (2008), 'From economy to ecology: a policy framework for creative labor', presented at Canadian Conference of the Arts, Ottawa, Canada, March.

Hall, D.T. (1976), *Careers in Organizations*, Glenview, IL: Scott, Foresman.

Handy, C. (1989), *The Age of Unreason*, Harvard, MA: Harvard Business School Press.

Heckathorn, D.D. and J. Jeffri (2001), 'Finding the beat: using respondent-driven sampling to study jazz musicians', *Poetics*, **28** (4), 307–29.

Hearn, G., S. Roodhouse and J. Blakey (2007), 'From value chain to value creating ecology', *International Journal of Cultural Policy*, **13**, 419–36.

Higgs, P. and S. Cunningham (2008), 'Creative industries mapping: where have we come from and where are we going?', *Creative Industries Journal*, **1** (1), 7–30.

Higgs, P., S. Cunningham and H. Bakhshi (2008), *Beyond the Creative Industries: Mapping the Creative Economy in the United Kingdom*, London: NESTA, available at http://www.nesta.org.uk/library/documents/beyond-creative-industries-report.pdf (accessed 29 July 2013).

Markusen, A. (2010), 'Organizational complexity in the regional cultural economy', *Regional Studies*, **44** (7), 813–28.

Morris, P., P. Higgs, S. Lennon and A. Kelleher (2007), *Perth's Creative Industries*, Perth: Perth City Council.

Pracsys (2011), *Cultural Ecology Mapping: Dance Sector*, Perth: Department of Culture and the Arts.

Stratton, J. (2008), 'The difference of Perth music: a scene in cultural and historical context', *Continuum: Journal of Media & Cultural Studies*, **22** (5), 613–22.

PART III

Education, learning and careers

Generation, learning and careers

11. Learning processes in Creative Services teams: towards a dynamic systems theory

Greg Hearn, José H.P. Rodrigues and Ruth Bridgstock

The fastest-growing segment of jobs in the creative sector are in those firms that provide creative services to other sectors (Hearn et al., Chapter 1 in this volume; Cunningham, Chapter 2 in this volume). There are also many Creative Services (architecture and design, advertising and marketing, software and digital content occupations) workers embedded in organizations in other industry sectors (Cunningham and Higgs 2009). Goldsmith (Chapter 9 in this volume) shows, for example, that the financial services sector is the largest employer of digital creative talent in Australia. But why should this be?

We argue it is because 'knowledge-based intangibles are increasingly the source of value creation and hence of sustainable competitive advantage' (Mudambi 2008, 186). This value creation occurs primarily at the R&D and the marketing ends of the supply chain. Both of these areas require strong creative capabilities in order to design for, and to persuade, consumers. It is no surprise that Rodgers (Chapter 7 in this volume), in a study of Australia's manufacturing sector, found designers and advertising and marketing occupations to be the most numerous creative occupations. Hearn and Bridgstock (2014, 83) suggest that

> the creative heart of the creative economy . . . is the social and organisational routines that manage the generation of cultural novelty, both tacit and codified, internal and external, and [cultural novelty's] combination with other knowledges . . . produce and capture value.

Moreover, the main 'social and organisational routine' is usually a team (for example, Grabher 2002, 2004).

The centrality of learning in knowledge service teams is now well accepted (Hearn and Rooney 2008; Tallman and Chacar 2011). However, fewer studies exist that specifically examine learning in Creative Services teams. We agree with Amabile et al. (1996) that there are complex and imprecise problems in what concerns the intertwined processes of creativity and learning in teams (ibid.). Here we utilize a family of complex systems theories to understand what might influence learning processes in teams composed of Creative Services occupations as identified in this volume (Hearn et al., Chapter 1 in this volume; Cunningham, Chapter 2 in this volume). We adopt this approach because we will argue Creative Services teams produce unpredictable and unexpected outcomes in response to fixed client constraints. Specifically, we adopt the communities of practice approach (Lave and Wenger 1991; Wenger 1998) and nonlinear pedagogy theory (see Chow et al. 2006; Chow et al. 2011) to advance a theory of learning in such creative teams.[1] In what follows, we first introduce the key ideas in each of these two schools of thought before applying them in order to theorize a model of learning in such creative teams. In doing so, we hope to make a contribution to this volume by explaining the importance of learning *in situ* for Creative Services work.

COMMUNITIES OF PRACTICE

Bridgstock (2013) studied small digital creative teams and found that a major challenge for these teams is the need for continual learning and relearning because of the sheer rate of change in the digital media industries. Three dialectical tensions are encompassed in this: currency versus best practice; diversification versus specialization of functions, roles and skills; and more learning opportunities versus fewer opportunities to learn. To address these challenges, informal learning strategies were the preferred approaches to acquire the majority of required knowledge and skills, for both ongoing and initial professional development. Informal learning has no 'curriculum' per se, and tends to be opportunistic, unstructured, pedagogically agile and far more self-directed than formal learning (Eraut 2004). The main strategy is what Bridgstock calls 'social informal learning strategies', which rely on social relationships (see Rooney and Schneider 2005) in either face-to-face or online modes. Face-to-face learning strategies tended to be employed along the lines of a 'community of practice' (CoP) (Wenger 1999), involving active relationship-building, and maintenance between individuals within and outside the organization with similar interests. A CoP involves repeated and extended reciprocal interactions, and is thus fairly time-and-energy-resource intensive. Despite the resource intensivity of CoPs, Bridgstock found that they were central to professional currency, career development and ideation, and were seen as very valuable.

In Bridgstock's study, the face-to-face learning communities ranged from fairly structured, regular group meetings with specific aims to casual, as-needed and fairly *ad hoc* modes of operation. Online modes of social informal learning were less likely to employ a CoP model, but rather a distributed learning network of professionals and other interested people (including users as well as producers) (Albors, Ramon and Hervas 2008). Professionals might not even know the people with whom they were interacting, or know them only slightly. These creative workers used informal learning to obtain 'just in time' quick-turnaround information and skills via social networking sites, finding information quickly and then passing it along.

Classically, a CoP is composed of groups of people who, on a regular basis, share knowledge and/or develop capabilities within a specific activity (Brown and Duguid 1991; Lave and Wenger 1991). This concept of knowledge sharing involves different levels of expertise along with individual action. Nevertheless, social interaction is a necessary component in this process of learning. Learners need to be involved in a specific context involving specific beliefs and behaviours (Borzillo, Aznar and Schmitt 2011). It is this interaction between practice, individuals and the environment that facilitates knowledge acquisition, resulting in learning (Lave and Wenger 1991). By this logic, learning is surrounded by context, activity and culture, and it can be unintentional (Hara 2009), informal (Wenger 1999) or deliberate (Borzillo, Aznar and Schmitt 2011). In essence, for learning to happen, information needs to be available from contexts where activity happens. This process was coined as legitimate peripheral participation by Lave and Wenger (1991). Several stages of development, different levels of interaction and different types of activities make up a CoP (Borzillo, Aznar and Schmitt 2011). It is through mutual engagement in practice that members establish norms and relationships, share a sense of joint enterprise, and produce a shared repertoire of resources (Wenger 1999). CoPs have been argued to be self-organizing systems because it is the community, not external requirements, that ultimately determines actions (Wenger and Snyder 2000; see also Dameron and Josserand 2009).

Theories of self-organization and dynamic systems suggest that such systems evolve over time as their components evolve. These self-emergent properties of dynamic systems inherent to a CoP have significant implications for learning. For example, in the course of specific goal-oriented actions, individuals interacting with environmental constraints may augment the potential for exploratory behaviour (Yanow 2004). Specific constraints might influence communities of practice to evolve in different ways and have specific intrinsic dynamics. It has been suggested that these spontaneous environmental interactions over time might promote cognition, action and the emergence of creative behaviour (Hristovski et al. 2012). Therefore the self-organization properties of a CoP (Wenger and Snyder 2000) may be a significant influence on the development of creativity (Coleman 1999).

NONLINEAR PEDAGOGY

Nonlinear pedagogy utilizes theory from ecological psychology and non-linear dynamics to understand and explain how learning propositions can be embedded in concepts such as self-organization, perception and action, meta-stability, multi-stability, constraints, variability and stability in complex neurobiological systems (Davids, Button and Bennett 2008; Handford et al. 1997; Kelso 1995). Learning is conceived in the course of ecological constraints: interactions that promote cognition, decision-making and the emergence of action. According to Gibson's (1986) theory of perception and action, contextual information creates a dynamic correlation linking the individual and the environment. This interaction fosters goal-oriented exploratory actions and detection of environmental affordances that allows for new perception and subsequent new actions (ibid.).

Gibson's ideas of affordance have been applied to architectural practice. Maier, Fadel and Battisto (2009) suggested that affordances can be used as a conceptual framework to comprehend the relationship between environments and occupants (particularly when addressing the aspects of form and function). In architectural design, the concept of affordance allows for a common theoretical basis to improve the design process. Affordances can be used as a means to explore the connection between design intentionality and functionality, and as a means to avoid design malfunction (ibid.).

The constraints perspective can explain and provide theoretical foundations in order to understand learners' behaviour because learners interact with each other, setting different time and space boundaries during their goal-oriented activities (Newell 1986). Constraints that unite the dynamics of learning and performance can be organized as environmental, task and individual (ibid.). Hristovski et al. (2012) suggested that creative behaviours may be developed under the influence of interacting constraints within the individual–environment system. Different 'constraints arrangements' promoted a discovery behaviour, which enabled a better fluency, flexibility and the search for new functional solutions to a task goal. Using team games, these authors emphasized that manipulations of system constraints might develop individual creative solutions. The context of the team's performance was of vital importance in creating possibilities for action.

Cross-functional teams (Lovelace, Shapiro and Weingart 2001) and several knowledge domain teams (Taylor and Greve 2006) have been suggested as frameworks for producing innovative products. These teams may assemble different individuals because creativity may be facilitated from combining different disciplines and functions (Woodman, Sawyer and Griffin 1993). A higher absorptive capacity has been associated with these types of teams, since an individual's expertise can make access to external information and knowledge possible (Cohen and Levinthal 1990; Jansen, Van Den Bosch and Volberda 2005). However, constraints such as budgets, group size and deadlines may generate discrepancy within functionally diverse teams; therefore these teams may not necessarily be efficient and innovative in respect of their goals (Lovelace, Shapiro and Weingart 2001). Furthermore, within specific environments tasks may be influenced by different constraints or the same constraint may have a different repercussion within different environments (Taylor and Greve 2006). These aspects suggest that, depending on how constraints are manipulated, they may have a critical influence on creativity and innovation (ibid.).

TOWARDS A MODEL OF LEARNING IN CREATIVE TEAMS

What would a theory of learning in creative teams based on the theories discussed above look like? In what follows, we use the language from complex systems-compatible theories of learning (principally nonlinear pedagogy and communities of practice) to advance a theory of learning in creative teams. By way of initial orientation, Table 11.1 provides a glossary of key theoretical terms and definitions.

A logical starting point for theory-building is to define the kinds of creative outcomes that creative teams (CTs) are required to produce. In Table 11.2, we use a taxonomy expounded by Kaufman and Beghetto (2009) and applied by Hristovski et al. (2012) to creativity in sports teams in order to specify the kinds of outcomes that creative teams are seeking to produce. These range from 'Mini c' individual team member adaptations in skills or knowledge, through to 'Big C' creative interventions that produce a completely new business model for an existing product (for example, Spotify) or even product class (for example, Dyson's bagless vacuum cleaners). The taxonomy also differentiates between 'Little C'

*Table 11.1   Glossary of terms and definitions of theoretical terms in
              creative teams*

Mini c creativity	Individual insights/discoveries/short-cuts (Kaufman and Beghetto 2009)
Little C creativity	Finding a solution in a known space of multiple functional solutions (Kaufman and Beghetto 2009)
Pro C creativity	Skilled, flexible and integrated emergent creative response to client need (Kaufman and Beghetto 2009)
Big C creativity	Invention of new solution paradigm (Kaufman and Beghetto 2009)
Creative fluency	Generation of a large number of alternate solutions to a problem (Torrance 1966)
Creative flexibility	Generation of a variety of classes of solutions (Torrance 1966)
Creative originality	Atypicality of solutions to the problem (Torrance 1966)
Knowledge architecture	Total network of contacts, capacities, tacit knowledge and technologies that enable a creative team to perform at the highest level (Tallman and Chacar 2011)
Knowledge componentry	Necessary but insufficient knowledge e.g. digital know-how (Tallman and Chacar 2011)
Affordances	Properties of the environment, specified in the information array (flow field) of the individual, that present possibilities for action and are available for an agent to perceive directly and act upon (Gibson 1986)
Effectivities	The agent's ability to perceive and use affordances of the environment (Turvey 1992)
Constraints	Boundaries that shape the emergence of behaviour. May be personal, environmental or task-related (Newell 1986)
Multistability	Briefs that are on the border of stable and unstable (Hristovski et al. 2012)
Meta-stability	'Peak Creative Flow before returning to more functional operating' (Hristovski et al. 2012; Kelso 1995)

novel aesthetic variations (for example, new-look packaging) and 'Pro C'
integrated creative solutions (for example, dynamic multiplatform advertising campaigns).

   In order to produce these outcomes, high-performing creative teams

Table 11.2   Types of creative team solutions

Creativity	Creative process	Product/service outcome	Outcome characteristic
Mini c	Team member insights/ discoveries/short-cuts	None	Novel only
Little C	Finding a solution in a known space of multiple functional solutions	E.g. aesthetic variation	Effective
Pro C	Skilled flexible integrated emergent creative response to client need	E.g. effective/novel marketing campaign	Novel and effective
Big C	Invention of completely new approach to creative solution	E.g. new business model enabled by creative solution	Innovative

are not seeking efficiencies under stable conditions, but are immersed in dynamic environments, going from phases of stability, to instability, to new stability (cf. Losada 1999). Variations in interaction pattern types play a functional role in the detection and exploration of stable boundaries, and facilitate the creation of fluid flexible novel solutions (Kylén and Shani 2002). Effective creative teams within dynamic environments become attuned to critical sources of information by being exposed to constraints and perceiving affordances (Hristovski et al. 2012). Consequently, these teams learn how to do this routinely (ibid.). Creative teams are able to fluently boundary-span different discipline or knowledge domains (cf. Ratcheva 2009) in order to make the necessary translations or transformations that link to their novel creative solutions. They both generate novelty and determine fitness for purpose with specific, though dynamic, task and outcome constraints (for example, market opportunity or financial constraints).

We propose two types of learning that are needed to fully explain the performance of creative teams:

> *Type 1 Creative Team Learning*   First, how does a creative team learn in the context of a single-task specification or brief? How do they master the brief and share knowledge within the team and mutually learn to produce novel responses? How do they understand what the client wants? How do the different disciplines learn from each other once one aspect of the creative solution has been formulated? How do they assemble the knowledge between team and client systems? What are the stages of learning across the demands of the task?

Type 2 Creative Team Learning   The second type of learning relates to how creative teams assemble what allows them to engage in Type 1 learning, for the long term, across a range of briefs. How does a CT go about assembling deep expertise (often tacit), and accessing the needed knowledge to engage talent and client systems, capacities and resources, relational and semantic stocks? Also, what constraints and affordances in the macro-creative ecosystem need to be present for this to occur? Of particular relevance to the current volume is the question of whether creative resources are insourced, outsourced or achieved via a combination of approaches.

These distinctions are adaptations of terms proposed by Tallman and Chacar (2011), who distinguish between the component knowledge (similar to our Type 1 Learning) and the knowledge architecture (similar to our Type 2 Learning). Component knowledge is 'typically a combination of explicit technology, which can be easily absorbed, and tacit understandings related to context and application, which require some degree of insight for absorption'. Knowledge architecture 'is defined as highly path-dependent (experiential) in nature, deeply embedded, tacit, and inherently immobile (sticky). It exists as a stock or body of knowledge developed and held at different levels of organization and separates units engaged in different practices' (ibid., 203). Individual tasks require the assembly of component knowledge, which may be tacit or codified and may reside in different organizational systems. On the other hand, firms or professional groups are communities of practice that build and share the same knowledge architecture over time (see also Grabher 2004 on temporary and permanent projects) (see Figure 11.1).

With this background, we will now develop complex systems theoretical descriptions of Type 1 and Type 2 Creative Team Learning, via an amalgam of the knowledge community of practice and nonlinear pedagogy paradigms.

TYPE 1 CREATIVE TEAM LEARNING

The nonlinear pedagogy paradigm has been applied primarily to team sports (Hristovski et al. 2012). Although the ratio of routinized interventions versus novel interventions is likely to be different between sporting and creative teams, we suggest that the framework is very useful here, because a complex dynamic systems approach is foundational to understanding Creative Team Learning. In fact, we suggest that understanding the balance of closed versus open task constraints is crucial to the model.

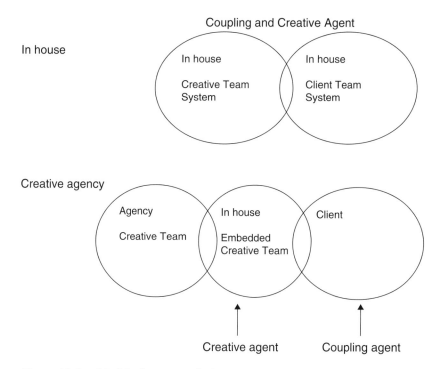

Figure 11.1   Model of system relations

For example, Grabher's (2004) study compared the project ecology of a software company in Munich and an advertising agency in London. He introduced the distinction between requirements for modularization versus originality in the former compared to the latter. The software company undertook projects that were essentially replicable. Learning was a step-by-step progression amongst similar combinations of partners. In the advertising company, the projects were more disruptive and often involved variations in relationships. We suggest that these are examples respectively of closed versus open task environments.

Our theory also builds on the prior work of Hearn, Rooney and Mandeville (2003), who applied complex systems theory to phenomenological problems in general. They proposed an approach to the study of innovation and creativity that focused not on creativity per se, but on complex knowledge systems that evolve through time. Furthermore, they argued:

> Knowledge systems, then, are not simply collections of data and information, although data and information are part of such systems. Knowledge systems are also systems of ideas and meanings – the nature of such a system is that actors

> must apprehend the meaning aspects of the system subjectively. Moreover, because such systems derive or create new meanings from the way one person's meanings are related to others' meanings, the system is inter-subjective in nature. Consequently, in an inter-subjective human system, imperfect and idiosyncratic awareness (consciousness) is a further complicating factor. The precise combination of intersubjectivity and awareness (the phenomenological) is to a large degree indeterminate, transitive and capable of considerable fluctuation. (Ibid., 232)

Extrapolating from Hristovski et al. (2012) and Hearn, Rooney and Mandeville (2003), we propose below that certain generalized systems theoretical terms may be helpful in explaining how creative teams arrive at solutions in a nonlinear way, rather than through practice and repetition or following due process. Shifts between stability and instability, between phases of confusion and interim creative solutions and so on, invoke the concepts of meta- and multi-stability in dynamic systems. Moreover, such variations may arise because of subtle perturbations in the creative 'space' that influence how teams respond to dynamic constraints, and assemble and deploy dynamic creative resources. Changes in the ecological dynamics (constraints, affordances and effectivities) can be hypothesized to underlie such processes.

    The core of this model is the idea that creative teams (compared with other task performance teams) face an environment that is radically open ideationally, while, at the same time, constrained in very specific ways (such as technology requirements, cost, intellectual property [IP]). Put another way, we can ask: how are the open and closed aspects of a constraining environment negotiated? Also, how is the resource mobilization and nonlinear nature of novelty production factored into negotiating this environment? Do teams move into open/closed solution-seeking modes? Are there different phases of providing a solution to a creative brief that have different modes and constraint environments, or is it better to think of processes rather than deterministic phases (cf. Dameron and Josserand 2009)? To answer these questions, Table 11.3 uses the ecological dynamics concepts of constraints, affordances and effectivities to describe and exemplify three processes that, we hypothesize, are involved in Type 1 Creative Team Learning. We refer to these as generative learning, evaluative learning and optimization. In addition, we propose that each of these processes includes variations in the types of creative outcomes ('Mini c' to 'Big C') and the operation of tacit versus codified knowledge.

> *Generative learning*   When a creative brief is obtained, there are some constraints that are relatively fixed, but other task features represent an open possibility space. For example, a creative response to a brief

Table 11.3 Processes in Creative Team Learning in response to a creative brief

Phases	Constraints	Affordances	Effectivities	Creativity	Tacit/codifed
Generative	No time constraints Task demands Client system values and culture	Networked digital creative ecosystem Creative team as community of practice, particularly tacit knowledge and peak creative expertise	Rapid possibility prototyping	Pro C Big C	Mainly tacit
Evaluative	Soft time constraints Client preferences Fit with technical systems IP issues Consonance with brand	Prior codified knowledge (e.g. templates) and tacit knowledge in the community of practice Deep expertise in multiple domains	Ability to manage open and closed aspects of the task simultaneously Understanding of client system (requirements, culture and preferences)	Mini c Little C Pro C	Tacit and codified
Optimizing	Hard time constraints Client requirements Accuracy of all text copy Optimal fit with technical systems Corporate sign-off on corporate identity requirements Legal sign-off on IP issues	Prior codified knowledge (e.g. project management methodologies) Some tacit knowledge in the community of practice Deep expertise in multiple domains	Ability to work fluidly across coding, look and feel and interaction design Understanding of client system (requirements, culture and preferences)	Mini c Little C	More codified than tacit

185

will not be successful because of its inherent efficiencies but, rather, because it satisfies functional requirements in an exceptionally novel way. Constraints are real, but broad, and might include client preferences and task guidelines. All four forms of creative outcome may be involved in generating a range of creative solution possibilities. Tacit knowledge may predominate over codified knowledge. Creative teams refer to such processes as 'rapid prototyping' and 'smoke and mirrors mock-ups'.

Evaluative Learning involves refining interim solutions and working out those that are suitable for a client. Constraints might include soft time deadlines, consonance with brand, client feedback and so on.

Optimization   In the third and final process, the solution is refined and delivered to high standards of execution. A number of constraints are key in this process, for example hard time constraints, accuracy of all text copy, optimal fit with technical systems, corporate sign-off on corporate identity requirements, and legal sign-off on IP issues. Equally in this process, 'tiny c' aesthetic variations can be trialled, whilst 'Big C' is, of course, now fixed and closed off. Codified project management procedures may be increasingly important in this process.

In summary, Type 1 Creative Team Learning, which is engaged in responding to briefs, is a complex systemic process that can be understood through the lens of ecological dynamics theory. A number of primary questions for future investigation are inherent:

1.   How and when are the different processes engaged in the task cycle?
2.   How is the boundary between open and closed constraints mediated?[2]
3.   How are the effectivities at each stage actually learnt?

TYPE 2 CREATIVE LEARNING

To understand Type 2 Creative Learning, which occurs as the architecture of learning is assembled, different issues need to be examined than for Type 1 Creative Learning. Often, creative teams are composed of executive producers and multidisciplinary creatives, as well as project and client management personnel. The core question to be answered is: how do they find people and integrate the team into a stable creative structure capable of flexible delivery of creative solutions? Put another way, how does the team assemble the capability and knowledge resources (including tacit and codified knowledge) located in different parts of a creative ecosystem?

A seminal study conducted by Grabher (2002) examines routines and regimes in the organization of creative services and the 'project ecology' of advertising services. Using the London advertising industry as a case study, Grabher describes its project ecology as

> a heterarchic form of social organization . . . that, despite dense patterns of interaction, is less systemic and less coherent than the more established territorial innovation models. Temporary collaboration in project ecologies . . . preserves the identities of a diverse spectrum of practices and organizational forms. Rather than being built on organizational coherence, project ecologies are driven by rivalry. (Ibid., 246)

Bowman and Swart's (2007) delineation of separable, embodied and embedded forms of capital is relevant here. In their study of professional services, including advertising, they make the point that some forms of capital, such as equipment or even patents and trademarks, can be held by companies completely separately from employees; hence the term separable capital. In contrast, embodied capital, such as knowledge and skills, cannot exist separately from the individuals or teams that deploy them. The third form of capital, 'embedded capital', occurs in the relationship between the two: 'embedded capital exists where there is ambiguity surrounding the rent creating contributions of human capital due to synergistic interactions between separable and embodied capital that are difficult to disentangle' (ibid., 494). For example, in creative teams proprietary software may have to be melded with dramatic content to produce an outcome for a client. In this case it is hard to say where the idea and the digital affordance start and end.

Building on these formulations, Swart and Kinnie (2010) distinguish three types of knowledge assets of relevance to creative teams. First, there is domain knowledge, skills and experiences of individual creative workers. Second, there are relational knowledge assets that are embedded within the external and internal social networks in which the team operates. Third, there is organizational capital, which is a function of the way the team organizes its creative processes. This could be anything from design methodologies to client workshop processes.

The beginning of theory-building for Type 2 Creative Learning is to imagine a firm negotiating a path through the dynamic creative ecosystem over time, assembling human capital and organizing it through social regimes. What is the appropriate form of contracting to achieve 'Mini c' through to 'Large C' outcomes? Some of the meta-capabilities are less easily secured and traded than the 'Mini c' creative resources that are easily substituted (see, for example, Hearn and Bridgstock 2014). Also, what kinds of organizational and social routines does the CT use in building its niche in the creative ecosystem? What is the creative team's survival strategy in the macro-creative ecosystem? How does it keep up with the game in a rapidly evolving ecosystem?

Hearn, Mandeville and Rooney (2003) describe three complex system trajectories in phenomenological systems that help us understand this process – they all involve learning (though different forms of learning in each case). We can use studies of design firms, especially Abecassis-Moedas et al. (2012) to describe each of these learning processes.

1. *Self-referencing*   Using autopoetic processes to define and maintain core creative identity. These creative teams are built around growing the reputation of a designer or designers. Ambitious creative projects are developed, leading to a house style. Industry awards and prizes cement the reputation of the team. Relationships with clients are often through a personal network.
2. *Self-organizing*   Learning through adaptation to fluctuating environmental conditions. This includes splitting and merging with other teams as well as attracting talent. Some creative teams grow through very close and responsive relationships with clients (for example, 'client intimacy processes'). Here the emphasis is on social and organizational routines that bind human capital to client needs in productive ways, perhaps by creating scenarios that can effect radical changes to products, services and brands. Sometimes the future of the creative team is tied to the future of its client systems in quite specific ways.
3. *Self-transforming*   A culture of constant in-house creative innovation, not in response to client environments that enhance sustainability. Some creative teams build a culture of curiosity and constant innovation, and manifest this in innovative methodologies deployed on behalf of clients. For example, IDEO has such a reputation and invents and deploys new methods regularly as well as creating them.[3] The embodiment of the design processes can be obtained by developing ad hoc tools able to support the interaction with clients. Client systems absorb these processes and thus the whole creative ecosystems of creative team and client grow in a culture of curiosity and innovation.

CONCLUSION

Creative teams operate in the realm of creative ideas. This realm is very dynamic and creative teams must become adept at routinely producing original and imaginative ideas that solve problems with quite fixed requirements from clients. In other words, creative teams need to learn to navigate within dynamic social and semantic systems that involve both novelty production and response to constraints. Because of this we have utilized a family of learning theories compatible with complex systems theory to build frameworks that can explain the processes involved. From perceptual and environmental psychology we utilized the theories of ecological dynamics and nonlinear pedagogy. These learning theories have been applied in a number of realms, from perception to sports performance, and we propose, here, that they are also useful in helping to explain creative constraints, novelty production and the notion of the creative ecosystem. From social anthropology and education psychology we utilized the idea of communities of practice to underscore the socially situated nature of creative team development.

These theoretical requirements apply, in different ways, to both learning about each individual problem brief (Type 1 Learning), and to learning to survive over the long term by cultivating creative assets and resources in the team (Type 2 Learning). In Type 1 Learning different kinds of creative outcomes are involved, ranging from aesthetic variation to business paradigm innovation. Further we propose that quite different types of learning are required for generative, evaluative and optimization tasks. In Type 2 Learning capability acquisition is the objective. This is enacted in a large and very dynamic social network milieu, comprising competitive and collaborative processes. Teams may survive by adaptation or by merging with other agents, scaling up through replication of solutions or operating methodologies, or by gaining competitive advantage through first-principles innovation. It is hoped that in this theoretical exercise we have begun to develop a language in which to talk about the phenomenon of learning in creative teams, and suggested questions that a theory would need to explain. It falls to future studies to operationalize and test these questions.

NOTES

1. Although we use the terms 'creative team' and 'creative services team' interchangeably, we restrict our focus here to creative service teams, but note that the theory may apply to other kinds of creative teams. As we define them, creative teams may be either microagencies, creative service teams in agencies, creative teams embedded in organizations or an amalgam of these.
2. For example, Staber (2008) proposes different path dependencies in networks of ideas to explain this.
3. IDEO 'is an award-winning global design firm that takes a human-centered, design-based approach to helping organizations in the public and private sectors innovate and grow' (IDEO 2013).

REFERENCES

Abecassis-Moedas, C., S.B. Mahmoud-Jouini, C. Dell'Era, D. Manceau, D. and R. Verganti (2012), 'Key resources and internationalization modes of creative knowledge-intensive business services: the case of design consultancies', *Creativity and Innovation Management*, **21** (3), 315–31.

Albors, J., J.C. Ramos and J.L. Hervas (2008), 'New learning network paradigms: communities of objectives, crowdsourcing, wikis and open source', *International Journal of Information Management*, **28** (3), 194–202.

Amabile, T.M., R. Conti, H. Coon, J. Lazenby and M. Herron (1996), 'Assessing the work environment for creativity', *Academy of Management Journal*, **39** (5), 1154–84.

Borzillo, S., S. Aznar and A. Schmitt (2011), 'A journey through communities of practice: how and why members move from the periphery to the core', *European Management Journal*, **29** (1), 25–42.

Bowman, C. and J. Swart (2007), 'Whose human capital? The challenge of value capture when capital is embedded', *Journal of Management Studies*, **44** (4), 488–505.

Bridgstock, R. (2013), 'Learning strategies of creatives in digital micro businesses', unpublished manuscript.

Brown, J.S. and P. Duguid (1991), 'Organizational learning and communities-of-practice: toward a unified view of working, learning, and innovation', *Organization Science*, **12** (2), 198–213.

Chow, J.Y., K. Davids, C. Button, R. Shuttleworth, I. Renshaw and D. Araújo (2006), 'Nonlinear pedagogy: a constraints-led framework for understanding emergence of game play and movement skills', *Nonlinear Dynamics, Psychology, and Life Sciences*, **10** (1), 71–103.

Chow, J.Y., K. Davids, R. Hristovski, D. Araújo and P. Passos (2011), 'Nonlinear pedagogy: learning design for self-organizing neurobiological systems', *New Ideas in Psychology*, **29** (2), 189–200.

Cohen, W.M. and D.A. Levinthal (1990), 'Absorptive capacity: a new perspective on learning and innovation', *Administrative Science Quarterly*, **35** (1), 128–52.

Coleman, H.J. (1999), 'What enables self-organizing behavior in businesses', *Emergence*, **1** (1), 33–48.

Cunningham, S. and P. Higgs (2009), 'Measuring creative employment: implications for innovation policy', *Innovation: Management, Policy and Practice*, **11** (2), 190–200.

Dameron, S. and E. Josserand (2009), 'The structural and relational development of a network', presented at European Academy of Management Conference, Liverpool, England, May.

Davids, K., C. Button and S. Bennett (2008), *Dynamics of Skill Acquisition: A Constraints-Led Approach*, Champaign, IL: Human Kinetics Publishers.

Eraut, M. (2004), 'Informal learning in the workplace', *Studies in Continuing Education*, **26** (2), 247–73.

Gibson, J. (1986), *The Ecological Approach to Visual Perception*, Hillsdale, NJ: Lawrence Erlbaum Associates.

Grabher, G. (2002), 'The project ecology of advertising: tasks, talents and teams', *Regional Studies*, **36** (3), 245–62.

Grabher, G. (2004), 'Temporary architectures of learning: knowledge governance in project ecologies', *Organization Studies*, **25** (9), 1491–514.

Handford, C., K. Davids, S. Bennett and C. Button (1997), 'Skill acquisition in sport: some applications of an evolving practice ecology', *Journal of Sports Sciences*, **15** (6), 621–40.

Hara, N. (2009), *Communities of Practice: Fostering Peer-to-Peer Learning and Informal Knowledge Sharing in the Work Place*, Bloomington, IN; Berlin; Heidelberg: Springer-Verlag.

Hearn, G. and R. Bridgstock (2014), 'The curious case of the embedded creative: managing creative work outside the creative industries', in S. Cummings and C. Bilton (eds), *Handbook of Management and Creativity*, Cheltenham, UK and Northampton, MA, USA: Edward Elgar, pp. 65–92.

Hearn, G. and D. Rooney (eds). (2008), *Knowledge Policy: Challenges for the 21st Century*, Cheltenham, UK and Northampton, MA, USA: Edward Elgar.

Hearn, G., D. Rooney and T. Mandeville (2003), 'Phenomenological turbulence and innovation in knowledge systems', *Prometheus*, **20** (2), 231–46.

Hristovski, R., K. Davids, P. Passos and D. Araújo (2012), 'Sport performance as a domain of creative problem solving for self-organizing performer-environment systems', *The Open Sports Sciences Journal*, **5** (Suppl. 1–M4), 26–35.

IDEO (2013), *About IDEO*, available at http://www.ideo.com/about/ (accessed 26 August 2013).

Jansen, J.J.P., F.A.J. Van Den Bosch and H.W. Volberda (2005), 'Managing potential and realized absorptive capacity: how do organizational antecedents matter?', *Academy of Management Journal*, **48** (6), 999–1015.

Kaufman, J.C. and R.A. Beghetto (2009), 'Beyond big and little: the four c model of creativity', *Review of General Psychology*, **13** (1), 1–12.

Kelso, J.A. (1995), *Dynamic Patterns: The Self-Organization of Brain and Behavior*, Cambridge, MA: The MIT Press.

Kylén, S. and A.B. Shani (2002), 'Triggering creativity in teams: an exploratory investigation', *Creativity and Innovation Management*, **11** (1), 17–30.

Lave, J. and E. Wenger (1991), *Situated Learning: Legitimate Peripheral Participation*, Cambridge: Cambridge University Press.

Losada, M. (1999), 'The complex dynamics of high performance teams', *Mathematical and Computer Modelling*, **30** (9–10), 179–92.

Lovelace, K., D.L. Shapiro and L.R Weingart (2001), 'Maximizing cross-functional new product teams' innovativeness and constraint adherence: a conflict communications perspective', *Academy of Management Journal*, **44** (4), 779–93.

Maier, J.R., G.M. Fadel and D.G. Battisto (2009), 'An affordance-based approach to architectural theory, design, and practice', *Design Studies*, **30** (4), 393–414.

Mudambi, R. (2008), 'Location, control, and innovation in knowledge-intensive industries', *Journal of Economic Geography*, **8** (5), 699–725.

Newell, K.M. (1986), 'Constraints on the development of coordination', in M.G. Wade and H.T.A. Whiting (eds), *Motor Development in Children: Aspects of Coordination and Control*, Boston, MA: Martinus Nijhoff, pp. 341–60.

Ratcheva, V. (2009), 'Integrating diverse knowledge through boundary spanning processes – the case of multidisciplinary project teams', *International Journal of Project Management*, **27** (3), 206–15.

Rooney, D. and U. Schneider (2005), 'The material, mental, historical and social character of knowledge', in D. Rooney, G. Hearn and A. Ninan (eds),

Handbook on the Knowledge Economy, Cheltenham, UK and Northampton, MA, USA: Edward Elgar, pp. 19–36.

Staber, U. (2008), 'Network evolution in cultural industries', *Industry and Innovation*, **15** (5), 569–78.

Swart, J. and N. Kinnie (2010), 'Organisational learning, knowledge assets and HR practices in professional service firms', *Human Resource Management Journal*, **20** (1), 64–79.

Tallman, S. and A. Chacar (2011), 'Communities, alliances, networks and knowledge in multinational firms: a micro-analytic framework', *Journal of International Management*, **17** (3), 201–10.

Taylor, A. and H.R. Greve (2006), 'Superman or the Fantastic Four? Knowledge combination and experience in innovative teams', *Academy of Management Journal*, **49** (4), 723–40.

Torrance, E.P. (1966), *Torrance Tests of Creative Thinking: Norms Technical Manual (Research Edition)*, Princeton, NJ: Personal Press.

Turvey, M.T. (1992), 'Affordances and prospective control: an outline of the ontology', *Ecological Psychology*, **4** (3), 173–87.

Wenger, E. (1990), *Communities of Practice: Learning, Meaning and Identity*, Cambridge: Cambridge University Press.

Wenger, E. and W. Snyder (2000), 'Communities of practice: the organizational frontier', *Harvard Business Review*, **78** (1), 139–46.

Woodman, R.W., J.E. Sawyer and R.W. Griffin (1993), 'Toward a theory of organizational creativity', *Academy of Management Review*, **18** (2), 293–321.

Yanow, D. (2004), 'Translating local knowledge at organizational peripheries', *British Journal of Management*, **15** (S1), S9–S25.

12. Translating creative skills: an example of Youthworx Media for marginalized youth[1]

Aneta Podkalicka

INTRODUCTION

'Youthworx Media' is a Melbourne-based youth project that capitalizes on the popularity of media production and training to support marginalized young people in re-entering education and employment markets. The delivery of accredited courses in Creative Industries (Certificates I to IV), through partnership with North Melbourne Institute of TAFE (NMIT) and Swinburne University, is the key facet of Youthworx's media training, alongside open access multimedia workshops and independent one-on-one mentoring. At Youthworx young people produce a variety of media content, such as digital storytelling, radio programs, short documentaries and fiction films. The processes of Cultural Production are organized as attractive but also purposeful, with built-in research activities, brainstorming, planning, teamwork and collegial feedback. Creative content is distributed through the youth community radio SYN MEDIA (Youthworx's partner), public screening events throughout the city, the program's website, and to external clients who commission work through Youthworx's social enterprise. This deliberately set up semi-formal context for digital media production is an example of an alternative education model directed towards developing general skills in order to facilitate youth transitions into further education and the labour market. Employment in the creative media sector is not the main objective of the project, although some Youthworx participants may go on to creative employment.

Existing academic and policy literature has noted the need to improve the understanding of participatory processes and a range of contributions delivered by media youth development initiatives with a social justice mission through empirical, longitudinal research (Slater et al. 2007; see also Sefton-Green 2008). Between 2008 and 2013 the Youthworx research has centred on documenting and analysing the nature of creative engagement and transitional outcomes for the youth involved.[2] This chapter focuses on answering a central research question of what happens to Youthworx graduates trained in Creative Industries skills after they leave the project, looking specifically at the types of education and employment they pursue. The main argument, reinforced by the data presented here, is that creative education is not a self-serving Creative Industry mechanism, but a multidirectional pathway[3] for disengaged young people towards inclusion in societal structures. This chapter draws on initial surveys with 45 students who officially enrolled in Youthworx-offered courses between 2009 and 2011. It also draws on 17 follow-up interviews with Youthworx graduates.

While other contributions in this book focus on models of creative work beyond the Creative Industries through the notion of the embedded workforce, our research examines a situation in which investment in building creative human capital generates social participation in broader spheres of formalized education and the labour market. Youthworx's experience demonstrates that semi-formal creative education can result not only in employment outside the Creative Industries, but also produces a range of social benefits and opportunities with wide applications for the participants. Therefore the chapter extends the discussion of the creative workforce beyond the distinctions between specialist and embedded forms of creative work by providing evidence about the positive impacts of creative skill development for a solid, if nonlinear, transition into education and employment across a variety of industry sectors for a group of disenfranchised youth.[4]

THE LITERATURE

The chapter intersects with important international debates on nonlinear youth transitions into education and employment (Furlong 2009; Fouad and Bynner 2008), and more generally the role of creative production as an alternative educational site for skill development (Buckingham 2007; Sefton-Green and Nixon 2009). Small, variously funded organizations delivering vocational training for the Creative Economy, and often directed to young people deprived of social opportunities, are seen as complementary to the mainstream schooling and important in 'remediating forms of social exclusion' (Sefton-Green 2008, 11). At the same time, the dominant tendency in youth research has been to frame the discussion of contemporary youth transitions as complex, nonlinear, often fragmented and erratic, with young people's career paths marked by phases of unemployment, delayed or extended transition into work, or changes in occupation. Theoretical debates have raged between the role of social class and structural factors *vis-à-vis* agency, lifelong choices and risk-taking as shaping educational and occupational aspirations and particular career trajectories (Goodwin and O'Connor 2013).[5] Significant attention has been paid to groups of disadvantaged youth as compelling examples to explore the validity of the concepts of transition, resilience, 'poverty of aspiration', or to suggest, after Furlong, the emergence of 'new mechanisms of exclusion' occurring in the situation of personal cultural, social and material scarcity and against the general context of 'protracted and individualized transitions' (Furlong 2010, 517). Available studies have recognized the risky, nonlinear experience and pathways of marginalized youth (see, for example, Furlong et al. 2003) who do not necessarily lack aspiration – contrary to previously held assumptions – but face the constraints of socioeconomic resources, geography or concrete opportunities to pursue their goals (Sinclair, McKendrick and Scott 2010). This sociological research into the precarious and casualized youth labour market (see, for example, Furlong and Kelly 2005) is paralleled by critical accounts of precarity associated with casualization, short-term or mixed employment in the Creative Industries (Bridgstock 2005; Deuze 2007; Ross 2009; Throsby and Zednik 2010).

This chapter presents our research material by drawing on these intersecting debates. It highlights nonlinear career paths to embedded work and precarity of the journey for a group of vulnerable young people engaged in alternative creative education. The findings of the nonlinearity and the precarity of creative transitions discussed here should be cautiously applied to similar cohorts. Thought should be given to who is studied and the contexts in which they operate.

YOUTHWORX MEDIA

Young people aged between 15 and 22 are referred to Youthworx Media through a network of social agencies, including the Salvation Army's Brunswick Youth Services (BYS), Melbourne City Mission, Anglicare or the Department of Human Services. Located in Melbourne's northern suburb of Brunswick, the program began its operation in 2008, introduced accredited courses in 2009, and launched its small-scale commercial media production company, Youthworx Productions, in 2010. In 2011 Youthworx added a full-time youth worker to strengthen its social service support (see Table 12.1).

Table 12.1   Youthworx Productions employees and staff (2010–2012)

Staff	Total
Core staff	6
Core trainees	6
Contracted industry professionals	20
Paid trainee assistants	24
Internships (through work placements)	6

Table 12.2   Number of accredited courses (Certs I–III) in Creative Industries

Year	2009	2010	2011	2012	2013	Total
Certificates	15	18	19	17	18	87

A total of 35 students of the 45 officially enrolled graduated with Youthworx certifications. Many students continued the training beyond the Certificate (CERT) I, progressing to obtain CERT II and CERT III (see Table 12.2). In addition, two further students obtained Victorian Certificate of Applied Learning (VCAL) diplomas during their time at Youthworx. Youthworx Productions's core trainees (three at one time) had enrolled in CERT IV, but have not completed.

THE STUDY

Between 2008 and 2010 we drew on qualitative, ethnographic techniques, such as regular participant observation, and semi-structured interviews with participants and Youthworx staff (for details see Podkalicka et al. 2013). We also employed survey-based techniques consisting of paper-based questionnaires filled out by students before participation in the course. Their function was to identify the participants' educational background, key areas of interest and educational and occupational plans. Between 2010 and 2013 we continued to track youth transitions through visits to the project site and a series of structured follow-up interviews that addressed the questions of the program's value and actual transitions from the point of view of Youthworx graduates.

This chapter draws on the sample of 45 students who officially enrolled in Youthworx-offered accredited courses in Creative Industries between 2009 and 2011.[6] Seven other young people started courses, but soon dropped out and never officially enrolled. In addition, between 2008 and 2012 over 400 young people came through Youthworx, participating in group-based media workshops without accreditation or in one-on-one independent training sessions. Two main sets of data are analysed: one sourced from entry questionnaires that students fill out before beginning their Youthworx course; the other based on follow-up interviews conducted between 2012 and 2013 with a group of young people who participated in the project between 2009 and 2011. Out of 45 former students contacted, we managed to interview 17; 11 were uncontactable either due to disconnected numbers or no response despite a number of attempts.[7] We were able to determine transition pathways for some of the remaining graduates through contact with Youthworx and BYS social workers. A few students appear to have disappeared beneath the radar. There is large variation between the interviewees in terms of the time that passed since they left Youthworx, ranging between three years and several months. The initial questionnaire demonstrates students' expectations from the course, as well as plans for further education and employment. The interviews focus on pathways and students' directions following Youthworx.

The rest of the chapter is structured in three sections. The first section sets the scene for the discussion of youth transitions and outcomes by revisiting the expectations and motivations of young people who initially engaged in the training. The second section addresses the main research question of how Youthworx-led creative and media training translates into the education and employment market for this demographic. This section combines quantitative and qualitative material from the follow-up interviews (2012 to 2013) to explore key areas of the project's value for participants. The final section discusses the relationships among creative skill development, creative employment and social change.

REASONS FOR DOING A YOUTHWORX COURSE IN CREATIVE INDUSTRIES

Of the 32 students who provided written answers in the initial questionnaire, the overwhelming majority (31) stated interest in media.[8] Roughly half (14) combined their answers on this topic with seeing the course as a pathway into employment in the Creative Industries, or more broadly as 'something that will help me get a job when I'm older', or that will offer 'different options and choices'. Only two students gave more general responses as seeking 'something to do with life' or 'because of social reasons'. Based on the responses provided, creative work is mostly regarded in a traditional sense of Cultural Production and corresponding sectors (for example, film, TV, music, publishing, marketing).[8] Their stated dream jobs referred mostly to glamorous or high-profile media jobs and included:

    actor
    band front man
    being on TV
    fashion photographer
    film director
    magazine editor working with celebrities
    model manager
    music producer
    radio presenter
    rapper
    songwriter
    TV star

Asked 'where they see themselves in five years', the majority of respondents (23) reported expectations to work in the Creative Industries, either generally or in specific areas, such as music-making, illustrating, graphics or film-making. A few (four) saw Youthworx creative/media training as an employment pathway more broadly: for example, to 'do[ing] a trade apprenticeship' (for example, as a plumber or electrician), youth work, office or administrative work, or more prosaically to 'find work in the city', or 'any work'. Two students saw their professional future in either 'filming or [a] building trade', or 'sampling or painting'; five declared they didn't know.

When asked about their education and employment plans, over one-third (12 of 32) of respondents emphasized an aspiration to take up further education post-Youthworx rather than seek immediate jobs. The respondents listed general courses such as Victorian Certificate of Applied Learning (VCAL), Technical and Further Education (TAFE) or media-specific courses ('Victorian Certificate of Education (VCE) in multimedia', or 'university photography course'), as well as 'working towards building computer and media skills'. In two cases, the plans combined both media and trade (as above), such as 'finish year nine, do media and VCAL, apprenticeship in building trade'. Seven respondents focused on creative employment plans, with nine stating general employment or other jobs. Three declared they weren't sure.

It is important that only a small number of respondents (seven) listed employment in Creative Industries as part of their plans, compared with 31 declaring interest in media (including creative employment) and 23 seeing themselves in Creative Industries job in the next five years. Acknowledging the limitations of the questionnaire-based data, while drawing on our ethnographic research, we suggest a couple of possible readings for the noted disjuncture between the strong interest/aspirations and weak plans.[10] First, the strong interest in creative media confirms the appeal of the program for this group of young people otherwise disengaged from formal education (Slater et al. 2007). The initial media-based allure of the program is critical, even if, as the data demonstrate, the enrollees do not see the Creative Industries course as a means in itself or final destination. The orientation towards further study might be explained by a level of awareness about difficult entry into the competitive Creative Industries sector, and the generally acknowledged precarity of securing a stable income, thus making media work an interesting, but remote, reality. This could explain why most of the enrolling students identified a number of glamorous jobs in the Creative Industries as their dream employment. Furthermore, the response 'I'd like to have some sort of part-time or casual work for the time being, until I can make something from making music' captures a related aspect that signals the perceived value of study in terms of 'cushioning' the risks taken with creative pathways. Numerous studies point to patterns of supplementing or subsidizing creative jobs with more stable non-creative employment alongside or across careers (Cunningham 2013), or the precarity of creative employment more generally (Bridgstock 2005; Deuze 2007; Ross 2009; Throsby and Zednik 2010). Our material suggests that further study has a similar auxiliary function for this demographic. Second, the focus on further education may be a reflection of a general trend, which has seen a steady decline of young people choosing the labour force rather than full-time education (Lamb and Mason 2008, ix). One graduate put it rather succinctly: 'I'm not interested in jobs, but more courses' – thus signalling the general value of education as continuing to 'work on oneself' beyond Youthworx.

When we cross-referenced the entry data with 17 follow-up interviews, we found that the majority of the interviewees (11) confirmed their interest in media, but here the answers are more weighted towards interest in media-making generally, rather than undertaking creative/media jobs. In addition, what underpins these responses is also an acute sense of the opportunity that the Youthworx course presented to them at the time – a finding consistent with our earlier analysis (Podkalicka et al. 2013). This leads us to reinforce the point that creative work training might be a particularly attractive option, over other courses, for those who have no clear direction in life. The following accounts illustrate it well:

I didn't really have anything to do, or life direction; was enrolled at VCAL (general high school curriculum); out of school for a year before VCAL (dropped out year nine); didn't know what to do with myself; initially not steering towards media but my engagement developed.

Just finished VCAL and was looking for next thing, Youthworx was right next to VCAL at the time, so just fell into it. And we would already use our breaks to get into the Youthworx studio.

FURTHER EDUCATION AND TRAINING FOLLOWING YOUTHWORX

Of the whole group of 46, more than half (25 students) have undertaken some type of further training and education following Youthworx. Of those 25, 22 students had previously completed Youthworx certificates, indicating a high rate of continuity between Youthworx and external further education. Twelve of these graduates moved on to full-time courses. The post-Youthworx courses can be clustered as types of education (apprenticeships, TAFE, VCAL) and as part of different industry sectors (see Table 12.3).

Table 12.3   Types of education and training across apprenticeships, TAFE and VCAL courses following Youthworx

Types of education
Bakery
Boiler making
Childcare
Disability training
Forklift
Graphic design
Hospitality
Instrument making and repair
Landscaping
Mechanic
Media/Arts
Painting
Personal training
Photography
Retail
Rendering
Screen writing
Social work
Warehousing

It is important to note that apprenticeships, as a form of on-the-job training, are reported as both 'education' and 'employment', meaning that the entries in both categories overlap. Its general popularity among the Youthworx graduates is consistent with an overall finding that apprenticeships are an important pathway to full-time employment for students who leave school before year 12 (Lamb and Mason 2008, ix).

Since leaving Youthworx, six former students are known to have undertaken more than one course. Five expressed interest in further study (for example, animal care, hospitality, business, retail, carpentry or travel agent), including those who had already completed courses post-Youthworx, or those who had a part-time job at the time of the interview.

Traditional trades proved popular (for example, painting, forklift operation for men, and retail or childcare for women), while social work seemed attractive for men and women. Personal training/fitness was considered a major growth area by the young people interviewed, and pursued by three of the Youthworx graduates. Occupations in fitness and social work were mentioned as attractive for their inherently social dimensions. They were viewed not only as tangible employment, but also as an altruistic form of 'giving back to the community'. This sense of indebtedness figured in several accounts, expressed as a result of the positive experience at Youthworx, or its social service partner the Salvation Army's Brunswick Youth Services. For similar 'social' reasons, a couple of students took up employment at a community centre, or as 'support for kids who fall behind with work' at a local school.

EMPLOYMENT FOLLOWING YOUTHWORX

Of 46 students, ten are currently employed in a variety of jobs (see Table 12.4).[11] A further seven had been employed after they left Youthworx, but their current employment status could not be verified.[12] Of those 17 interviewed, five were engaged in full-time jobs, with a couple working part-time and studying simultaneously.

Of the 45 former students, three are currently in specialist creative employment. One of these graduates is working as a freelance specialist creative. One is in full-time specialist creative employment and undertaking additional freelance work. Another is studying media full-time on top of specialist employment. An additional graduate is employed part-time as a specialist or embedded creative (survey results were unclear about the place of employment). We also know that one graduate was employed intermittently and on a casual basis as an assistant in an advertising company during his enrolment in Youthworx. In addition, Youthworx

Table 12.4   Employment following Youthworx

Creative Industries employment (some graduates have multiple forms of employment).	Film and photography editing
	Film making
	Guitar making
	Jeweller
	Events organizing
	Musician
	Photography
Other employment	Car wreckage
	Community centre
	Diesel mechanic
	Disability services
	Equipment hire
	Factory/warehouse
	Fitness training
	Hospitality
	Landscaping
	Painting
	Rendering
	Retail
	School support
	Beauty professional

Productions offers paid traineeships to its core trainees in filming, editing and design, as well as occasional casual work for current or former students. Since mid-2010 over 20 young people had been employed as paid assistants on short-term commissioned media projects, undertaking filming, editing and web design.

Although falling outside the suggested definitions of creative work and sectors (Cunningham 2013; Cunningham, Chapter 2 in this volume), trade occupations such as painting or landscaping, depending on the exact characteristics of the job, can be viewed as reliant on creative decisions and inputs. Cultural texts, such as Sennett's *The Craftsman* (2009) or Crawford's *Shop Class as Soulcraft* (2010), have sought to reinstate the value of manual labour, demonstrating how operational intelligence, material transformation and expressive work are all constitutive elements of craftsmanship that can be applied to various sectors, including work as laboratory technicians (Sennett 2009) or car mechanics (Crawford 2010).

Of the 17 students interviewed, seven reported ongoing aspirations in creative or media work but pointed out a number of barriers (see below). A few expressed no interest in creative work (a change from the initial engagement in Youthworx), but stressed the value of media training, suggesting that it had acted as a social lubricant for their existing and new circles of friends. The same number (three) declared no interest whatsoever, as they have moved into trade employment that they are enjoying and are keen to pursue in future.

For those with an ongoing interest in creative jobs, including the former core Youthworx Productions trainees, a transition towards employment in the creative sector is tedious and long. It involves a series of part-time jobs alongside creative courses, possible unpaid internships or casual freelance stints. The following account gives a good illustration:

> I was waitressing while studying after Youthworx to get by. Not working at the moment, but have been freelancing since leaving Youthworx. I had an ad on Gumtree [a classified ads website] advertising my media skills and have been getting jobs through that. This is work for arts students, and I can get between $50–100 for a session, which is good enough. Lately, I've been thinking about working in a travel agency, so I'm planning to do a full-time six-month course soon.

The recognition of the tough entry conditions and the precarity of the sector have oriented such students towards other courses post-Youthworx with the view of getting, in their own words, a 'concrete' and 'well-paid job'. Those who stayed at Youthworx the longest, including the former core trainees in Youthworx Productions, have opted to 'do something else first', 'save money' and 'then come back to media work'. Three graduates commented:

> [I'm doing] a fitness course now because it's hard to find something in media, without the same network and support as through Youthworx. The Youthworx experience was life changing but you [need to be realistic too].

> It's hard [finding a job] because I don't have any other qualifications except media, and of course it's difficult to find some media-related work, so I'm thinking about doing a full-time hospitality [course] soon.

> I'm looking into internships, as I would like to get back into media.

Financial considerations feature strongly in the graduates' accounts. During and after their participation in the program, several students dropped out of the course, citing the need to pay rent and bills. This is no different after they leave. In a pointed critique of the internship system in the US, Perlin (2011) observes that people from low socioeconomic groups cannot afford to do internships, which puts them at a disadvantage in the new labour market where internships are the norm, reinforcing Furlong's (2010) observation about new forms of exclusion.

YOUTHWORX'S VALUE: SKILLS AND PATHWAYS BEYOND CREATIVE WORK

All 17 respondents affirmed that they benefited from Youthworx. The identified benefits encompassed personal, social and vocational skills. Young people, especially those involved in the paid traineeships at Youthworx's social enterprise, reported having learned basic work-based capabilities such as regular attendance, punctuality, commitment to seeing a project through to completion, improved time management, communication and networking skills, alongside more specialized media literacies. Many noted the value of the improved self-confidence as a prerequisite for capitalizing on social and professional opportunities, including invitations to create promotional media material for friends in an expert capacity, enrolling in further educational courses or successful liaising with external clients on commissioned media projects. This is well captured by one graduate:

> One thing for sure is [that the Youthworx experience] boosts your confidence because you are thrown in a lot of situations people call a deep end. I wouldn't at all. But you are put in situations where you need to talk, you have to network with people, you might be filming at a location where you don't have your bosses with you, so you're on your own, and you're in charge. After a while you start to get a hang of it and you turn out to be a different person leaving that place. After a while of having to do this, it suddenly [becomes] natural.

This comprehensive skill development was achieved by embedding young people's digital media production work within the organizational and pedagogic structure of Youthworx.[13] The program cultivates basic 'employability' principles such as attendance and communication, enhanced by the close partnership with the youth community radio SYN MEDIA or through business relationships with clients in the case of Youthworx Productions. As Jenkins observes, 'the new media literacies should be seen as social skills, as ways of interacting within a larger community, and not simply an individualized skill to be used for personal expression' (2009, 20). At Youthworx, young people produce, broadcast and deliver media content to clients, learning, in the process, 'new social skills' that are critical for the workplace and participation in the broader economy.

'YOUTHWORX HAS STARTED IT ALL'

> Youthworx has kick-started all other things for me. It is one of the best things I ever did; I absolutely loved it.

This chapter takes the question of creatives beyond the Creative Industries further than the Creative Trident of core, support and embedded, and considers how Creative Industries education can empower a group of marginalized youth and assist them in participating in social spheres, broader education and the economy. The study also demonstrates the socioeconomic contribution of a specific area of the Creative Industries: an area where resources are invested towards improving skills and employment prospects of marginalized youth through creative training. Across evaluation studies, there is a common consensus that the contribution of projects for marginalized youth should be measured using an integrated approach that accounts for both formal and informal outcomes (Slater et al. 2007; Myconos 2012). The data analysed here confirm this strongly. In addition to 'hard' outcomes represented in the number of completed courses and jobs attained, young people's accounts attest to a spectrum of intangible values derived from the project, such as increased self-worth, communication and social skills, applicable in professional and social contexts. These skills are interconnected and conducive to young people's participation in the broader economy (Slater et al. 2007; see also Podkalicka et al. 2013).

What our follow-up data bring into sharper focus is a nonlinear model governing creativity-led youth transformation and its outcomes. Of 46 former students, ten are currently employed across a range of industries, with a further seven known to have been employed post-Youthworx. At the same time, 25 have been involved in further education, ranging from accredited TAFE, VCAL courses, apprenticeships and university degrees, all from various fields. The majority of those pursuing further education had graduated from Youthworx with an accredited diploma in Creative Industries, many with a couple of certificates.

In a general overview of higher-level vocation training, Foster et al. (2007, 10) argue that 'employment outcomes are partially related to graduates' aspirations and the nature of the qualifications held. However, the skill requirements and employment practices of employers determine the final employment outcomes.' This observation sheds light on the two dimensions explored in our analysis. On the one hand, we noted the unanimous interest in media work at the entry point into the program, but a greater emphasis on educational rather than employment plans. In short, Youthworx students' main aspirations are oriented towards educational pathways, and Youthworx is successful in supporting them. Given a high level of prior disengagement from education by the Youthworx demographic, this is an important, transformational and generative outcome.

On the other hand, the broader context of the labour market in a particular sector and at a particular time determines employment outcomes.[14] While the oversupply of graduates and resulting competition within the creative sector is definitely an important factor (Sefton-Green 2008), creative sector employers (especially in multimedia and design) have been found to often prefer university graduates over VET graduates, even those with high-level VET qualifications (Certificate IV or diplomas) (Foster et al. 2007). In addition, entries into post-Year 12 education, university degrees and the labour market are strongly dependent on socioeconomic status and parents' education, with students from low socioeconomic backgrounds strongly disadvantaged (Lamb and Mason 2008, 20). These structural conditions leave Youthworx graduates in a difficult position. And yet, of ten, four are currently in creative employment: one in full-time specialist creative employment and undertaking additional freelance work; one in part-time specialist creative employment while continuing study; one undertaking freelance specialist work; and one is employed part-time as a specialist or embedded creative (survey results were unclear about the place of employment). This is a very promising outcome. With the rise of the Internet, the growing segments of the Creative Industries are located in the embedded workforce and Creative Services occupations such as designers, content developers, communicators, advertising and marketing (Cunningham 2013, 135). While our data show creative employment outcomes in mostly 'traditional' Cultural Production areas, with casual work gained in photography, film editing and web design, there is perhaps potential to strengthen the areas of online production, design and communications as part of the Youthworx accredited courses. There are signs that online creative production and distribution are starting to be included in the training in a more sustained way.

There is also a broader point about disadvantaged youth and precarity. A number of Youthworx's former students indicate that traditional, non-creative jobs are often fraught with problems. Many of those in jobs post-Youthworx expressed the instability of their employment: some were laid off because of organizational restructure, unattractive working culture or because the pay was very low. Importantly, precarity is ever present in these young people's lives. Our follow-up interviews confirmed the picture painted earlier (Podkalicka et al. 2013; Podkalicka and Wilson forthcoming): young people struggle to stay afloat due to their marginalized social milieu, challenging families and frequently serious health issues that some of them reportedly sustained at work, either as early teens or as adults. Other factors negatively affecting their education and employment during and after Youthworx are: housing; social or family issues; substance abuse; illegal activities; and new parenthood. These factors have meant that they put job seeking or completing study on hold, move back and forth between far-flung suburbs of Melbourne (including a one-way commute to Youthworx that takes over one-and-a-half hours), frequently rely on informal support from siblings and friends, or relocate interstate. As noted earlier, many students were no longer contactable at the time of the follow-up interview (some second-hand information was available about these students from Youthworx staff), while a few appear to have totally fallen through the cracks.

As suggested elsewhere (see, for example, Podkalicka and Thomas 2010; Podkalicka et al. 2013), the most significant lesson from the Youthworx case study is the project's capacity to 'kick-start other things'. This needs to be acknowledged theoretically and in a practical sense. Indeed, as Fouad and Bynner (2008, 244) observe, 'One notable test of the effectiveness of a country's institutions for managing transitions is their effectiveness in continuing to help individuals make the right choices and keep their lives on track.' The data presented here provide strong evidence for successful re-engagement and pathway building into formalized education and training beyond Youthworx, even if some gaps and cracks remain. Revisiting the entry responses helps to establish the departure points and horizons of the journey made by this group, while an overview of the broader class structures and political economy of the labour markets provides an additional backdrop to contextualize these transitions.

All 17 graduates interviewed considered Youthworx a highly beneficial experience, and the majority saw it as directly useful to other employment opportunities. For some participants, the project has ignited passion for creative endeavours that reportedly does not subside despite the lack of immediate work prospects in Creative Industries. For many, the project led them to develop competencies that are wide-ranging and applicable across further education and employment. This finding adds to the Centre of Excellence for Creative Industries and Innovation's body of work on university graduate transitions arguing that training in the humanities and Creative Industries offers generic, transferable skills that facilitate transitions into the workplace (Cunningham and Bridgstock 2012). While general social skills may be developed through other forms of social programs and interventions, such as sports, craft or art, digital media creation provides a strong platform for the initial engagement and valued alternative learning. Youthworx augments this creative production experience by direct links to real-life professional networks and media segments, such as community radio or media-based social enterprise.

The contribution of Youthworx, and similar media-based initiatives, can be thus defined 'less [by] the service of reshuffling the deck of who succeeds in professional careers in media' (Ito and Lange 2010, 252), but rather, as Sefton-Green (2008, 17) observes, through 'achieving policy objectives around social exclusion, diversity, and social justice'. Combining qualitative and quantitative evidence about youth transitions, this research provides more clarity about an otherwise elusive category of 'social inclusion' deployed in the developmental field. It documents the translation of skills acquired through creative education into formalized further education and employment.

NOTES

1. Many thanks to the research participants – the Youthworx participants for their time and reflections – and the Youthworx staff, especially Jon Staley. Thanks also to Ellie Rennie, David Mackenzie and Julian Thomas for comments on the early drafts, and to Jenny Kennedy for research support.
2. This chapter reports on the research conducted by a team of researchers: Chief Investigators Professor Denise Meredyth, Professor Julian Thomas, Associate Professor David MacKenzie, also Associate Professor Ellie Rennie, and PhD candidates Chris Wilson and Jon Staley.
3. This finding is consistent with Sefton-Green's (2008, 17) analysis of the non-formal learning sector in the UK. In addition to the discussion of the relationship between creative education and youth transitions in this chapter, our previous work has noted Youthworx's operation within a niche media market based on media for social justice. Our work-in-progress is also examining the role of the youth media creative workforce.
4. Those who participate in the Youthworx program have experience of homelessness, alcohol or drug abuse, dysfunctional families or interrupted education.
5. See Goodwin and O'Connor (2013) for proposing an alternative framework of 'ordinary' and 'typical' in relation to youth transitions.
6. Certificates I–III are conducted in partnership with NMIT TAFE at the Youthworx site, while Certificate IV in Multimedia and IT is run in partnership with Swinburne University at Swinburne University.
7. One student enrolled but never attended.
8. It is important to note that the high number of those who originally stated their media and Creative Industries job-related motivations was not reflected in subsequent interviews conducted during the fieldwork or later during the follow-up interviews. Given that the entry interviews are designed to gauge the suitability of a student for the Youthworx courses, it seems natural for students to answer in this way.
9. For elaboration of the definition and measurement of creative activities see Cunningham (2013; Chapter 2 in this volume).
10. The composite nature of the question might have compromised the clarity in providing responses. Additionally, the entry interviews were co-designed by researchers and Youthworx staff, but administered by Youthworx staff and handed over to the researchers for analysis, which precludes a more contextual interpretation of the responses at the point of collecting data. However, we are able to draw on broader ethnographic work to make the presented reading.
11. Some jobs, as noted earlier, correspond with apprenticeships.
12. As noted earlier, we endeavoured to contact all the students for the follow-up interviews. However, 11 remained either uncontactable or unavailable for interview.
13. For a detailed qualitative study of a similar US-based youth media program and its contributions to work ethic and media skill development, see Soep and Chavez 2010.
14. For analysis of factors influencing transition outcomes for young people in post-recession Australia in general see Department of Education, Employment and Workplace Relations (2012) and Graduate Careers Australia (2011).

REFERENCES

Bridgstock, R. (2005), 'Australian artists, starving and well-nourished: what can we learn from the prototypical protean career?', *Australian Journal of Career Development*, **14** (3), 40–48.

Buckingham, D. (2007), *Beyond Technology: Children's Learning in an Age of Digital Culture*, Cambridge: Polity.

Crawford, Matthew B. (2010), *Shop Class as Soulcraft: An Inquiry into the Value of Work*, London: Penguin.

Cunningham, S. (2013), *Hidden Innovation: Policy, Industry and the Creative Sector*, St Lucia, Queensland: University of Queensland Press and Lexington Books, an imprint of Rowman & Littlefield.

Cunningham, S. and R. Bridgstock (2012), 'Say goodbye to the fries: graduate careers in media, cultural and communication studies', *Media International Australia Incorporating Culture and Policy*, **145**, 6–17.

Deuze, M. (2007), *Media Work*, Cambridge: Polity.

Department of Education, Employment and Workplace Relations (2012), *Interim Evaluation of the National Partnership on Youth Attainment and Transitions*, available at http://foi.deewr.gov.au/documents/interim-evaluation-national-partnership-youth-attainment-and-transitions (accessed 4 June 2013).

Foster, S., B. Delaney, A. Bateman and C. Dyson (2007), *Higher-Level Vocational Education and Training Qualifications: Their Importance in Today's Training Market*, Adelaide: NCVER.

Fouad, N.A. and J. Bynner (2008), 'Work transitions', *American Psychologist*, **63** (4), 241–51.

Furlong, A. (2009), 'Revisiting transitional metaphors: reproducing inequalities under the conditions of late modernity', *Journal of Education and Work*, **22** (5), 343–53.

Furlong, A. (2010), 'Transitions from education to work: new perspectives from Europe and beyond', *British Journal of Sociology of Education*, **31** (4), 515–18.

Furlong, A. and P. Kelly (2005), 'The Brazilianization of youth transitions in Australia and the UK?', *Australian Journal of Social Issues*, **40** (2), 207–25.

Furlong, A., F. Cartmel, A. Biggart, H. Sweeting and P. West (2003), 'Youth transitions: patterns of vulnerability and processes of social inclusion', *Social Research: Research Findings*, **8**, available at http://www.scie-socialcareonline.org.uk/repository/fulltext/socrfind8.pdf (accessed 27 July 2013).

Goodwin, J. and H. O'Connor (2013), 'Ordinary lives: "typical stories" of girls' transitions in the 1960s and the 1980s', *Sociological Research Online*, **18** (1), 4.

Graduate Careers Australia (2011), *Graduate Destinations 2011: A Report on the Work and Study Outcomes of Recent Higher Education Graduates*, available at http://www.graduatecareers.com.au/wp-content/uploads/2012/08/Graduate-Destinations-2011-secured.pdf, (accessed 7 May 2013).

Ito, M. and P.L. Lange (2010), 'Creative production', in M. Ito, S. Baumer, M. Bittanti, D. Boyd, R. Cody, B. Herr-Stephenson, H. A. Horst, P.G. Lange, D. Mahendran, K.Z. Martínez, C.J. Pascoe, D. Perkel, L. Robinson, C. Sims, L. Tripp, with contributions by J. Antin, M. Finn, A. Law, A.Manion, S. Mitnick, D. Schlossberg and S. Yardi (eds), *Hanging Out, Messing Around, and Geeking Out: Kids Living and Learning with New Media*, Cambridge, MA: MIT Press, pp. 252–93.

Jenkins, H. (2009), *Confronting the Challenges of Participatory Culture – Media Education for the 21ˢᵗ Century*, Chicago, IL: MacArthur Foundation. Available at http://digitallearning.macfound.org/atf/cf/%7B7E45C7E0-A3E0-4B89-AC9C-E807E1B0AE4E%7D/JENKINS_WHITE_PAPER.PDF (accessed 1 July 2013).

Lamb, S. and K. Mason (2008), *How Young People Are Faring: An Update about the Learning and Work Situation of Young Australians*, Melbourne: The Foundation for Young Australians, available at http://www.fya.org.au/wp-content/uploads/2012/10/FULL_DIGITAL_HYPAF2012.pdf (accessed 4 June 2013).

Myconos, G. (2012), *Re-Engagement, Training and Beyond*, Fitzroy, Melbourne: Brotherhood St Laurence, LINK.

Perlin, R. (2011), *Intern Nation: How to Earn Nothing and Learn Little in the Brave New Economy*, London: Verso.

Podkalicka, A. and J. Thomas (2010), 'The skilled social voice: an experiment in creative economy and communication rights', *International Communication Gazette*, **72** (4–5), 395–406.

Podkalicka, A. and C. Wilson (forthcoming), 'Engaging youth in a professional media production community of practice: opportunities and tensions in intervening in the social through the creative industries', *International Journal of Learning and Media*.

Podkalicka, A., D. Meredyth, D. MacKenzie, E. Rennie, J. Staley, J. Thomas and C. Wilson (2013), *Youthworx Media: Youth Media and Social Enterprise as Intervention and Innovation* (report).

Ross, A. (2009), *Nice Work If You Can Get It: Life and Labor in Precarious Times*, New York: New York University Press.

Sefton-Green, J. (2008), *What Future for the Non-Formal Learning Sector?: An Analytic Review Commissioned by the London Development Agency*, available at http://www.julianseftongreen.net/wp-content/uploads/2008/07/seftongreen_NFLS_essay.pdf (accessed 25 July 2013).

Sefton-Green, J. and H. Nixon (2009), 'Reviewing approaches and perspectives on "digital literacy"', *Pedagogies: An International Journal*, **4** (2), 107–25.

Sennett, R. (2009), *The Craftsman*, London: Penguin.

Sinclair, S., J. McKendrick and G. Scott (2010), 'Failing young people? Education and aspirations in a deprived community', *Citizenship and Social Justice*, **5** (1), 5–20.

Slater, J., B. Gidley, T. Dowmunt, S. Rowe, I.C. MacWeeney, R. Smith, A. Rooke and P. Cardullo (2007), *Inclusion Through Media: Beyond the Numbers Game*, London: Centre for Urban and Community Research, Goldsmiths, University of London, available at http://inclusionthroughmedia.org/ITM%20Evaluation/BTNG_Report.pdf (accessed 4 June 2013).

Soep, E. and V. Chavez (2010), *Drop that Knowledge: Youth Radio Stories*, Berkeley: University of California Press.

Throsby, D. and A. Zednik (2010), *Do You Really Expect To Get Paid? An Economic Study of Professional Artists in Australia*, Australia Council for the Arts, available at http://www.australiacouncil.gov.au/__data/assets/pdf_file/0007/79108/Do_you_really_expect_to_get_paid.pdf (accessed 25 July 2013).

13. Developing agency in the creative career: a design-based framework for work integrated learning

Oksana Zelenko and Ruth Bridgstock

INTRODUCTION

Research (Freeman 2007; Higgs, Cunningham and Bakhshi 2008; Andrews, Yeabsley and Higgs 2009; Higgs and Freebody 2010) shows that approximately half of all creative practitioners operate as 'embedded creatives' – that is, they secure creative employment in organizations located in fields beyond the Creative Industries. However, it is also known that creative workers move between embedded and specialist roles over the course of their career (see, for example, Vinodrai 2006; Bridgstock and Hearn 2013). These career circumstances foreground the significance of having the necessary skills to successfully cross disciplinary boundaries in order to negotiate a professional role. An implication of this for emerging creative practitioners is the need to be able to identify and successfully target shifting professional and industry standards while remaining responsive to change. A further implication involves creative practitioners engaging in a continuous cycle of renegotiation of their professional identities. This makes the management of multiple professional selves, along with creating and recreating a meaningful frame of reference (such as the language around their emerging practice), a necessary skill.

This chapter presents a framework for work integrated learning (WIL) experiences, in which undergraduate Creative Industries (CI) students develop the skills necessary to manage their emerging professional identities with agility. Agility is required in the face of rapidly changing work contexts. Central to the framework is the use of ideas and processes from the field of design practice (for example, architecture, industrial design, interaction design). Students are encouraged to think of their internship role and their professional identity as things they must design. They are also encouraged to see their career as moving through design cycles. The use of such design-related ideas and processes promotes the value of agency and autonomy as skills necessary for creative practitioners. The chapter draws upon the authors' reflections on the WIL program in the Creative Industries Faculty at the Queensland University of Technology, which was the first program created specifically for a faculty-wide Creative Industries context. This program offered students a range of industry placement and advanced specialized projects in the field for academic credit (Collis 2010). The CI WIL program is a final-year capstone program that, in 2012, had six subjects, over 700 enrolments across 13 disciplines (from journalism to fashion to performance studies), and nearly 30 academic and professional staff supporting it. The program operates as an interface connecting Creative Industries students with industry partners and academics.

UNCERTAINTY, AGENCY AND NEW CAREER IDENTITIES

Creative Industries graduates emerge from university into an increasingly dynamic, unknowable and ontologically unfamiliar world (Barnett 2004). This leads to a form of personal uncertainty that recognizes that we can never hope to satisfactorily describe the world, 'let alone act with assuredness in it' (ibid., 250). The lack of a clear understanding of conceptual boundaries around the new type of professional suggests being 'employable in more than one place' (Geurts in Meijers 1998), which is often seen as negative due to the perceived dilution of disciplinary boundaries. Meijers (1998) has framed this as 'despecialisation of the work' and discusses the resulting need to either create or renegotiate roles in response to 'work-related insecurity' and the rapidly changing conditions of the work environment. Post-industrial fragmentation perpetuates despecialization of professional roles, but also breaks down traditional – or fixed – boundaries around the notion of a 'career'. Professional futures are uncertain, and individuals must navigate this uncertainty as a necessary skill. In the working world of the twenty-first century, the meta-level critical capacity to transform ambiguity and uncertainty into opportunity and possibility becomes significant.

The diversity of the Creative Industries student cohort and economic changes affecting the number and types of available internship opportunities have highlighted the significance of students negotiating the parameters of the role. Further, the majority of organizations taking CI interns are small to medium enterprises with a high turnover of creative staff. This chapter presents the argument that a lack of clarity in the context of CI practice creates the potential for practitioners to actively generate new roles and shape new professional pathways within the industry: shifting from a deficit- or risk-oriented framing towards a strength- or agency-based approach. Central to this argument is Arthur and Rousseau's (1996) concept of a 'boundaryless career'. The experience of uncertainty this concept addresses shifts from a risk society (Beck 1986) to a change in perception: uncertainty is the necessary trigger for generating 'new [professional] opportunities' (Bolles 1996). This lens frames the lack of clarity around a creative professional role not as an indicator of failure, but as a catalyst for assuming a greater degree of control over determining its boundaries. Assuming agency over the professional pathway requires ongoing cultivation of the skills necessary to intentionally generate – or design – variations on career identity. This capacity is furthered by the additional agility to shift freely between multiple roles in response to changes in the industry contexts (Bridgstock and Hearn 2012).

WORK INTEGRATED LEARNING AND EMBEDDED CREATIVE INTERNS

Work integrated learning refers to learning in the workplace and can take many forms, including internships, practicums, fieldwork and moot court, to name a few. WIL programs can now be found in many university courses. The justification for WIL is that students learn in a deeper, more meaningful way and are better prepared professionally when theory is integrated with practice (Boud and Solomon 2003). Thus WIL can potentially be of great value to students, providing opportunities to experience and make sense of professional practice with all its attendant 'unpredictable, immediate, unique, transient' and transdisciplinary knowledge requirements, and its 'competing interests' (Orrell 2007; Franz 2007).

However, Creative Industries WIL programs, like the bulk of university curricula, place great emphasis on archetypal specialist roles, with disproportionately little emphasis on embedded roles involving creative practitioners working outside the Creative Industries, despite growing evidence of the importance of embedded roles in creative careers (see, for instance, Bridgstock and Cunningham, Chapter 14 in this volume). Examples of embedded creative practitioners include: an interaction designer working in health developing interfaces for e-health applications, or a creative writer working in education developing interactive digital literacy resources. Thus Creative Industries students enrolled in embedded WIL placements will often be working with people far outside their disciplinary specialisms, providing creative–cultural expertise in 'non-creative' contexts.

For Creative Industries students, defining career pathways using embedded WIL experiences is partly an opportunity to actively shape new roles within organizational structures. This process necessarily involves a complex set of negotiations, with students assuming increasing agency. The new set of skills involves the capacity to successfully balance and navigate the existing and prospective professional opportunities. It involves a deeper engagement with the established (or tangible) boundaries of vocation (Cope and Kalantzis 2011), as well as prospective (or intangible/yet to be defined) boundaries. The process of crossing disciplines and fields necessarily involves reconsidering the existing boundaries, while the process of creating new boundaries is inherently a creative, meaning-making process. It is at the intersection of the personal, the academic and the professional that an opportunity to harness the emergence of new professional configurations, and the formation of a new role, arises.

TOWARDS A NEW FRAMEWORK FOR WORK INTEGRATED LEARNING

We argue that traditional 'top–down' approaches to WIL, comprising predefined and predetermined roles and activities, do not address the growing challenge of navigating the world of work and constructing a career identity in times of rapid economic change and uncertainty. They do not yet fully appreciate the need for students to have control over their professional pathway, potentially leading to a lack of reciprocity between industry and academia. There is a need for a WIL framework that structurally enables greater reciprocity and dialogue between stakeholders, and facilitates students to develop the skills necessary to create and maintain it.

Despite existing programs providing support to students in finding industry and community placements, those instances where students take part in co-determining the parameters of the placement have the potential for better outcomes, particularly in regard to becoming prepared for managing their careers into the future. A new framework proposed in this chapter places agency at centre stage in creating and renegotiating a professional role at the core of the WIL experience, building on the notion of 'internal locus of control'. Originally introduced by Julian Rotter in 1954 in the context of psychology, this concept relates to an individual's perception of control over their life, in regard to their inner self or their external environment. The framework has a wide application across a number of fields, including academia and tertiary education (Watkins 1987, 222). This approach to WIL pedagogy further aligns with the broader societal 'shift in the balance of agency' (Cope and Kalantzis 2011), which frames professionals more strongly as 'self-steering units' (Meijers 1998, 191).

We are beginning to see a shift in WIL programs to more inclusive, dynamic and reciprocal models. Franz (2008), for instance, developed an action-based pedagogical framework for WIL in the discipline of built environment and engineering. A higher level of responsiveness and an inclusive cooperative dynamic among key stakeholders is also argued by Smith and Smith (2010), who further highlight the contribution of the industry-partner perspective to WIL.

AN ITERATIVE, DESIGN-BASED FRAMEWORK FOR WORK INTEGRATED LEARNING

Design can be defined as a meaning-making process (Krippendorff 2006). It is a capacity for criticality and creative synthesis that shifts from top–down traditional control towards what Cope and Kalantzis call the experience of 'agentive autonomy' (Cope and Kalantzis 2011, 58). Through a design-based framework, agency and intentionality in shaping a professional career pathway are brought to the fore. A design-based approach also foregrounds meta-level capacities and facilitates agile/creative learning (as opposed to reproductive learning) required to navigate and negotiate an embedded role. Agile/creative learning is defined by van Peursen (1992) as the process whereby, through interaction, the learner connects new knowledge with existing knowledge and, through that, intentionally develops new learning processes that are self-directed and self-reflexive. This results in the acquisition of meta-level capabilities.

The framing of design as a meta-level practice, and transferability of design thinking and processes to WIL, involves conceptualizing the professional role as a designed object or artefact. Perceptions of the professional self as an iteratively created malleable structure involve the act of articulating and re-articulating that role. However, the process of classification and labelling, by definition, has the capacity to simultaneously define, 'lock in' (and, therefore, give access to an idea by giving it conceptual boundaries, in this case linguistic) and restrict access to future iterations of the professional self. For an internship role to be framed as a designed object, it needs to be reconceptualized not as singular and fixed, but as an iteratively emergent and perpetually renegotiable set of parameters.

Reframed as an artefact, the WIL role is simultaneously a designed object with conceptual boundaries and a process of iterative design through interaction with others. The parameters of the professional role are dialogic and integrate multiple voices: those of the learner's career aspirations, the academic standards and the affordances to accommodate these within the organizational structure of the industry partner. Weaving the voices of multiple stakeholders is an interactive participatory process of managing the complex and continuously changing heteroglossic dynamic formed by the multiple contributors to the shape of the internship role. By framing the internship role as a multiplicity, we argue against overinvestment by creative practitioners in a single career pathway, and instead for generating many simultaneously rising prospective roles.

In assuming responsibility for designing their professional pathways, Creative Industries interns necessarily become co-designers of their WIL experience, acting as agents of change in shaping the internship role. When applied to WIL, the iterative phase, core to the design process, translates into the process of purposefully renegotiating a professional role – a role that is perpetually involved in synthesizing personal, academic and industry parameters and expectations (which are, in turn, subject to change). Within this framework, it is not the persistence of role boundaries that could potentially hinder its future reconceptualizations, but rather the lack of creative agility and imaginative foresight into new relational possibilities and the interfaces that would enable new roles to emerge. Krippendorf's definition of 'interface' as a dynamic object could be applied to the professional role in order to reconceptualize it as processual. It can be seen as a cycle of assimilation and adaptation and a new kind of artefact, a product with a configurable and reconfigurable interface (Krippendorff 2006). Scaffolding this approach across WIL pedagogy will help to achieve better results for emerging creative practitioners by cultivating their capacity to construct, renegotiate and sustain a dynamic multiplicity of actual and conceptualized professional identities.

The advantages of using a dynamic framework based in philosophical and pedagogical principles of design practice include access to a set of new understandings that can further be explored in the context of WIL. For example, 'empathy' and 'equity' (principles of participatory design) can be used as foundations for building sustainable industry partnerships through WIL programs. In negotiating a role, reciprocity and collaboration create space for mutual impact through closer relationships and fostering deeper understanding. The transferability of a design-based framework implies a 'value-based approach to WIL' that opens up the possibility of sustained mutual benefit and reciprocity critical to the formation of sustainable long-term partnerships (Zelenko and Creyton 2012).

AGENCY-BASED CRITERIA FOR WORK INTEGRATED LEARNING

What might evidence of the developmental processes and outcomes we propose in this chapter look like? To address this question, we developed a new set of agency-based criteria founded on the principles of design practice presented in this chapter, and trialled them using a set of reflective blogs completed by CI WIL students. The new criteria utilize some aspects of an existing set of criteria by Krumboltz (1993). The criteria were initially selected and reworked significantly to better capture and respond to meta-level agency-driven attributes evident and practiced by emerging creative practitioners.

To pilot-test these criteria, we analysed a set of reflective internship blogs written by Creative Industries students in order to track the degree of agency, and locate their 'locus of control' in their experience of constructing an internship role. The blogs were written as part of formal assessment by final-year students from three disciplines: creative writing, media and communication (mediacomm), and interactive and visual design. Four blogs from each discipline were selected – two embedded interns and two specialist interns. The disciplines were selected on the basis of their potential to illustrate the application and value of a design-based agency-led approach to WIL.

The six criteria used are listed and described below:

1. *Setting parameters for the role and assessing the malleability of organizational structure to accommodate these* Evidence of understanding the role, reflection on the scope of the role and the structure to evaluate potential for change and growth (starting point/ trigger).
2. *Setting the parameters for aspirational professional identity/end goals* Including explicit references to professional aspirations; identifying and setting priorities (as markers for change); enacting change by problem-solving.
3. *Explicit assessment or awareness of degree of agency over pathway(s) through the role* Setting the intent to plan/co-plan and manage/co-manage the role; type and quality of mentor feedback.
4. *Willingness and attempts (rather than existing capacity) to adapt to change* Attempts at creating new role/new tasks/new direction beyond original role description; intentional attempts at reframing own goals to accommodate the predetermined role proposed by the organization (category exists in title, but is substantially modified to differentiate between an innate capacity and the intent to identify a need for and develop a new skill or ability).
5. *Intentional managing of relationship dynamic to serve the end goal/ aspirational coordinates of career identity* Planning or ceasing opportunities to carry out higher level of operational control where called upon and/or where appropriate.

6. *Iterative evaluation, planning and seeking opportunities to evaluate change against set goals/markers* Independently reflecting on and identifying factors contributing to change; receive and use both positive and negative feedback (existing category, Krumboltz 1993); provide constructive feedback.

INSIGHTS, REFLECTION AND DISCUSSION

Analysis in response to the first criterion showed that a value-based alignment creates greater trust, freedom and agency to drive creative decision-making within the role. Control over the role at a meta-level of alignment of personal values with an organization's values – as opposed to experience of control at the level of managing tasks day to day – results in a more meaningful professional outcome. Interestingly, embedded internship roles did not necessarily result in a greater degree of control over the role or in greater value for the intern, although specialist roles did so in instances where greater experience of creative freedom and decision-making within the role was afforded.

Analysis using the second criterion addressed the varying degrees of agency in shaping the role, and raised questions about the differing levels of technical specialization needed to fulfil role objectives. Responses show that these variations in technical skill determined the malleability of roles. Technical specialization leads to more rigidly defined roles that are prescriptive. In these instances, professional success is determined by sustaining consistency and continuity of the pre-established role boundaries. Change or variation on standard processes is perceived as risky or erroneous. Strategies for managing expectations and readiness for unanticipated change within the role have been linked to having a sense of an aspirational/career identity in place: 'my expectations of my role as a media researcher differ to my expectations of the workplace' (mediacomm specialist).

The blogs also show that the process of engaging critically with a pre-determined/predefined internship role could lead to the establishment of a career identity (participant response). In this context, embedded roles may not necessarily offer interns more control over shaping the professional role. Across both the specialist and embedded contexts, a strongly matched professional/internship role with a career identity/broad direction enables more flexibility at the granular level of tasks and responsibilities (participant response). Ability to articulate and align an internship role with their aspirational career identity prompts them to consider and reflect on professional possibilities and the potential value of their practice. For embedded creatives, articulating practice across disciplines creates tangible boundaries to the intangible possibility of enacting that role in the future. The process of articulating the aspiration becomes the mechanism through which the value of the role and the direction are formulated. In the context of embedded creative practice, a professional role may be the final destination (participant response). Here, the boundaries of a career identity often consist of meta-level, as opposed to concrete role-specific, attributes and aspirations. These attributes and aspirations are agency-enablers as they provide orientational clarity. Reflective blogs show that the opportunity and the act of articulating a career identity in a workplace context is an experience of agency and control in itself (participant response).

For embedded creatives, agility in venturing beyond established role boundaries may facilitate the emergence of a new career identity (participant response), and a clear sense or articulation of a career identity may in itself provide an impetus for its emergence. Too broad a career identity has the risk of resulting in a lack of direction, as boundaries can be too abstract, universal/open-ended or all-encompassing. An indeterminable professional pathway must fall back on existing organizational pathways and dynamics in order to gain definition. For specialist practitioners, a predetermined role is more meaningful precisely because it is experienced as more manageable, with clearer boundaries, and anchored by a career identity.

Analysis of one's awareness of the degree of flexibility and variation within the role – the third criterion – has overall been found to facilitate a greater experience of control over the concrete aspects of the role (for example, daily tasks), as well as assessing the potential for changing its direction. Joint negotiation of the scope within the role directly enables agency and facilitates the possibility of growth and transformation within the role. Successfully leveraging value from an apparent lack of role definition is the ultimate experience of agency and control, and bridges towards an aspirational identity, as one intern reports:

> during my internship I learnt to place myself as not only a 'graphic designer' but as a valuable creative practitioner in the industry, with a wide and varied array of skills and an enthusiasm to 'dip my toe in every pool' so to speak and undertake any task that would fit my client's needs. By doing so you increase your self worth, can adapt to technological and creative advances and make yourself indispensable to any company. (interactive and visual design specialist)

It was found that the experience and skill of agility and adaptation to changing work conditions remains regardless of the context, which could include either professional or personal circumstances. In embedded roles, creatives were able to identify the lack of explicit instruction and structured guidance as an opportunity to extend parts of the role or propose a new direction – a willingness to reach beyond the established roles leading, in some instances, to taking on a key role in a creative project.

The observations from the fourth criterion are that willingness to adapt and change is critical for building professional resilience. This willingness arises when interns are pushed to operate on, or beyond, the boundary of previously acquired knowledge, skills and experience. This was seen as a trade-off between rigid constraints (for example, deadlines) and compromising one's own creative vision and values for the benefit of a project. Individual compromise resulting from a value-based alignment with the project team – as opposed to fulfilment of individual tasks at hand – opened new professional experiences and required interns to build links between previously unconnected skill sets. Despite the initial apparent 'misalignment' of personal aims with industry-based roles, the outcome is evaluated as an opportunity for growth: 'Though my initial aims were changed, I feel like in the end I have learnt a number of valuable insights about the industry and myself' (mediacomm specialist). Another student reported a similar outcome: 'My role within the company has multiple focuses and requires me to adapt to tasks which I have not attempted as part of my undergraduate degree' (creative writing specialist). Initial feelings of discomfort from facing the unknown are accompanied by negative expectations and 'disappointment', but ultimately judged to result in professional value and 'a number of new skills which weren't in [the] initial plan but are still beneficial for [the] future' (interactive and visual design embedded). Where embedded practice was initially deemed 'irrelevant', upon completion of the internship it was re-evaluated as 'very beneficial', as it provided important insights into the broader industry context (mediacomm embedded).

Unanticipated professional growth resulting from applying knowledge in new and unfamiliar or uncertain contexts or circumstances where no clear pathway is outlined does not form part of the intended plan or objective. It is perceived as a 'challenging', negative or undesirable experience while it is occurring, but as an 'integral' and 'valuable' part of the role when evaluated in retrospect. For students interning in specialist roles, this process required a significant change to their individual 'way of thinking' and an explicit re-evaluation of difference as value-add. One student reflected on their engagement with workplace practice at a meta-level in order to articulate the value arising from their experience of difference: 'changing my way of thinking to stop pointing out the differences in our opinion and start recognizing the value was rather difficult' (creative writing specialist). For interns in core creative roles, the apparent lack of continuity and alignment between academic and industry contexts frames any 'misalignment' or disruption as erroneous or evidence of deficiency in one's capacities – rather than an opportunity to shape new professional pathways. Assuming agency in shaping the role is perceived as the last resort due to the disruptive experience of change.

For embedded interns, an internship is an opportunity for iteratively redirecting their practice and for meta-level conceptions of their learning: 'This internship is not only a chance to learn, but to reshape knowledge I already possess, and apply it from a new perspective or for a different purpose' (interactive and visual design embedded). Additionally, interns in embedded roles allowed the role to change by consciously surrendering the locus of control over its boundaries in order to be open to influence from external factors (for example, clients, other practitioners). The shift from core creative practice into an interdisciplinary embedded context is seen as 'a positive marker of . . . developing interdisciplinarity as a practitioner, which is both valuable and an unexpected bonus'. In conclusion, a lack of continuity between academia and industry is framed in a 'positive' light as a significant learning opportunity. Generally, embedded contexts are seen as providing a more valuable professional experience due to a broader application of core skills (creative writing embedded).

Observations from applying the fifth criterion on managing relationship dynamics showed that the degree of reciprocity from knowledge transfer between interns and the industry was one where the industry affected students rather than students bringing new knowledge to industry. Instances of leadership and initiative were not sought, anticipated or explicitly planned by interns, but where the initiative was taken, results had an impact on the organization. Agency and creative control were seen by interns as a last resort, and the authority to generate ideas was assumed only if no explicit instruction was available, resulting in a falling back on pre-existing solutions. Perceptions of creative freedom are experienced as simultaneously desirable yet restrictive: 'In a perfect world, designers have 100 per cent of creative control over any given project' (interactive and visual design specialist).

The final criterion produced highly granular and detailed accounts that exemplify problem-solving unfolding on a day-to-day operational level. Overall, there was an indication that an explicit evaluation of role leads to a greater awareness of one's capacities, skills, knowledge and, ultimately, the value of one's professional contribution. The ongoing feedback received by both core and embedded creatives from internship supervisors formed the foundation of their professional confidence and resilience, and ultimately led to the experience of thriving in the workplace. A recurring theme throughout responses among all creatives was the value-based alignment of individual aims and organizational ethos. Students experienced a greater sense of value from immersion (and subsequent dilution of role boundaries) within collaborative 'decentralized' dynamics. The resulting sense of belonging to a group was interpreted to lead to 'greater opportunit[ies] for professional success as a valued contributor than at university, where [their] work is for individual gain' (creative writing specialist).

Importantly, the practice of explicit and ongoing self-assessment (a part of traditional WIL program design) and an articulation of professional development outcomes (new knowledge and skills) proved a critical factor for both core and embedded creatives' self-perception and awareness of their value as creative practitioners. Without explicit evaluation/reflection on learning curves, this value remains tacit. The process of identifying and explicitly relating one's own professional value to a real-world workplace raises internal awareness and external perception of this value.

CONCLUSIONS AND IMPLICATIONS FOR WIL PEDAGOGY

The experience of agility and adaptation – the iterative reframing/ redesigning of the role – within an internship is not necessarily maximized within embedded contexts (as opposed to specialist contexts). Instead, it is strongly linked to the ability to activate and sustain the reciprocity between the meta-level value-based aspirations and the concrete (or predetermined by industry) role boundaries. Disciplinary differences have emerged from the analysis, suggesting that the value of an agency-driven model for embedded WIL may not be uniformly transferable. Although the responses included in this chapter are limited (that is, the number and types of disciplines and practices represented, the sample size; three disciplines [media and communication, creative writing, interactive and visual design] were included with four blogs [two specialist and two embedded] from each discipline), the analysis has produced insights into the experiences and competencies required for creative practitioners to thrive in the workplace. These can be distilled into a number of principles that support agency in an embedded WIL context, including:

- value-based (as opposed to skill-based) alignment to facilitate reciprocity and potential for mutual impact;
- self-reflexivity and an ongoing synthesis of predetermined and aspirational or prospective aspects of the role to enable articulation of one's value as a creative practitioner; and

- future-orientedness or meta-level approach to managing a career pathway.

The framework has further implications for the development of curriculum and learning materials. Of particular significance is the emerging difference – and dynamic relationship – between more complex meta-level learning resources (that are necessary because they provide that common denominator to a diverse and fragmented set of practices and disciplines) and the relationship of these to the roles situated within the specific discipline-embedded creative processes (where students independently ground and apply these meta-level principles in ways appropriate to their respective fields). The primary benefit of structuring content this way is that meta-level concepts – by virtue of not being tied to the parameters of a given practice – have the potential to be of value and reused across a number of contexts and fields.

The aim of this chapter has been to use the insights from the process-based design field as a lens through which to view WIL programs catering to a diverse and dispersed set of disciplines in order to inform future developments that prepare creatives for the world of work. New developments in WIL pedagogy supporting embedded creative practitioners need to take into account the principles that frame work integrated learning. The attributes of agency, critical and leadership capacities, and self-reflexivity (as shown in this chapter) are contributors to generating new professional experiences and opportunities for emerging creative practitioners. These principles could be further extended to guide the design of corresponding frameworks for evaluating embedded WIL pedagogies in the Creative Industries, of which the set of criteria developed specifically for use in this case study is only one example.

ACKNOWLEDGEMENTS

We would like to thank the editorial board and the reviewers for the insightful critique of this chapter and the Australian Research Council Centre of Excellence for Creative Industries and Innovations for support in publishing this volume and the opportunity to contribute. Thanks also to the meticulous attention to detail by the research assistant throughout the data collection and analysis stages.

REFERENCES

Andrews, G., J. Yeabsley and P. Higgs (2009), *The Creative Sector in New Zealand: Mapping and Economic Role: Report to New Zealand Trade and Enterprise*, Thorndon: New Zealand Institute of Economic Research.

Arthur, M.B. and D.M. Rousseau (1996), *The Boundaryless Career: A New Employment Principle for a New Organizational Era*, Oxford: Oxford University Press.

Barnett, R. (2004), 'Learning for an unknown future', *Higher Education Research & Development*, **23** (3), 247–60.

Beck, U. (1986), *Risikogesellschaft. Auf dem Weg in eine andere Moderne*, Frankfurt a.M: Suhrkamp.

Bolles, R. (1996), *Welke kleur heeft jouw parachute?* Amsterdam: Nieuwezijds.

Boud, D. and N. Solomon (2003), '"I don't think I am a learner": acts of naming learners at work', *Journal of Workplace Learning*, **15** (7/8), 326–31.

Bridgstock, R. and G. Hearn (2012), 'A conceptual model of capability learning for the 21st century knowledge economy', in D. Rooney, G. Hearn and T. Kastelle (eds), *Handbook on the Knowledge Economy* (Vol. 2), Cheltenham, UK and Northampton, MA, USA: Edward Elgar, pp. 105–22.

Collis, C. (2010), 'Developing work-integrated learning curricula for the creative industries: embedding stakeholder perspectives', *LATHE: Learning and Teaching in Higher Education*, (4–1), 3–19.

Cope, B. and M. Kalantzis (2011), '"Design" in principle and practice: a reconsideration of the terms of design engagement', *The Design Journal*, **14** (1), 45–63.

Franz, J.M. (2007), 'Work integrated learning for design: a scholarship of integration', in R. Zehner (ed.), *ConnectED Conference on Design Education 2007* (Conference Proceedings), n.p.

Franz, J.M. (2008), 'A pedagogical model of higher education/industry engagement for enhancing employability and professional practice', in *Work Integrated Learning (WIL): Transforming Futures, Practice . . . Pedagogy . . . Partnerships* (Conference Proceedings), pp. 164–9.

Freeman, A. (2007), *London's Creative Sector: 2007 Update*, London: Greater London Authority.

Higgs, P. and S.P. Freebody (2010), *Auckland's Creative Workforce Report 2010*, Auckland.

Higgs, P., S. Cunningham and H. Bakhshi (2008), *Beyond the Creative Industries: Mapping the Creative Economy in the United Kingdom*, London: NESTA, available at http://www.nesta.org.uk/library/documents/beyond-creative-industries-report.pdf (accessed 29 July 2013).

Krippendorff, K. (2006), *The Semantic Turn: A New Foundation for Design*, Boca Raton, FL: CRC Press.

Krumboltz, J.D. (1993), 'Integrating career and personal counselling', *Career Development Quarterly*, **42** (3), 143–8.

Meijers, F. (1998), 'The development of a career identity', *International Journal for the Advancement of Counselling*, **20** (3), 191–207.

Orrell, J. (2007), 'Keynote address', ACEN-Q WIL Symposium, Brisbane, February.

Rotter, J.B. (1954), *Social Learning and Clinical Psychology*, Englewood Cliffs, NJ: Prentice-Hall.

Smith, J.E. and R. Smith (2010), 'Work integrated learning: an industry partners' perspective', in *Proceedings of Australian Vocational Education and Training Research Association (AVETRA)*, n.p.

van Peursen, C.A. (1992), *Verhaal en werkelijkheid – een deiktische ontology*, Kampen: Kok Agora.

Vinodrai, T. (2006), 'Reproducing Toronto's design ecology: career paths, intermediaries, and local labor markets', *Economic Geography*, **82** (3), 237–63.

Watkins, D. (1987), 'Academic locus of control: a relevant variable at tertiary level?', *Higher Education*, **16** (2), 221–9.

Zelenko, O. and M. Creyton (2012), 'Using value-based partnerships to support community engaged learning: benefits, challenges, stakeholder perspectives', presented at AUCEA: Engagement Australia Conference on Community Engaged Learning, Brisbane, July.

14. Graduate careers in journalism, media and communications within and outside the sector: early career outcomes, trajectories and capabilities

Ruth Bridgstock and Stuart Cunningham

INTRODUCTION

This chapter reports findings from a study of ten years of graduates from Queensland University of Technology's (Brisbane, Australia) courses in journalism, media and communication studies, using a 'Creative Trident' lens to analyse micro-individual survey data. The study findings engage with creative labour precarity discussions, and also assertions of creative graduate oversupply suggested by national graduate outcome statistics. We describe the graduates' employment outcomes, characterize their early career movements into and out of embedded and specialist employment, and compare the capability requirements and degree of course relevance reported by graduates employed in the different Trident segments, with a view to making recommendations about the role of higher education in preparing students for diverse and multiple careers inside and outside the Creative Industries.[1]

CREATIVE LABOUR: PRECARIOUS OR NOT?

The dominant corpus of contemporary literature relating to creative labour rests on descriptions of the creative career as precarious. The precarity account of creative careers indicates that workers tend to be under-employed overall, that they hold piecemeal creative and non-creative jobs in a 'portfolio career' pattern, that they undertake short-term project-based work, which is often conducted on a self-employment basis, and that their overall career prospects are highly uncertain at best (see, for instance, Banks and Hesmondhalgh 2009).

According to cultural labour economists, part of what underlies the precarity phenomenon is an oversupply of creative workers (Menger 2006). These creative workers tend to have strong intrinsic motivations for their career, perhaps alongside high hopes of a lucky break leading to outstanding success (Taylor and Littleton 2008), which lead them to 'self-exploit'. Rather than exiting the field in search of better employment prospects in other industries, they persevere and work for free or at reduced rates (Hesmondhalgh and Baker 2010).

Both precarity and self-exploitation would appear to be even worse among graduates of creative degrees as they attempt to enter the creative workforce than among creative workers in general. Researchers have reported that creative graduates often experience extended education to work transition periods involving multiple entry attempts, unpaid internships and reliance on non-career jobs, family or social security for financial support (Galloway et al. 2002). McRobbie (2002) and Baumann (2002) both highlight that informal and social processes involved in finding or creating creative work are key barriers to breaking into a creative career. Because finding or creating work is often contingent on 'who you know' in various ways, and much is dependent on experience and the quality of previous work outputs, it can take a significant length of time to become established in a creative career.

In striking contrast to the commentary around precarity in creative careers is a parallel body of literature that provides evidence that creative work, and creative workers, are vital to economic development in post-industrial economies, via the contribution of essential creative and cultural expertise (human capital) to national innovation systems through a process of 'culturalization' of industry and the economy more broadly (Hearn and Bridgstock 2010; Lash and Urry 1994; Müller, Rammer and Trüby 2009). Empirical support for these arguments can be found in the continued growth of the size of the Creative Industries as a group of industry sectors, and in the size and financial contribution of the creative workforce.

Over the first decade of the 2000s, the ARC Centre of Excellence for Creative Industries and Innovation (CCI) was engaged in measuring the creative workforce in various countries using census data (see Cunningham, Chapter 2 in this volume for more details). This 'Creative Trident' research has shown that the creative workforce is growing at a significantly faster rate than the general economy, and that overall the creative workforce earns salaries above the national average. The mapping work has also found that more of this workforce is 'embedded' in the general economy than is found as 'specialists' inside the Creative Industries sectors.

CAREERS IN JOURNALISM, MEDIA AND COMMUNICATIONS

So what can be said of journalism, media and communication (JMC) occupations, included in all major definitions of the Creative Industries (Department for Culture Media and Sport 1998), and mapped as part of CCI's creative workforce research? To what extent do these occupations follow the 'precarious labour' pattern? To what extent are they contributors to the cluster of creative activity driving economic growth? To what extent are JMC occupations embedded throughout the economy, and where within these occupations and industries is there evidence of growth or decline?

There is certainly a high level of volatility in these industries and workplaces because of influences such as digitization and convergence, regulatory reform, globalization and changing industry/market structures, and this has certainly had an impact on individual careers and patterns of work (Elefante and Deuze 2012), but overall demand for media products and services continues to rise (Compton and Benedetti 2010). Creative Trident mapping work using Australian census data from 2006 and 2011 shows that, in 2011, JMC professionals accounted for 11.9 per cent of the 310 056 people employed in creative (embedded and specialist) occupations in Australia. A total of 22 per cent of these were embedded workers; the proportion of embedded media and communications workers was higher than for journalism workers (26 per cent versus 18 per cent).

Table 14.1 documents the relative growth rates of embedded and specialist occupations between 2001 and 2006, and 2006 and 2011 in JMC. We can see that in this ten-year period the number of journalism jobs stayed approximately constant, and that between 2006 and 2011 embedded journalism positions actually declined. Over the ten years, media and communications jobs (comprising advertising, marketing, copywriting, and non-video media production roles) grew much faster than the rest of the economy. Growth was strong in both specialist and embedded media and communications occupations between 2006 and 2011; between 2001 and 2006, the number of embedded media and communications jobs more than doubled.

The Creative Trident mapping work indicates that the creative labour

Table 14.1   *Annual growth rates 2001–2006, 2006–2011, Australian journalism, media and communications occupations*

	2001–2006			2006–2011		
	Specialist (%)	Embedded (%)	Total (%)	Specialist (%)	Embedded (%)	Total (%)
Journalism	0.9	0.5	0.9	1.1	–1.5	0.6
Media & Communications	0.2	23.0	4.3	5.4	3.3	4.9
Total JMC	0.4	12.03	2.6	3.3	1.1	2.7
Creative workforce overall	0.5	3.4	1.7	3.2	1.8	2.8
Economy at large			2.4			2.0

Note: The ASCO classification was changed to ANZSCO in 2006, and advertising occupation codes were amended at this time. At the level of aggregation presented in this chapter ('journalism', 'media and communications'), the changes do not affect the figures. The growth of the 2001–2006 embedded media and communications figure was due to a 138 per cent increase in embedded media producers between 2001 and 2006, to 3310 in total.

force is heterogeneous in terms of levels of embeddedness and also occupational growth rates. The most recent iteration of mapping research thus differentiates between high-growth 'Creative Services' occupations and 'Cultural Production' occupations, which have exhibited much less occupational growth over the last five years. Cultural Production encompasses film, television and radio, publishing (including journalism), music, performing arts and visual arts. Creative Services are business-to-business activities including design, architecture, digital content, software development, advertising and marketing (see Cunningham, Chapter 2 in this volume for more details).

Survey research supports the notion that Creative Services and Cultural Production occupations may be quite distinct from one another in terms of labour market characteristics, and goes further to describe experiences of career in the two as being quite different. Bridgstock (2011) used a longitudinal survey method to examine the predictive value of career self-management capability to early career success over one year (as measured by creative employment and employability, creative income and career satisfaction) across a range of creative disciplines. She found a bi-modal clustering of graduate outcomes that complement the Creative Trident mapping outcomes, with Creative Services graduates finding work much more quickly and earning significantly more than Cultural Production graduates. Bridgstock also found evidence of high levels of intrinsic career motivation among the Cultural Production graduates, which predicted perseverance in the industry despite relatively low levels of objective career success among the cohort.

JMC GRADUATE TRAJECTORIES AND EXPERIENCES

So what can we say about the early career experiences and destinations of JMC graduates of university courses? The Australian Graduate Destination data collection, or GDS (Graduate Careers Australia 2013), provides annual national survey-based statistics on graduate outcomes, and is thus the first port of call. However, it must be noted that the GDS is conducted a few months after university course completion, and as such gives a rosier employment outlook for graduates from courses that are strongly aligned with compulsory post-course-completion internships (such as pharmacy) and established salaried professions where transitions to the workforce are relatively immediate. Second, the GDS uses full-time employment as a key positive outcome indicator. As we know from the previous literature review, full-time ongoing employment is often less likely among even established creative professionals than those from other fields. Third, the GDS aggregates arts, humanities and other creative course outcomes into a single set of average figures that do not permit the kind of close analysis required to gain sufficient results for the employment outlook for graduates from each disciplinary grouping. Fine-grained analyses of graduate movements into the world of work, their capability requirements in various employment destinations, and the degree to which university courses are relevant to the graduates and their work, are of course beyond the scope of the GDS.

Of general applicability is the Australian Council of Educational Research *2008 Graduate Pathways Survey* report (Coates and Edwards 2009). This study reported on the five-year career outcomes of 9000 graduates from Australian degree programs in 2002. It included 'society and culture' graduates, broadly defined, and surveyed 2300 graduates from social sciences and humanities courses in a single category. At five years after course completion, nearly seven in ten society and culture graduates (68 per cent versus all graduates 75 per cent) had full-time work, expressed positive course satisfaction and gave course relevance ratings.

A cluster of journalism graduate tracking studies, published from the mid-1990s to about 2002, attempts to address concerns of the time that journalism courses and enrolments were proliferating far beyond the demand from the sectors that employ journalists (Alysen 2001; Green and McIlwaine 1999; Patching 1996). At the same time, Becker et al. (1997) were conducting survey-based studies of graduates of 92 US schools of journalism. Becker and colleagues found that in 1996, 87 per cent of bachelors graduates surveyed had obtained employment of some sort by the time of graduation, and six to eight months later, 73.3 per cent were in full-time employment. The Australian studies were also finding that graduates were indeed finding full-time work and embarking on professional careers. However, they were also finding that a significant proportion of the graduates were not working in traditional newsrooms, but rather working in a wide range of industries that drew upon their research, analytical and communication skills, particularly media and communications jobs (Alysen 2001; Patching 1996; Putnis et al. 2002).

There are few studies of JMC graduate destinations since this cluster of research, and the job market and journalism courses have both changed remarkably over the last decade. There is some research that suggests that the characteristics of journalism jobs are changing to match the volatility in the industry, and that graduates may not be keeping up with these changes. In 2009, Cokley and Ranke conducted a comparative study of advanced journalism students' employment expectations, and Journalism job opportunities in Australia. They concluded that more paid employment is now available for journalists outside the 'Big Media' of established news publishers than for those within. They recommended that journalism educators should prepare candidates for a more flexible, independent and competitive working environment.

In summary, we know relatively little that is discipline-specific and up to date about the career trajectories of graduates from JMC courses, although the industry transformations and studies such as that of Cokley and Ranke suggest that JMC graduate careers may have changed somewhat since the comprehensive tracking work of Becker in the US in 1996–1997 and of Green and McIlwayne in Australia in 1999. We know even less about when and how these graduates move into embedded work (which has never been studied explicitly before now), what they do when they get there, and what their initial and preparatory professional education requirements are in the twenty-first century. Given that Creative Services activities are argued to be vital contributors to the knowledge economy and society, it seems important to gain an understanding of these issues.

The aims of the present study were to document early career destinations and career paths of graduates from JMC courses, and to investigate the degree of congruence between skills developed during such courses, and capabilities required in the workforce. This chapter also reports on comparative statistical analyses between graduates engaged in embedded work versus those engaged in specialist work in terms of career trajectories and skill/course relevance.

METHODOLOGY

Alumni database contact records were obtained for all 1820 graduates from Queensland University of Technology undergraduate and post-graduate JMC studies-related courses (JMC courses) from 2001 to 2010. Of the original sample of 1820 records, 36 per cent ($n = 655$) of the supplied contact numbers were either disconnected, or the participant was no longer contactable at that number. Of the 1165 live phone numbers supplied, 403 surveys were conducted, 71 declined to participate, and 569 were not able to be contacted in three attempts (answering machine or numbers rang out). A further 122 were overseas. The overall response rate, calculated as the percentage of potentially contactable participants who were actually surveyed, was a statistically robust 34.59 per cent.

Graduates from a total of 28 courses were included in the sample, of which 15 courses were 'vocational' with clear professional pathways, such as journalism, and 13 were 'non-vocational' courses, such as mass communication and media/communications.[2] The top ten most common vocational and non-vocational courses included are presented in Table 14.2. In addition, 87 of the 403 study participants graduated from dual/double degrees – most commonly B Journalism/B Business ($n = 25$) and BCI (Media Communications)/B Business ($n = 27$), but also a small number of double degrees with Law.

Table 14.2   Top ten most common vocational and non-vocational courses included in the study by number of participants

'Vocational' courses	'Non-vocational' courses
Bachelor of Journalism $n = 80$	Bachelor of Mass Communication $n = 54$
Bachelor of Creative Industries (Journalism) $n = 57$	Graduate Certificate of Creative Writing $n = 23$
Graduate Certificate of Journalism $n = 13$	Bachelor of Creative Industries (Media and Communications) $n = 10$
Graduate Diploma of Journalism $n = 8$	Bachelor of Creative Industries (Interdisciplinary) Honours $n = 9$
Master of Journalism $n = 5$	Bachelor of Creative Industries (Interdisciplinary) $n = 7$

Data Collection

The survey was conducted by telephone over a one-week period. A team of research assistant interviewers made up to three contact attempts (home phone, mobile phone, work phone) for each alumni database contact record. If contact was successfully made and permission granted to conduct the interview, interviewers read out survey questions and entered participant answers verbatim onto an online form.

The survey instrument asked graduates to document details of their last six jobs, including job role name, company, basis for employment, region, length of tenure, whether the job was a concurrent job or overlapped with another job, whether the job was a government job or private sector one, and whether the job was 'embedded', 'specialist' or 'support' (as per the previous research by CCI on measuring the creative workforce). The instrument also contained questions about unemployment and time out of the workforce, any study at certificate level or higher undertaken since graduation, graduate perceptions of the degree of course relevance and of skills used, and any perceived gaps in course provision.

Responses to open-ended questions relating to job titles and skills were coded post hoc. Job titles were coded using standard ANZSCO codes (Australian Bureau of Statistics 2006), and special codebooks were developed for the skills questions.

RESULTS

The survey captured predominantly recent graduates (the modal graduation year was 2008, with 72 graduates), but also contained graduate outcomes going back to 2001, with 201 graduates from the year 2007 or earlier, enabling comparisons between recent graduates and those with more established careers. Three-quarters of the participants (74.7 per cent) were female, and the median age was 26.

In general, graduates maintained an ongoing career commitment to journalism, media and communications fields. Unlike other occupations in the Creative Industries (particularly Cultural Production fields), it seems that there are full-time, career-level positions available to JMC graduates. Four in five (80 per cent) of the participants were employed full-time, 70 per cent were employed in jobs requiring a degree, and 62 per cent were employed in jobs they regarded as related to their JMC courses. There was no difference between vocational and non-vocational course graduates in terms of likelihood of full-time employment or course–job relatedness ($\chi^2(1) = 0.51$, $p > 0.05$). There was a fairly low percentage unemployment rate among the study participants – although 24 per cent had been unemployed at some point since graduation, the average length of time unemployed was only two months. Only 4 per cent of the cohort had been unemployed more than once since graduation.

About one-quarter of the study cohort (26 per cent) had engaged in further formal study at certificate level or higher. A significant proportion of those who did engage in further study stayed within the discipline cluster (29 per cent), and continued to more advanced levels of study, which suggests strong satisfaction with, and commitment to, JMC career trajectories. A further 18 per cent of those who went on to further study engaged in courses in business/management fields.

Specialist, Embedded and Support Jobs

One-quarter (24.9 per cent) of the participants in this study were engaged in embedded jobs – that is, employed in JMC jobs outside the media, journalism and communication sector, and 38.7 per cent were specialists, that is, employed in JMC jobs within the JMC sector. Just 3 per cent were in JMC support roles. There was a total of 110 different destination job titles across the 403 participants. Embedded roles accounted for a disproportionate 37.3 per cent of these job titles. Specialist roles accounted for only 16.5 per cent.

Non-vocational graduates were much more likely to be embedded or support, and much less likely to be specialist, than vocational graduates ($\chi^2(1) = 29.05$, $p < 0.0001$), with 59.2 per cent embedded and 5.4 per cent support among non-vocational graduate current main positions, and 25.3 per cent embedded and 1.3 per cent among vocational graduates (see Table 14.3). Although comparative data on graduates of other disciplines are not available, a seemingly high proportion of the cohort – nearly one-third (29.5 per cent) – were employed in government positions, of whom the majority were non-vocational graduates (73.9 per cent), and in PR, marketing and communication-related roles (67.22 per cent).

Table 14.3   Embedded, specialist and support current main job by vocational and non-vocational courses

	'Vocational' courses (%)	'Non-vocational' courses (%)
Embedded	25.3	59.2
Specialist	76.0	35.2
Support	1.3	5.4

Table 14.4   Most common specific recent job roles and broad fields of work (n = 250)

Specific job roles – ANZSCO 6-digit codes	Specialist (%)	Embedded (%)
Television Journalist	13.2	0
Print Journalist	13.2	0
Media Producer	9.9	2.0
Journalists and Writers nec	6.0	3.1
Public Relations Manager	6.0	20.4
Marketing Specialist	4.6	21.4
Advertising Specialist	4.6	1.0
Communication Officer	2.0	8.2
Public Relations Professional	2.0	12.2

Broad fields of work – ANZSCO 2-digit codes	Specialist (%)	Embedded (%)
Arts and Media Professionals	60.1	8.8
Business, Human Resource and Marketing Professionals	15.9	45.1
Specialist Managers	10.9	31.9

Table 14.4 presents the most common recent job roles and broad fields of work by ANZSCO 2- and 6-digit codes. The most common specialist roles were television and print journalist, followed by media producer. There were no embedded journalism roles, although there was a small number of embedded media producer roles. The most common embedded occupations were in public relations and marketing.

Career Trajectories

For many in the study cohort, the first year after course completion involved a period of transition to the workforce involving multiple job-holding, higher levels of casual work, voluntary work, work not related to the JMC course, non-Creative Trident roles and non-degree level work.

This pattern resolved in years one to two after course completion, and we see a consistent pattern of full-time, JMC-related work requiring a degree. This finding corroborates McCowan and Wyganowska's (2008) observation, from their telephone survey of QUT Creative Industries graduates across all disciplines, that at 12 months after course completion Creative Industries graduates tend to be at the same point of development, career-wise, as graduates from other areas at three months out.

Between one and two years after course completion, graduates were relatively more likely to move into specialist or embedded roles than at other times. Experienced graduates (five-plus years post-course completion) tended to be occupied in specialist roles or higher-level non-Trident roles, such as outside Creative Industries sector management (see Table 14.5).

While full-time employment was equally likely among specialist and embedded graduates, all the self-employed graduates in creative occupations were specialist creatives (a necessary condition of embedded employment is, of course, that the creative must be an employee of a 'non-creative' firm).

Course Relevance, Use of Learned Skills, and Skills Gaps

Those employed as specialist creatives reported the highest course relevance and use of skills learned during their degrees (means 4.09 and 3.74 on 1–5 scales ranging from 'not at all relevant' to 'extremely relevant' and 'not used at all' to 'used constantly'), followed by embeddeds (3.74 and 3.68), followed by support creatives (2.81 and 2.69) and non-Trident graduates (2.77 and 2.62). Regardless of employment category, the most commonly mentioned skill developed during courses seen as relevant to work was written communication (33.6 per cent). Both specialists and embeddeds also commonly mentioned discipline-specific knowledge and skills (21.4 per cent). Embeddeds were more likely than specialists to talk about the importance of verbal communication and interpersonal skills, particularly interdisciplinary communication skills and team management skills.

When asked to list required skills that were not covered in their QUT JMC courses, participants tended to emphasize specific industry- and practice-based skills arising from internships and work experience (41 per cent of comments), and indicated that more industry exposure would have been helpful during their degrees. They also wanted courses to include digital skills development relating to the specific software packages used most commonly in industry (17.8 per cent of comments), employability/ entrepreneurship skills (15.4 per cent of comments) and social networking/ social media (8.2 per cent of comments).

There were differences in reported course skill gaps by recent (less than one year) and less recent (more than one year) graduates. Recent graduates (less than one year) were significantly more likely than less recent graduates to report course gaps in terms of industry-based digital and software skills (37.0 per cent versus 14.4 per cent of comments). Recent graduates were less likely to report course gaps in practice-based industry knowledge and experience (19.6 per cent versus 45.0 per cent of comments) and social networking and social media (0 per cent versus 9.7 per cent of comments).

Table 14.5 Graduate trajectories of JMC graduates by years after course completion

	> = 1 year out	1–2 years out	2–3 years out	3–4 years out	4–5 years out	5+ years out
% multiple concurrent or overlapping jobs	23.0	16.8	18.7	17.7	16.5	15.9
% casual work	19.7	9.6	4.1	7.3	6.3	7.2
% full-time work	61.8	76.8	80.3	80.5	81.8	80.9
% voluntary/unpaid work	5.9	0.8	1.6	1.2	1.3	0.9
% work related to JMC fields	55.1	69.6	65.3	70.7	68.7	64.1
% work requiring a degree	55.3	68.8	67.2	67.1	68.5	67.2
% specialist	35.5	36.8	41.0	49.4	50.2	44.7
% embedded	19.7	29.6	25.4	23.5	20.7	19.5
% support	9.2	6.4	3.3	4.9	6.5	9.4
% non-Trident	35.5	27.2	30.3	22.2	22.6	26.4

Participants who were employed in specialist roles were more likely than those employed in embedded roles to mention technical disciplinary skills and employability/entrepreneurship skills as gaps (6.3 per cent versus 2.1 per cent and 20.3 per cent versus 12.3 per cent). The absolute number and variety of skills gaps mentioned by embeddeds were also much higher than for specialists (embedded average number per participant 4.1, total different skills mentioned 46, specialist average number per participant 1.6, total different skills mentioned 21).

DISCUSSION

The data in this study support the creative workforce mapping findings that JMC professionals are found throughout the economy. In this study, this can be said particularly of those graduates employed in public relations, marketing and communications roles, whereas early-career journalists tend to be employed within the core media sectors. Overall, the graduates in this study enjoyed high levels of employment and gave positive accounts of the relevance of their courses to working life. In these particular Creative Industries disciplines at least, and despite significant recent volatility in the media sectors, there is evidence of minimal precarity of employment, with about 1 per cent of participants undertaking unpaid or voluntary work after the first year after course completion, only 16 per cent holding multiple jobs and 80 per cent employed on a full-time basis.

The proportion of PR, marketing and communications graduates who found destinations as embedded workers in this study was actually significantly higher than the 2011 Census data suggest might be the case, with more than half of 'non-vocational' graduates employed in embedded roles. This finding may be a function of several factors. First, the group under study is not representative of the Census cohort data, in that all possessed degrees, and were all early-career professionals (that is, within ten years of course completion). The graduate trajectory data in this study suggest that embeddedness peaks quite early on in careers, and that graduates are more likely to take on specialist roles as they become more experienced in the workforce.

The finding that non-vocational JMC graduates are more likely than not to be embedded may also be reflective of the geographical region in which the participants of this study live and work. The majority of study participants remained in Brisbane after completing their degrees, which has relatively fewer specialist PR, marketing and communications firms than the Australian media centres of Sydney and Melbourne. It makes sense that there might be geographical variations in degree of embeddedness, which in turn will have implications for educational and professional infrastructure in different locations. For instance, if the majority of graduates from Brisbane-based, non-vocational JMC courses can look forward to full-time embedded local work, the composition of their initial degrees may need to be quite different from that of Sydney-based courses, where graduates can expect specialist work, which the present findings suggest may require somewhat different skill sets.

In terms of movements outside specialist and embedded JMC work, the year-by-year graduate trajectory data show that, approximately five years after course completion, graduates are increasingly likely to take on support and non-Trident roles as they move progressively into managerial positions. This means that, in some instances when specialists move into roles involving management of other JMC professionals, they are able to be counted as 'support' within the Trident, whereas some equivalent management roles outside the sector (for example, communications managers) are 'non-creative' according to the Creative Trident methodology and are no longer counted within the Trident at all.

It seems that, by and large, the JMC courses in this study were successful in delivering the capabilities, skills and orientations that facilitated graduate employability, irrespective of eventual employment type. The wide variety of job destinations points to the ongoing importance of transferable/generic skills, such as written and verbal communication, to employability; these are a core component of JMC degrees. Study participants indicated that these generic/transferable capabilities were both key strengths of their university courses and highly relevant to their careers, echoing the sentiments of health communications graduates from Edgar and Hyde's (2005) US-based study, and the cluster of journalism graduate tracking studies of a decade ago (Alysen 2001; Patching 1996; Putnis et al. 2002).

The differences between embeddeds and specialists with respect to course relevance and skills gaps suggest that university programs may not fully appreciate, or cater for, embedded roles, which represented more than half of the graduates of non-vocational programs in this study. The greater number and magnitude of reported skills gaps for embedded graduates imply that, while the ANZSCO codes for an embedded creative and a specialist creative may be identical, embedded creatives are engaged in a somewhat different, and perhaps a wider, range of activities at work. For instance, Hearn and Bridgstock (2014) argue that embeddeds may be more likely than specialists to be involved in commissioning, managing or brokering creative work, in addition to undertaking it themselves. It would be beneficial to undertake further study of embedded JMC work in order to enhance understanding of the professional capabilities it requires, perhaps using an ethnographic approach, or a large-scale content-analytical procedure comparing specialist and embedded JMC job advertisements, as per Rodgers, Hearn and Bridgstock's (forthcoming) study of recently advertised Australian PR and communications positions.

The findings of the present study point to opportunities to build curricula that better address the capability needs in embedded careers, particularly in courses that are likely to feed into embedded employment, such as those concerned with mass communication, media, public relations and advertising. Some of this can be achieved by increasing the number of embedded internship opportunities available in capstone programs, which traditionally privilege specialist roles. Thus students will have situated and authentic learning experiences that support the development of specific professional, adaptive and reflective capabilities for embedded work (see Zelenko and Bridgstock, Chapter 13 in this volume).

However, this approach should be complemented by a more comprehensive inclusion of embedded career possibilities, and indeed diverse potential career trajectories, throughout programs of study. Journalism programs, in particular, tend to make strong and explicit links between journalism study and building a career in the newsroom of a newspaper, television or radio station (Cokley and Ranke 2009; Cullen and Callaghan 2010), when a significant proportion of graduates will end up in unanticipated jobs in unanticipated sectors.

Learning engagement while at university and graduate employability outcomes are both improved by the development of realistic and adaptable working life horizons, informed by building student knowledge about labour market possibilities (Penttinen, Skaniakos and Lairio 2013). One approach that has been used successfully with undergraduate students of Creative Industries programs (Bridgstock et al. 2012) is the use of enquiry-based career development learning in the first year, in which students research opportunities and capability requirements for careers of interest, and then develop learning and career plans for themselves.

LIMITATIONS OF THE STUDY

There are several methodological limitations to this study that must be acknowledged and addressed when interpreting its findings. First, while the sample was relatively large and the survey response rate respectable (Dillman et al. 2009), the sampling frame included only contact records for JMC graduates from one university, and, therefore, the generalizability of the results to JMC graduates more broadly is somewhat limited. This limitation might be ameliorated if the study were to be replicated in other

Australian universities offering similar courses. Second, the study took a retrospective approach to surveying. Participants were asked to recall their employment and study experiences as far back as a decade before the survey. Some inaccuracies in responses can therefore be expected, particularly among participants who graduated several years ago. Third, the survey was necessarily not anonymous, and was conducted by interviewers from QUT. Responses could have suffered from bias due to social desirability and other measurement effects. The potential effect of this third shortcoming was minimized by the inclusion of interview scripting, which separated the research project from QUT Creative Industries Faculty, and indicated that only aggregated findings would be shared.

NOTES

1. Embedded refers to creative workers and occupations in non-Creative Industries, such as a designer in manufacturing or a PR professional in healthcare. Specialist refers to creative workers and occupations inside the Creative Industries, such as an actor in a television program or a software developer in a software company.
2. Here we take 'vocational' courses to mean those with clearly delineated occupational destinations, such as pharmacy, law or nursing, rather than courses delivered by the vocational education and training sector. 'Non-vocational' courses are not associated with a clear professional pathway, and include humanities/ liberal arts and science.

REFERENCES

Alysen, B. (2001), 'Tertiary journalism education: its value in cadet selection at Metropolitan Media', *Asia Pacific Media Educator*, **1** (10), 100–111.

Australian Bureau of Statistics (2006), *1220.0 – ANZSCO – Australian and New Zealand Standard Classification of Occupations*, Catalogue, ABS.

Banks, M. and D. Hesmondhalgh (2009), 'Looking for work in creative industries policy', *International Journal of Cultural Policy*, **15** (4), 415–30.

Baumann, A. (2002), 'Informal labour market governance: the case of the British and German media production industries', *Work, Employment & Society*, **16** (1), 27–46.

Becker, L.B., G. Kosicki, L. Porter and D. Watson (1997), *1997 Annual Survey of Journalism & Mass Communication Graduates*, Athens, GA: Henry W. Grady College of Journalism & Mass Communication.

Bridgstock, R. (2011), 'Skills for creative industries graduate success', *Education & Training*, **53** (1), 9–26.

Bridgstock, R., A. Thomas, K. Lyons, L. Carr and O. Zelenko (2012), 'Putting the cart before the horse? Driving student engagement through first year career identity development in a large multidisciplinary creative industries cohort', presented at the First Year in Higher Education Conference, Brisbane, Queensland, June.

Coates, H. and D. Edwards (2009), *The 2008 Graduate Pathways Survey: Graduates Education and Employment Outcomes Five Years After Completion of a Bachelor Degree at an Australian University*, Australian Council for Educational Research, available at http://www.acer.edu.au/research/projects/graduate-pathways-survey-gps/ (accessed 5 December 2011).

Cokley, J. and A. Ranke (2009), 'The long tail evident in journalism employment opportunities, but students unaware', presented at the Future of Journalism, Cardiff, September.

Compton, J.R. and P. Benedetti (2010), 'Labour, new media and the institutional restructuring of journalism', *Journalism Studies*, **11** (4), 487–99.

Cullen, T. and R. Callaghan (2010), 'Promises, promises: are Australian universities deceiving journalism students?', *Australian Journalism Review*, **32** (2), 117–29.

Department of Culture, Media and Sport (DCMS) (1998), *Creative Industries Mapping Document 1998*, London: DCMS, available at http://webarchive.nation alarchives.gov.uk/+/http://www.culture.gov.uk/reference_library/publications/4740.aspx (accessed 29 July 2013).

Dillman, D.A., G. Phelps, R. Tortora, K. Swift, J. Kohrell and J. Berck (2009), 'Response rate and measurement differences in mixed-mode surveys using mail, telephone, interactive voice response (IVR) and the Internet', *Social Science Research*, **38** (1), 1–18.

Edgar, T. and J.N. Hyde (2005), 'An alumni-based evaluation of graduate training in health communication: results of a survey on careers, salaries, competencies, and emerging trends', *Journal of Health Communication*, **10** (1), 5–25.

Elefante, P.H. and M. Deuze (2012), 'Media work, career management, and professional identity: living labour precarity', *Northern Lights: Film and Media Studies Yearbook*, **10** (1), 9–24.

Galloway, S., R. Lindley, R. Davies and F. Scheibel (2002), *A Balancing Act: Artists' Labour Markets and The Tax and Benefit Systems*, London: Arts Council of England.

Graduate Careers Australia (2013), *Gradstats 2012: Employment and Salary Outcomes of Recent Higher Education Graduates*, available at http://www.graduatecareers.com.au/wp-content/uploads/2011/12/GCA-GradStats-2012_FINAL1.pdf (retrieved 3 June 2013).

Green, K. and S. McIlwaine (1999), 'Where do all the graduates go?' *Australian Journalism Review*, **21** (2), 134–41.

Hearn, G. and R. Bridgstock (2010), 'Education for the creative economy: innovation, transdisciplinarity and networks', in D. Araya and M.A. Peters (eds), *Education in the Creative Economy: Knowledge and Learning in the Age of Innovation*, New York: Peter Lang, pp. 93–116.

Hearn, G. and R. Bridgstock (2014), 'The curious case of the embedded creative: managing creative work outside the creative industries', in S. Cummings and C. Bilton (eds), *Handbook of Management and Creativity*, Cheltenham, UK and Northampton, MA, USA: Edward Elgar.

Hesmondhalgh, D. and S. Baker (2010), 'A very complicated version of freedom: conditions and experiences of creative labour in three cultural industries', *Poetics*, **38** (1), 4–20.

Lash, S. and J. Urry (1994), *Economies of Signs and Space*, London: Sage.

McCowan, C. and J. Wyganowska (2008), 'Gathering the real data from creative industries graduates one year out', *Australian Journal of Career Development*, **17** (1), 29–39.

McRobbie, A. (2002), 'Clubs to companies: notes on the decline of political culture in speeded up creative worlds', *Cultural Studies*, **16** (4), 516–31.

Menger, P.-M. (2006), 'Artistic labor markets: contingent work, excess supply and occupational risk management', in V.A. Ginsburg and D. Throsby (eds), *Handbook on the Economics of Art and Culture*, Vol. 1, Oxford: Elsevier, pp. 765–811.

Müller, K., C. Rammerand J. Trüby (2009), 'The role of creative industries in industrial innovation', *Innovation: Management, Policy & Practice*, **11** (2), 148–68.

Patching, R. (1996), '900 into 300 won't go: are Australia's journalism courses producing too many graduates?', *Australian Journalism Review*, **18** (1), 53–65.

Penttinen, L., T. Skaniakos and M. Lairio (2013, forthcoming), 'Supporting students' pedagogical working life horizon in higher education', *Teaching in Higher Education*, n.p.

Putnis, P., B. Axford, L. Watson and W. Blood (2002), 'Communication and media studies in Australian universities', *Australian Journal of Communication*, **29** (1), 1–20.

Rodgers, J., G. Hearn and R. Bridgstock (forthcoming), 'Is embedded creative work as precarious as core creative work? A content analysis of job advertisements for Design and PR/Marketing employment'.

Taylor, S. and K. Littleton (2008), 'Art work or money: conflicts in the construction of a creative identity', *The Sociological Review*, **56** (2), 275–92.

Index

influences on development 178, 179
London, as world stage of 13, 79
long association with healthcare 96
as source of competitive advantage 159
types of, for teams 180, 181, 185
Creativity: London's Core Business 82, 83, 84, 88
Csíkszentmihályi, M. 55–6
"cultural capital" 28, 168
cultural diversity of London 78, 84
cultural ecology map (CEM) 169–70
cultural identity of Perth 158–9
cultural occupations 169, 171
cultural perspectives in healthcare 103, 105
Cultural Production
  as Creative Industries sub-category 2
  employment figures 37
  employment growth 4, 38–40, 165
  and health therapists 106
  as 'icing on the cake' 38
  incomes 165–6
  managing precarity 43
  motivation among graduates 229–30
  occupations 2, 36, 134, 229
    within digital typology 137–8, 141
    traditional 198, 206
  processes at Youthworx 193
culturalization 5–6, 25, 26, 30, 41, 227
Cunningham, S. 1, 5, 6, 7, 8–9, 13, 18, 29, 31, 32, 33, 34, 35, 41, 43, 50, 62, 97, 101, 102, 103, 104, 105, 111, 129, 130, 131, 133, 135, 141, 160, 165, 166, 169, 170–71, 175, 199, 202, 206, 207, 208, 211
customer centred design (CCD) 149, 152–3

Dameron, S. 177, 184
data mining 69, 101
de Peuter, G. 7, 8
Deloitte Access Economics 128, 148
Denham, J. 80
Department of Broadband, Communications and the Digital Economy 61, 128
Department of Communications, Information Technology and the Arts 130, 131, 132

Department of Culture, Media and Sport (DCMS) 30, 31, 80, 82, 130, 131, 134–6
Department of Industry, Innovation, Science, Research and Tertiary Education 111, 115
design
  and affordance 178
  in all digital typology groupings 137–8
  as Creative Services segment 2, 36, 134
    employment figures 37
    employment growth rates 38–40
  design studio 13, 78
  designers 6
  digital, in banking 145–55
  in healthcare 98, 99, 100, 104–5, 107
  illustrating learning processes 188
  in manufacturing 14, 87, 113–23, 125, 175
  occupations
    degree of embeddedness 42
    demand for 7
    by industry sector 3–4
    sub-sectors 43
  in Perth 161, 165, 166
design-based framework for learning 211–23
Deuze, M. 26, 195, 199, 228
device fragmentation 146–7
digital content
  Australian studies 131–2, 141–2
  in banking 145–6
  as Creative Services segment 2, 36, 61, 134
    employment figures 37
    employment growth rates 38–40
  in healthcare 14, 98–103, 106–7
  in manufacturing 113, 115–16, 117, 123
  occupations by industry sector 4
  in Perth 161, 165
  policy 128–9
  skills shortages 10
digital creative employment, definitional changes 134–6
digital creative services
  case studies
    education 63–7

creative resource, defining 84
creativity as human resource 88–9
governance, intelligence, policy and
    research 79–81
introduction 13, 78–9
political climate changes 85–6
product definition and consumer
    identification 83–4
questions and issues 86–8
service and the city 89–90

Malossi, G. 28, 29
Mandeville, T. 62, 72, 183, 184, 188
manufacturing industry
  case studies
    digital development 64, 70–72
    fans and pumps 118–20
    lighting solutions 120–21
    smart weighing 117–18
  embedded creatives
    challenges 122–4
    value-add 115–17, 121–2
  introduction 14, 111–12
  methodology 112–15
  study conclusions 124–5
market failure approach 85–6, 87
marketing
  as Creative Services segment 2, 36,
    134
    employment figures 37
    employment growth rates
      38–40
  in healthcare 98, 99, 100, 103, 107
  in manufacturing 113, 114, 115–16,
    119–23, 125, 175
  in media and communications
    228–9, 235, 238
  occupations by industry sector 4
  in Perth 161, 165
  in Semi-Digital grouping 15, 136,
    138, 139
MARVIN 102
Marxist theory of labour 8, 27
Mason, K. 199, 201, 206
McGuigan, J. 27, 28
McIlwaine, S. 231
McRobbie, A. 26, 227
measurement issues
  Creative Trident 32–41
  overview 11–13

question of size 26
statistics 30–32
media
  barriers to working in 202–3
  interest in 197–200, 205
  progressing in 204, 207–8
  see also journalism, media and
    communications (JMC)
medical research 101
Meijers, F. 212, 214
Menger, P.-M. 9, 227
mentoring 10, 17, 73, 193
Miller, T. 27
minimal viable product (MVP) 65, 66
mining case study 64, 67–70
Misys and Finextra 148, 155
mobile banking 15, 147–9, 150, 155
mobile platforms 15, 102, 148, 150,
    155
Montez, T. 148, 155
Morris, P. 159–60
Mudambi, R. 6, 72–3, 175
Müller, K. 62, 74, 227
Murphy, P. 169, 171
music
  as Cultural Production segment 2,
    36, 134
    employment figures 37
    employment growth rates 38–40
  as dream jobs 198, 199
  in healthcare 98, 99, 100, 105–6, 107
  incomes 34, 35, 42
  in manufacturing 113, 115, 116
  occupations by industry sector 3
  in Perth 161, 165
  self-employment rates 41
  in Semi-Digital grouping 138

Nakamura, J. 55–6
Naro, S. 28, 29
National Endowment for Science,
    Technology and the Arts
    (NESTA) 34, 36, 80, 91, 135, 154
NeuroSmart 65–7
Newell, K.M. 178, 180
Nissan 78, 89
Nixon, H. 17, 194
non-creative occupations (NCO)
  within JMC 213, 235–6, 239, 241
  job security and satisfaction 49–58